PSALMS

A Song for Every Situation
Each Summarized on One Page

G. Michael Cocoris

PSALMS

A Song for Every Situation
Each Summarized on One Page

G. Michael Cocoris

© 2014 by G. Michael Cocoris

All rights reserved. This publication may not be reproduced (in whole or in part, edited, or revised) in any way, form, or means including, but not limited to, electronic, mechanical, photocopying, recording or any kind of storage and retrieval system *for sale*, except for brief quotations in printed reviews, without the written permission of G. Michael Cocoris, 2016 Euclid #20, Santa Monica, CA 90405, michaelcocoris@gmail.com, or his appointed representatives. Permission is hereby granted, however, for reproduction of the whole or parts of the whole without changing the content in any way for *free distribution,* provided all copies contain this copyright notice in its entirety. Permission is also granted to charge for the cost of copying.

Unless otherwise indicated, all Scripture quotations are taken from the New King James Version ®, Copyright © 1979, 1980, 1982 by Thomas Nelson, Inc. Used by permission. All rights reserved.

TABLE OF CONTENTS

PREFACE 1
PSALM 1: WHEN YOU WANT TO BE HAPPY 3
PSALM 2: WHEN YOU SEE REBELLION 4
PSALM 3: WHEN THOSE WHO TROUBLE YOU MULTIPLY 5
PSALM 4: WHEN YOUR FRIENDS BECOME YOUR FOES 6
PSALM 5: WHEN YOU ARE FACING A DEADLY FOE 7
PSALM 6: WHEN YOU FEEL GOD IS ANGRY WITH YOU 8
PSALM 7: WHEN YOU ARE SLANDERED 9
PSALM 8: WHEN YOU GAZE AT THE STARS 10
PSALM 9: WHEN PRAYING ABOUT YOUR PROBLEM 11
PSALM 10: WHEN THE WICKED SEEM TO BE WINNING 12
PSALM 11: WHEN YOUR VERY FOUNDATION IS SHAKEN 13
PSALM 12: WHEN YOU LIVE AMID VILE SPEECH 14
PSALM 13: WHEN YOU FEEL FORSAKEN BY GOD 15
PSALM 14: WHEN YOU ARE PEOPLE WATCHING 16
PSALM 15: WHEN YOU SEEK GOD'S FELLOWSHIP 17
PSALM 16: WHEN YOU ARE FACING DEATH 18
PSALM 17: WHEN YOU FACE VICIOUS ENEMIES 19
PSALM 18: WHEN GOD DELIVERS YOU 20
PSALM 19: WHEN YOU SEE GOD'S REVELATION 21
PSALM 20: WHEN YOU ARE FACING A BATTLE 22
PSALM 21: WHEN YOUR BATTLE IS WON 23
PSALM 22: WHEN YOU FEEL ABANDONED BY GOD 24
PSALM 23: WHEN THE LORD IS YOUR SHEPHERD 25
PSALM 24: WHEN YOU SEEK TO APPROACH GOD 26
PSALM 25: WHEN YOU NEED FORGIVENESS 27
PSALM 26: WHEN YOU ARE FALSELY ACCUSED 28
PSALM 27: WHEN YOU ARE FACING A FEARFUL DANGER 29
PSALM 28: WHEN YOU DEAL WITH WICKED ENEMIES 30
PSALM 29: WHEN YOU ARE WATCHING A THUNDERSTORM 31
PSALM 30: WHEN YOU ARE DELIVERED FROM DEATH'S DOOR 32
PSALM 31: WHEN YOU ARE IN AGONY 33
PSALM 32: WHEN YOU CONTEMPLATE FORGIVENESS 34

- **PSALM 33: WHEN YOU CONSIDER GOD'S WORD AND WORKS** 35
- **PSALM 34: WHEN YOU SAVED FROM A FEARFUL SITUATION** 36
- **PSALM 35: WHEN YOU ARE TREATED UNJUSTLY** 37
- **PSALM 36: WHEN YOU READ GOD'S REVELATION** 38
- **PSALM 37: WHEN YOU FRET OVER THE WICKED** 39
- **PSALM 38: WHEN YOU ARE DEALING WITH THE EFFECTS OF SIN** 40
- **PSALM 39: WHEN YOU ARE SICK BECAUSE OF SIN** 41
- **PSALM 40: WHEN COUNTLESS PROBLEMS OVERWHELM YOU** 42
- **PSALM 41: WHEN YOU ARE SICK, LIED ABOUT, AND BETRAYED** 43
- **PSALM 42: WHEN YOU LONG FOR GOD AND HIS PEOPLE** 44
- **PSALM 43: WHEN ATTACKED BY A DECEITFUL ENEMY** 45
- **PSALM 44: WHEN YOU ARE INNOCENT AND SUFFER DEFEAT** 46
- **PSALM 45: WHEN YOU CONTEMPLATE A ROYAL WEDDING** 47
- **PSALM 46: WHEN YOU ARE IN PHYSICAL DANGER** 48
- **PSALM 47: WHEN YOU ARE CALLED TO PRAISE THE KING** 49
- **PSALM 48: WHEN GOD HAS PROTECTED YOU** 50
- **PSALM 49: WHEN YOU ARE INTIMIDATED BY THE WEALTHY** 51
- **PSALM 50: WHEN GOD JUDGES YOU** 52
- **PSALM 51: WHEN YOU COMMIT SERIOUS SINS** 53
- **PSALM 52: WHEN SOMEONE LIES ABOUT YOU** 54
- **PSALM 53: WHEN YOU OBSERVE PEOPLE** 55
- **PSALM 54: WHEN YOUR ENEMIES DO EVIL** 56
- **PSALM 55: WHEN A FRIEND TURNS AGAINST YOU** 57
- **PSALM 56: WHEN YOU FEAR FOR YOUR LIFE** 58
- **PSALM 57: WHEN PEOPLE TRY TO TRAP YOU LIKE AN ANIMAL** 59
- **PSALM 58: WHEN YOU DEAL WITH AN UNJUST JUDGE** 60
- **PSALM 59: WHEN YOU NEED A BODYGUARD** 61
- **PSALM 60: WHEN A SETBACK CAUSES YOU TO BE CONFUSED** 62
- **PSALM 61: WHEN YOU FEEL OVERWHELMED** 63
- **PSALM 62: WHEN YOU ARE VERBALLY ATTACKED** 64
- **PSALM 63: WHEN YOU CANNOT SLEEP** 65
- **PSALM 64: WHEN YOU DEAL WITH A SECRET PLOT** 66
- **PSALM 65: WHEN YOU SEE GOD'S POWER IN THE WORLD** 67
- **PSALM 66: WHEN YOU HAVE BEEN TESTED** 68
- **PSALM 67: WHEN YOU WANT TO SEE PEOPLE CONVERTED** 69

- PSALM 68: WHEN YOU ARE DEALING WITH GOD'S ENEMIES 70
- PSALM 69: WHEN YOU SUFFER FOR YOUR ZEAL FOR THE LORD 71
- PSALM 70: WHEN YOU NEED IMMEDIATE HELP 72
- PSALM 71: WHEN YOU ARE ELDERLY AND IN TROUBLE 73
- PSALM 72: WHEN YOU PRAY FOR THE GOVERNMENT 74
- PSALM 73: WHEN YOU SEE THE PROSPERITY OF THE WICKED 75
- PSALM 74: WHEN YOU SEE DIVINE DISCIPLINE 76
- PSALM 75: WHEN YOU CONTEMPLATE GOD'S JUDGMENT 77
- PSALM 76: WHEN GOD GIVES YOU THE VICTORY 78
- PSALM 77: WHEN YOUR PROBLEMS KEEP YOU AWAKE 79
- PSALM 78: WHEN YOU READ THE OLD TESTAMENT #1 80
- PSALM 79: WHEN YOU THINK VENGEANCE IS APPROPRIATE 81
- PSALM 80: WHEN YOU NEED SPIRITUAL RESTORATION 82
- PSALM 81: WHEN YOU WANT TO CELEBRATE THE LORD 83
- PSALM 82: WHEN YOU ARE FACING AN UNJUST JUDGE 84
- PSALM 83: WHEN YOU PRAY FOR YOUR ENEMIES 85
- PSALM 84: WHEN YOU ARE ON YOUR WAY TO CHURCH 86
- PSALM 85: WHEN YOU NEED RESTORATION AGAIN 87
- PSALM 86: WHEN YOUR LIFE IS THREATENED 88
- PSALM 87: WHEN YOU CONTEMPLATE THE CITY OF GOD 89
- PSALM 88: WHEN YOU FEEL ALONE AND ABANDONED 90
- PSALM 89: WHEN YOU QUESTION GOD'S FAITHFULNESS 91
- PSALM 90: WHEN YOU REFLECT ON THE BREVITY OF LIFE 92
- PSALM 91: WHEN YOU ARE EXPOSED TO DANGER 93
- PSALM 92: WHEN YOU SEE THE DEFEAT OF YOUR ENEMIES 94
- PSALM 93: WHEN YOU SEE THE WORLD OUT OF CONTROL 95
- PSALM 94: WHEN YOU SEE THE WICKED TRIUMPH 96
- PSALM 95: WHEN YOU PRAISE THE LORD AS KING 97
- PSALM 96: WHEN YOU REFLECT ON THE FUTURE OF THE WORLD 98
- PSALM 97: WHEN YOU REFLECT ON THE COMING OF THE LORD 99
- PSALM 98: WHEN YOU ARE CALLED TO SING TO THE LORD 100
- PSALM 99: WHEN YOU SEE AN ANSWER TO PRAYER 101
- PSALM 100: WHEN YOU COME TO GOD'S HOUSE 102
- PSALM 101: WHEN YOU ARE PUT IN CHARGE 103
- PSALM 102: WHEN YOU SUFFER AFFLICTION 104

PSALM 103:	WHEN YOU BLESS THE LORD	105
PSALM 104:	WHEN YOU CONTEMPLATE THE CREATION	106
PSALM 105:	WHEN YOU READ THE OLD TESTAMENT #2	107
PSALM 106:	WHEN YOU READ THE OLD TESTAMENT #3	108
PSALM 107:	WHEN YOU SEE GOD'S WONDERFUL WORKS	109
PSALM 108:	WHEN YOU WAKE UP IN THE MORNING	110
PSALM 109:	WHEN YOU ARE WOUNDED BY WICKED WORDS	111
PSALM 110:	WHEN YOU WANT A PICTURE OF THE MESSIAH	112
PSALM 111:	WHEN YOU PRAISE THE LORD FOR HIS WORKS	113
PSALM 112:	WHEN YOU COUNT YOUR BLESSINGS	114
PSALM 113:	WHEN YOU SEE THE LORD DO THE UNUSUAL	115
PSALM 114:	WHEN YOU SEE THE LORD IS PRESENT	116
PSALM 115:	WHEN YOU HEAR GOD HAS BEEN INACTIVE	117
PSALM 116:	WHEN YOU FACE TROUBLE, SORROW, AND DEATH	118
PSALM 117:	WHEN ALL ARE CALLED TO PRAISE THE LORD	119
PSALM 118:	WHEN YOU ARE IN DISTRESS	120
PSALM 119:1-8:	WHEN YOU SEE THE BENEFITS OF OBEYING	121
PSALM 119:9-16:	WHEN YOU DESIRE A PURE LIFE	122
PSALM 119:17-24:	WHEN YOU WANT TO KNOW THE WORD	123
PSALM 119:25-32:	WHEN YOU FEEL DISCOURAGED	124
PSALM 119:33-40:	WHEN YOU WANT TO BE OBEDIENT	125
PSALM 119:41-48:	WHEN YOU HAVE BEEN REPROACHED	126
PSALM 119:49-56:	WHEN YOU ARE MOCKED	127
PSALM 119:57-64:	WHEN YOU ARE ENCIRCLED BY ENEMIES	128
PSALM 119:65-72:	WHEN SOMEONE LIES ABOUT YOU	129
PSALM 119:73-80:	WHEN YOU ARE MISTREATED BY OTHERS	130
PSALM 119:81-88:	WHEN YOUR DELIVERANCE IS DELAYED	131
PSALM 119:89-96:	WHEN YOUR WORLD IS UNSTABLE	132
PSALM 119:97-104:	WHEN YOU WANT TO BE WISE	133
PSALM 119:105-112:	WHEN YOU ARE IN A SEVERE TRIAL	134
PSALM 119:113-120:	WHEN YOU ARE FACED WITH EVILDOERS	135
PSALM 119:121-128:	WHEN YOU ARE OPPRESSED	136
PSALM 119:129-136:	WHEN YOU SEE WONDER IN THE WORD	137
PSALM 119:137-144:	WHEN YOU ARE DESPISED	138
PSALM 119:145-152:	WHEN YOUR ENEMIES DRAW NEAR	139

- PSALM 119:153-160: WHEN YOU ARE PERSECUTED 140
- PSALM 119:161-168: WHEN YOU ARE PERSECUTED WITHOUT CAUSE 141
- PSALM 119:169-176: WHEN YOU SPIRITUALLY GO ASTRAY 142
- PSALM 120: WHEN YOU ARE LIVING AMONG LIARS 143
- PSALM 121: WHEN YOU TRAVEL 144
- PSALM 122: WHEN PRAYING FOR THE CITY 145
- PSALM 123: WHEN YOU ARE TREATED WITH CONTEMPT 146
- PSALM 124: WHEN YOU ARE DELIVERED FROM ANNIHILATION 147
- PSALM 125: WHEN YOU CONTEMPLATE YOUR SECURITY 148
- PSALM 126: WHEN YOU ARE RESTORED #1 149
- PSALM 127: WHEN YOU WORK HARD 150
- PSALM 128: WHEN YOU REFLECT ON HAPPINESS 151
- PSALM 129: WHEN YOU SUFFER A SEVERE ATTACK 152
- PSALM 130: WHEN YOU ARE FORGIVEN 153
- PSALM 131: WHEN YOU TRUST THE LORD 154
- PSALM 132: WHEN YOU CONTEMPLATE GOD'S COVENANT 155
- PSALM 133: WHEN YOU CONTEMPLATE LIVING IN UNITY 156
- PSALM 134: WHEN YOU SEE PEOPLE SERVING THE LORD 157
- PSALM 135: WHEN YOU ARE CALLED TO PRAISE 158
- PSALM 136: WHEN YOU THANK GOD 159
- PSALM 137: WHEN YOU EXPERIENCE SEVERE DISCIPLINE 160
- PSALM 138: WHEN YOU ARE IN THE MIDST OF TROUBLE 161
- PSALM 139: WHEN SOMEONE WANTS YOU DEAD 162
- PSALM 140: WHEN YOU ARE FACED WITH A SLANDERER 163
- PSALM 141: WHEN YOU NEED PROTECTION 164
- PSALM 142: WHEN YOU ARE FORSAKEN 165
- PSALM 143: WHEN YOU ARE DEVASTATED 166
- PSALM 144: WHEN YOU ARE DOING BATTLE WITH LIARS 167
- PSALM 145: WHEN YOU PRAISE GOD AS KING 168
- PSALM 146: WHEN YOU PRAISE THE LORD FOR HIS HELP 169
- PSALM 147: WHEN YOU ARE RESTORED #2 170
- PSALM 148: WHEN YOU ARE STRENGTHENED 171
- PSALM 149: WHEN YOU REJOICE IN THE LORD 172
- PSALM 150: WHEN YOU PUBLICLY PRAISE THE LORD 173

PREFACE

The book of Psalms is the hymn book of the Bible. In virtually all the psalms, the psalmist is in a specific situation. Just about every kind of situation is covered in the book. Hence, the title of this material is "A Song for Every Situation." To capture the situation of each psalm, each one is given a title that begins with "when."

By design, this treatment of the psalms summarizes each psalm in one page or less. The purpose is to explain each psalm briefly. The major way that is done is by giving an *explanatory outline* of the psalm. Most of what is said in the psalms is self-evident. ("Praise the Lord" needs no explanation; it just needs to be practiced.) At the same time, when the meaning of a statement or phrase is not obvious, an explanation is given. The summary statement at the end of each psalm puts the situation and what the psalmist had to say about it in one sentence.

Students of the Psalter have pointed out that the psalms can be categorized by type. Various suggestions have been made about how many types there are and which psalms are examples of which types. This study mentions the type of each psalm in the introduction. Here is one explanation of the types of psalms with some of the psalms under each type.

    Laments psalms. Some are individual and some are communal laments.
    Thanksgiving psalms. Some are individual and some are communal thanksgiving.
    Praise psalms. Some are general praise and others are descriptive praise.
    Ascent psalms (84; 120-134). Song sung while ascending up to Jerusalem.
    Royal psalms (2; 18; 20;9; 21; 45; 72; 89; 101; 110; 132; 144).
    Wisdom psalms (1; 14; 37; 73; 91; 112; 119; 128).
    Acrostic psalms (9; 10; 25; 34; 37; 111, 112; 119; 145).
    Penitential psalms (6; 143).
    Flight from Saul (34; 52; 54; 56; 57; 59; 63; 142).
    Imprecatory psalms (7; 35; 55; 58; 59; 69; 79; 109; 137; 139). "Imprecatory" means "to invite a curse on someone." The author leaves vengeance up to the Lord. This is also a request for God to honor a provision of the Abrahamic covenant in which God promised to curse those who curse Abraham's descendants (Gen. 12:2-3).
    Enthronement psalms (93:1; 96:10; 97:1; 99:1). Whereas the Royal psalms use a secular King as a figure for the Lord, the Enthronement psalms speak directly of God as King. Four psalms contain the phrase "the Lord reigns." One psalm says, "God reigns" (47:1-9). One psalm says the Lord is "the great King above all gods" (95:3). One psalm simply calls Him "the King" (98:6). See also Ps. 20:9 and Ps. 24.
    Messianic psalms (2; 8; 16; 22; 31; 40; 41; 45; 68; 69; 102; 110; 118). A Messianic psalm foreshadows the Messiah, the "anointed One."

The subject of the Psalms is praise. The Hebrew Bible appropriately entitled the book "Praises" (Our title "Psalms" comes from the LXX; it is a Greek word that means a song sung to the accompaniment of musical instruments.) The message is that God's people lament, trust God, hope in God's future blessings, and praise God.

One purpose of the Psalms is to provoke worship. Psalms is the inspired song/worship book of prayer and praise. The children of God praise God amid their doubts and fears, longings and hopes, joys and sorrows. They trust God to bless the righteous and punish the wicked.

Another purpose of Psalms is to provide prophecy. At least thirteen psalms are proven to be Messianic by New Testament quotations (2; 8; 16; 22; 31; 40; 41; 45; 68; 69; 102; 110; 118). Most would agree that other psalms undoubtedly refer to Christ as well. The future glory of Israel and of the world is also a subject of prophecy in the Psalms. However uncertain the times, the Lord will establish His kingdom through the future Messiah. That reassurance might not stabilize the time, but it will certainly stabilize the heart.

A name in parenthesis is the name of the commentator who was commenting on that verse. "BDB" stands for Brown Driver and Briggs, the authors of their Hebrew lexicon (dictionary).

May the Lord use this material to provoke trust and praise in those who read it.

Hmmm G. Michael Cocoris
Santa Monica, California

Psalm 1: When You Want to Be Happy

Psalm 1 is a wisdom psalm written by an unknown author. It describes the happy in contrast to the ungodly (1:1, 4).

The Way of the Righteous (1:1-3) The people described in the first three verses are called righteous (1:5-6) and blessed (1:1). The righteous know the Lord (1:5-6). They reject the suggestions for how to live life, the sin, and the scorn of the unrighteous (1:1). They delight in and meditate in God's Word (1:2), implying they order their lives according to it. Consequently, they are righteous and happy (1:1). The Hebrew word translated "blessed" (1:1) means "happy" and the way it is written in the Hebrew text, it should be translated "Oh, how completely happy." Righteous/happy people are like a tree planted by the water; they are stable, fruitful, attractive, and successful (1:3).

The Way of the Unrighteous (1:4-6) The people described in the last three verses are called ungodly (1:1, 5, 6) and sinners (1:1, 1:5). They are not like the righteous at all. In the first place, they don't know God (1:5-6). They do not delight in nor meditate on God's Word to order their lives according to it (1:4). Consequently, they are ungodly (1:4). They are like chaff blowing in the wind; they are unstable, unfruitful, unattractive, and unsuccessful (1:4). Therefore, they will not be able to stand in the judgment or be numbered in the congregation of the righteous (1:5) and their *way* will perish (1:6; that is, their hopes and dreams will come to naught; they will be unhappy).

Summary: When you want to be happy, meditate on the Word of God, which leads to godliness, fruitfulness, and happiness and remember that the way of the unrighteous (to ignore God and His Word) leads to unhappiness and judgment.

A point to ponder: The really happy believers delight in and meditate on God's Word day and night to order their lives according to God's will.

Psalm 2: When You See Rebellion

Psalm 2 is a royal psalm written by David (see Acts 4:25). A royal psalm is about the Supreme King, the Messiah (18, 20, 21, 45, 72, 89, 101, 110, 132, and 144). Psalm 2 describes people in rebellion (2:1-3).

The Rebellion of the World (2:1-3) Psalm 2 begins by asking, "Why do the nations rage; why do the people plot vain things?" (2:1). The Hebrew word rendered "plot" means "to meditate, muse." It is the same word used in Psalm 1:2. Only here the object of meditation (or content) is different. In Psalm 1, it was the Word. Here, it is a vain thing. The kings of the earth set themselves against God and His Anointed (2:2-3). The Anointed is the Christ, the Messiah. The rulers of the world are determined to rid themselves of all divine restraint (2:3). In prayer in Acts 4:25-27, this is applied to the Gentiles and Jews, Herod, and Pilate in that they crucified Christ. In David's day, in Christ's time, and today, the people of the earth are in rebellion against God. Actively and passively, overtly and subtly, they are bent on throwing off all divine law.

The Decree of God (2:4-6) God decrees His Anointed will rule. He laughs at the absurdity of people rebelling against Him (2:4). He holds them in derision (2:4). He speaks in wrath and when He does, they are "distressed" (2:5). The Hebrew word rendered "distress" means "disturbs, dismays, terrifies them" (BDB). They "quake with fear" (Alexander). It is what He says that causes them to tremble: "Yet I have set My King on My holy hill of Zion" (2:6). In other words, He says, "You have 'set' yourselves against Me (2:2). Let me tell you what I have done. I have set My King on Zion" (2:6). History makes no mention of a king of Israel being anointed on Zion to rule all the nations on earth (2:8). Therefore, this is a reference to the Messiah. Christ shall rule the earth from Zion.

People want to dethrone God so they can enthrone themselves. God has decreed there is only one king is worthy to rule, His Son Jesus Christ (Phil. 2:9-11). It will take a while, but it will happen.

The Declaration of the Son (2:7-9) Next, the Messiah says, "The LORD has said to Me, 'You are My Son, Today I have begotten You'" (2:7). This Old Testament verse says God has a Son! This verse is quoted in Acts 13:33 and in Hebrews 1:5, 5:5 to prove the deity of Christ: "God sent forth His Son, born of a woman" (Gal. 4:4). The Messiah also says God will give Him all the nations of the world as an inheritance (2:8) and He will put down all rebellion (2:9). This will be fulfilled in the Millennium.

The Admonition of the Psalmist (2:10-12) The psalmist tells the rulers of this world to "be wise" (2:10), "serve the Lord" (2:11), and kiss the Son (2:12). A kiss was an ancient mode of showing allegiance to a king (1 Sam. 10:1). The last verse says, "Kiss the Son, lest He be angry, and you perish in the way when His wrath is kindled but a little. Blessed are all those who put their trust in Him" (2:12). In other words, submit to escape destruction, for His wrath will soon burn. The way to happiness and heaven is to trust the Son.

Summary: When you see people rebelling against God, remember God is going to establish His Son as King of the earth, so all should abandon their rebellion and submit to the rule of Christ.

A point to ponder: Get smart; serve the Lord.

Psalm 3: When Those Who Trouble You Multiply

Psalm 3 is an individual lament psalm written by David. The superscription indicates that the occasion was David's flight from his son Absalom (2 Sam. 15:13-17:22), who wanted to take over the throne contrary to God's will. Three times David addresses God (3:1, 3, 7). He laments that his troubles have multiplied (3:1-2).

David Laments (3:1-2) David begins by lamenting that those who trouble him have increased; many have risen against him (3:1; see 10,000 in verse 6). A whole army was after him. The odds were overwhelmingly against him. On top of that, many told David that not even God could "help" (Hebrew: save) him (3:2). They were saying David's situation was hopeless. Thus, David laments to God. We complain to other people.

David Praises (3:3-6) David's kingdom has been taken from him. Yet, he praises God for being his shield (3:3a), glory (3:3b), and encourager (3:3c). David felt defenseless, despised, and dejected. Still, he says God is the defense for the defenseless, honor for the despised, and joy for the comfortless. Today, we would say God is my bodyguard, my audience to applaud me, and my therapist.

Moreover, driven from Jerusalem, David was separated from God's holy hill (3:4), the place of the ark (2 Sam. 6:17), the presence of God. Nevertheless, David says, "I cried to the LORD with my voice, and He heard me from His holy hill. Selah" (3:4). "Selah" means "Think about that." The Lord hears our plea. He is the defense for the defenseless, honor for the despised, and joy for the comfortless.

Having fled his palace in Jerusalem, David was probably forced to sleep in an open field under the canopy of heaven. Yet he could say. "I lay down and slept" (3:5a). Amid his multiplied miseries, he went to sleep! The Lord protected him that night. Hence, the statement, "I awoke, for the LORD sustained me" (3:5b). He adds, "I will not be afraid of ten thousand of people who have set themselves against me all around" (3:6). He does not underestimate the enemy. Rather, he says, I will trust the Lord; He is my peace when I sleep at night and face my enemy during the day. Numbers are not everything. Absalom had the crowd, but David had the Lord, and one with God was the majority.

David Prays (3:7-8) David asks the Lord to save him by defeating his enemies (3:7) and to bless His people. In the midst of his trouble, he prays not only for himself but for others as well. When David says, "Salvation belongs to the LORD" (3:8) and "save me" (3:7), he is talking about being *delivered* from his troubles.

Summary: When those who trouble you multiply and contrary to the will of God, they pursue you, praise God for His many provisions and ask Him to deliver you.

A point to ponder: Stop fretting; praise the Lord and ask Him to deliver you from your troubles.

Psalm 4: When Your Friends Become Your Foes

Psalm 4 is an individual lament psalm written by David and expresses great trust in the Lord. Psalms 3 and 4 are closely related (see 3:3 with 4:7 and 3:6 with 4:9). Like Psalm 3, the backdrop is that Absalom wanted to sit on his father's throne. So, he gathered an army and prepared to march on Jerusalem. David fled with his friends, fellow countrymen, and his own family members against him. In that situation, David wrote Psalms 3 and 4. So, in this psalm, David's friends have become his foes (4:2).

Cry to God (4:1) Addressing God as "my Righteousness," David asks God to hear his prayer, reminding Him of His past deliverance and seeking His mercy in the present situation (4:1). In other words, "God hears me; You are just, faithful, and merciful."

Counsel to His Enemies (4:2-5) Turning his attention to his enemies ("sons of men"), David asks them how long they will turn his glory to shame, love to worthlessness, and seek falsehood (4:2). Then David tells his enemies they need to know that the Lord will hear his prayer because the godly are set apart to the Lord (4:3; David was set apart as king). He counsels them to 1) be angry and sin not (quoted by Paul in Eph. 4:26), 2) meditate (think about what you are doing), 3) be still, 4) offer the sacrifice of righteousness, and 5) trust the Lord (4:4-5). In short, trust the Lord. Do not sin. Do what is right. Thus, David does not cry to God for vengeance on his enemies but counsels them to make sure they are right with the Lord!

This passage gives a prescription for dealing with anger: 1) Be still. Calm down. 2) Get alone. 3) Think. Meditate. Reflect. 4) Don't sin. Do what is right. 5) Trust the Lord for the strength to do what is right.

Confidence of the Psalmist (4:6-8) In answer to those who ask, "Where is the good?" David asks the Lord to be gracious to "us" (4:6). Then he acknowledges that the Lord gives him joy (4:7), peace, and safety (4:8). Confident the Lord will keep him safe, David falls asleep (4:8). David was able to go to sleep because he was trusting the Lord to protect him.

Summary: When your friends become your foes, counsel them to trust in the Lord and you do the same. You will have joy and peace, even if they do not.

A point to ponder: Love your enemies (seek their good) and trust the Lord so that you can have peace and joy, even if they don't.

Psalm 5: When You Are Facing a Deadly Foe

Psalm 5 is an individual lament psalm written by David. As in Psalms 3 and 4, David is faced with deadly foes who desire to do him harm (5:8-9).

Hear Me (5:1-3) David piles one expression on top of another in asking God to hear him, including "give ear to my words" (5:1a), "consider my mediation" (5:1b), "give heed to the voice of my cry" (5:2), "You shall hear my voice in the morning" (5:3a). In the process, David addresses God as "Lord" (5:1) and as "King" (5:2). He is not approaching God as mere Creator but as Ruler. David, a king, comes to God, the King, knowing it was the king's function to protect His subjects. Notice David started his day with prayer. David concludes with "and I will look up" (5:3b), meaning, I will expectantly look for Your answer.

After the request (5:1-3), David gives the reason for his request (5:4-7), namely God's displeasure with sin (5:4) and His destruction of sinners (5:5-6). The sinners God will punish include the boastful (5:5), all workers of iniquity (5:5), liars (5:6), the murderers (5:6), and deceivers (5:6). An old proverb says, "Bloody and deceitful men dig their own graves."

David adds, "But as for me, I will come into Your house in the multitude of Your mercy; in fear of You I will worship toward Your holy temple" (5:7). In contrast to sinners who are headed to judgment, David will come to the Lord, who is merciful, fear the Lord, and worship the Lord. David will escape the destruction of sinners, not of his own merit, but because of God's mercy.

Lead Me (5:8-9) David prays that God will lead him in righteousness (5:8) and "make Your way straight before my face" (5:8), which refers to a path of protection. Thus, David asks God to protect him spiritually and physically.

After the request (5:8), David gives the reason for his request (5:9): that his enemies are evil and wicked men. Their mouth, heart, throat, and tongue are all instruments of sin. Paul quotes Psalm 5:9 to prove that all are sinners (Rom. 3:13). The point is that David prayed for protection because his enemies were wicked men who desired his destruction (5:9).

Judge Them (5:10) David asks God to "pronounce them (his enemies) guilty," "let them fall," and "cast them out" because "they have rebelled against You" (5:10). They were not just rebelling against David; they were rebelling against God. Again, David is praying for protection.

Bless Believers (5:11-12) David's fourth and final request is, "But let all those rejoice who put their trust in You; let them ever shout for joy, because You defend them; let those also who love Your name be joyful in You" (5:11). David's experience can be the experience of all who have David's heart. Anyone who trusts God shall rejoice. Notice those who love Him will be joyful in Him, not in their deliverance. Believers shall rejoice because the Lord will bless them with protection. He shall surround them with a shield (5:12).

Summary: When facing deadly foes who desire your harm, you will rejoice and not fear if you trust the Lord (ask the Lord) for your protection and their destruction.

The surprise in this psalm is not that David prayed for personal protection but that he prayed for the destruction of his enemies. It is not sinful to pray for the destruction of some people. David is not seeking revenge. He is praying for God's judgment of his enemies because they were the enemies of God (5:10).

A point to ponder: Those who trust the Lord will rejoice.

Psalm 6: When You Feel God is Angry with You

Psalm 6 is an individual lament Psalm, with elements of a penitential Psalm, written by David. A penitential psalm is a psalm of repentance (32, 38, 51, 102, 130, 143). In this case, the sin is not known. In this psalm, David feels God is angry with him (6:1).

Plea for Relief David pleads, "O Lord, do not rebuke me in Your anger nor chasten me in Your hot displeasure" (6:1). Although the specifics are not known, what is clear from this psalm is that David had sinned. God was angry and was disciplining him. David pleads for relief (6:1), mercy, and healing (6:2). Not all weakness and sickness are a result of God's chastening, but that is one form it can take (1 Cor. 11:31).

Prayer for Deliverance (6:4-5) Facing death, David gives two reasons why God should deliver him: 1) God's mercy and 2) God's praise so that David can praise God in this life.

Psalm 6:5, "For in death there is no remembrance of You; in the grave who will give You thanks," has been used to support the idea of "soul sleep." That is not a Scriptural concept (Eccl. 12:7; Lk. 16:19-31; 2 Cor. 5:8; Phil 1:23). In the context of Psalm 6, David is simply saying, "If you save me, spare me, I'll praise you. If you don't, I won't be able to thank you for deliverance now or after death for the simple reason that you didn't deliver me." "Only the living can publicly give thanks to God here on earth" (Ryrie Study Bible).

Lament Over Illness (6:6-7) David cried all night (6:6). His bed became a swimming pool ("I made my bed swim"). He sighed and sobbed so much he was worn out and weary (6:7). Part of the problem was his enemies (6:7).

Warning to His Enemies (6:8-10) Assured that God would answer his prayer, David tells his enemies to depart from him (6:8-9). Jesus quotes part of Psalm 6:8 in the Sermon on the Mount (Mt. 7:23). On the Day of Judgment, He will tell sinners (His enemies) to depart from Him, as David told his enemies to leave his presence.

David also declares, "Let all my enemies be ashamed and greatly troubled. Let them turn back and be ashamed suddenly" (6:10). Who these enemies were and why they were David's enemies is not known, except that they were workers of iniquity (6:8). The Hebrew word translated "ashamed" means "to be ashamed, disconcerted, disappointed" (BDB). They wanted his death; he says they will be disappointed. The Hebrew word translated "troubled" is the same one David used to describe the ailment in his bones (6:2) and soul (6:3). It means "to be disturbed, dismayed, even terrified" (see also 6:2). They wanted his death; he says let them be greatly dismayed.

Thus, David implores the Lord not to be angry but to be merciful and deliver him. He also urges his enemies to depart from him.

Summary: When you feel God is angry with you and when facing disease, distress, and death, plead God's mercy and trust Him to deliver you.

A point to ponder: No matter how dark your day is, no matter how diseased your body, no matter how depressed your spirit, plead God's mercy. He is merciful. Trust Him. "Beyond the trouble is the triumph, and beyond the gloom is the glory. Believe it" (Scroggie).

Psalm 7: When You Are Slandered

Psalm 7 is an individual lament psalm written by David. In it, David is dealing with being slandered (see the superscription; 7:14).

Plea for Deliverance (7:1-2) David addresses God as "Lord God" (7:1). "God" is used of Him as Creator. "Lord" (Yahweh) is His covenant name. "God" speaks of His power; "Lord" speaks of His love. David is going to the One who has the power to deliver him and is concerned to do it.

The Hebrew word translated "persecute" (7:1) means "pursue, persecute." Declaring his trust in the Lord to save him from those who pursue him, David pleads for deliverance (7:1), lest his enemies capture him and tear him in pieces like a lion does its prey (7:2). David, who was a shepherd, felt like a helpless lamb about to be slaughtered by a lion.

Proclamation of His Innocence (7:3-5) David proclaims that if he has iniquity in his hand (7:3), has repaid evil to those who are at peace with him (7:4), or has plundered his enemies without cause (7:4), let his enemies overtake him, trample him in the ground, and lay his honor in the dust (7:5). Apparently, Cush slanderously accused David of some sort of iniquity, injuring the innocent, and injustice. David is saying, "If I am guilty, let the Lord use my enemies to punish me with death and dishonor," which is another way of saying, "I am innocent."

Petition for Vindication (7:6-10) Since he is innocent and his adversaries are guilty, David assumes that God is angry with them (7:11). So he asks God to rise to intervene on his behalf (7:6), for the sake of His people (7:7), that is, to show them that He is a just Judge (7:11). David also asks God to judge him according to his integrity (7:8). He is innocent of the slander (7:3-4).

Since God tests the hearts and minds, David asks God to bring the wickedness of the wicked to an end and establish the righteous (7:9). David declares that God is his defense and God delivers the upright in heart (7:10).

Prayer for Judgment (7:11-16) After declaring that God is a just Judge who is angry with the wicked every day (7:11), David says that if the wicked do not turn to the Lord, He will judge them (7:12-13). Like a warrior preparing to battle, God will sharpen His sword, bend His bow (7:12), prepare instruments of death, and make fiery arrows (7:13).

Using the imagery of childbirth, David describes the wicked. They conceive trouble and give birth to iniquity and falsehood (7:14). They dig a pit and fall into it (7:15). The trouble and violence they conceive return upon their own head (7:16). The Hebrew word translated "trouble" in verse 14 is the same one that is translated "trouble" in verse 16. The wicked conceive trouble (7:14) and it returns on their head (7:15-16). Sin is self-destructive.

Promise to Praise God's Righteousness (7:17) Confident that the Lord will answer his prayer, David promises to sing the praises of His righteousness and to praise His name as "the Lord Most High" (7:17).

Summary: When slandered, trust God to deliver you and vindicate you by justly judging those who do evil to you.

A point to ponder: In Psalm 6, David said, "I'm guilty (6:1-2). In Psalm 7, David said, "I'm innocent" (7:3-4, 8). In Psalm 6, David pleads God's mercy (6:2, 4). In Psalm 7, David pleads God's justice (7:11). In both cases, David prayed. Learn a lesson about prayer from David. When you have sinned, plead God's mercy. When you are innocent, plead God's justice.

Psalm 8: When You Gaze at the Stars

Psalm 8 is a praise psalm written by David. It defies "divisions," except that it opens with praise (8:1-2) and closes with the same expression of praise (8:9). In between, David gazes into a night sky; he is gazing at the stars (8:3).

Praise (8:1-2) David says, "O LORD, our Lord, how excellent is Your name in all the earth, who have set Your glory above the heavens!" (8:1). David addresses God as "LORD" (Hebrew: Yahweh, the personal name of God), our Lord (Hebrew: Adonai, the sovereign over creation). He also calls God "our" Lord. He is the Lord of all mankind ("all the earth").

God's name is excellent all over the earth. The Hebrew word translated "excellent" means "wide, great, glorious, majestic." The preposition "above" should be translated "on" or "upon." This verse does not say God put His greatness "above" the heavens; His greatness and glory are displayed *in* the heavens. Because the heavens reveal God's greatness and glory, His name is great in the earth. Even the youngest children instinctively admire the greatness of God's power in creation, and by doing so, they silence the railings of the enemies of God (8:2). When the priests and scribes wanted to stop the people from praising Jesus with the words of Psalm 118:26, Jesus quoted Psalm 8:2 (see Mt. 21:16). The children get it when the adults don't.

Ponder (8:3-8) When David contemplated the heavens on a starry night (8:3), he asks, "What is man that You are mindful of him and the Son of man that You visit him?" (8:4). Here the word "man" refers to humanity. The greatness of the night sky reminded David of his smallness as compared to the universe. The Hebrew word for "man" here comes from a root meaning "weak, sick." Weak, frail, puny man seems like nothing before the vastness of the universe. David also asked, "What is ... the Son of man that You would visit Him?" This time, the Hebrew word used for "man" comes from the word for "ground." Seeing that man is the product of dust and dirt, why should a great God like the Creator of the universe visit (Hebrew: "attend to") him?

This part of the question reveals that the inquirer had more information beyond what was learned from creation. The one reflecting on a starry sky now has a Bible in his hand. He knows who the Creator is (see "LORD" in 8:1) and that the Creator pays attention to man.

David explains (see "for" at the beginning of verse 5) that God has given humanity dignity. God made man "a little lower than the angels" and "crowned him with glory and honor" (8:5). The writer to the Hebrews uses this of Jesus (Heb. 2:9), but that does not mean that the subject of this psalm is Jesus. The author of Hebrews only *applies* these words to Jesus.

God has also given humanity dominion over the earth (8:6-8). God has not only made man a king (see "crown" in verse 5), He has given him a kingdom. He has made man ruler over the works of God's hands; He has put all things under man's feet. Twice in the New Testament, Paul applies these words to Jesus (1 Cor. 15:27 and Eph. 1:22). As the representative of the human race, Christ will do in the future what God originally intended when He gave Adam dominion over the earth.

Praise (8:9) David concludes with a repetition of verse 1, but now it is richer and fuller. God's name is great on the earth not only because of His glory, which is revealed in the heavens, but also because of His goodness which is extended to humanity.

Summary: When you gaze at the stars (creation), you should praise God for His greatness as revealed in the heavens and His goodness as revealed in His dealings with people.

A point to ponder: Praise God for His greatness and His goodness to people.

Psalm 9: When Praying About Your Problem

Psalm 9 is a praise psalm written by David. In the Hebrew text, Psalm 9 and Psalm 10 form an alphabetic acrostic (almost every verse begins with the succeeding letter of the Hebrew alphabet). The Greek translation of the Old Testament (the Septuagint) combines them, but the Hebrew text and the English translations make them two separate psalms. In Psalm 9, David is praying about his trouble (9:13).

Praise (9:1-12) David resolves to praise the Lord (9:1-2). He says "I will" four times in the first two verses. He will praise God wholeheartedly, publicly proclaim His marvelous works, rejoice in Him and sing praises to His name.

Addressing the Lord, David rehearses God's righteous judgment of his enemies in the past (9:3-5). David's enemies have fallen (9:3) because the Lord judged them (9:4). The Lord has rebuked the nations, destroyed the wicked, and blotted out their names forever (9:5).

Speaking directly to his enemies, David tells them that their destructions are forever finished. They have destroyed cities, but their memory has perished (9:6).

Then David exalts the Lord (9:7-10). In contrast to David's enemies whose destruction is forever, the Lord will endure forever (9:7a). The Lord has prepared His throne for judgment (9:7b). The Lord will judge the world in righteousness, administer judgment for the people in uprightness (9:8), and will be a refuge for the oppressed in times of trouble (9:9). The Hebrew word translated "refuge" means "secure, height, retreat." In the Old Testament, people sought security by taking refuge in a fortress in high places. David said the Lord is his fortress.

Again addressing the Lord directly, David says, "And those who know Your name will put their trust in You; for You, Lord, have not forsaken those who seek You" (9:10). Obviously, people do not trust the Lord just because they know His name; they trust Him because they know something about Him, which His name represents. In this case, David knew the Lord as the God of Israel, faithful to His promises and people (see the last half of verse 9).

David exhorts the people to praise the Lord (9:11-12). Praise the Lord and publicly declare His deeds (9:11), because the Lord does not forget the cry of the humble; He remembers them and avenges their blood (9:12). Note, the Lord avenges (Deut. 32:35; Rom. 12:19).

Petition (9:13-20). David prays for mercy to be delivered from his present enemies, those who hate him (9:13). He promises to public praise the Lord when He does (9:14). He asks to be delivered from the "gates of death" (9:13) that he may praise God in the "gates" of the daughter of Zion, a term for the city of Jerusalem (9:14; Jerusalem was called God's daughter).

David describes the kind of judgment that God executes on his enemies (9:15-18). The wicked are snared in their own traps (9:16; see 7:15-16). They fall into the pit they dug for others and they get caught in the net they set for others (9:15). The wicked, all the nations that forget God, will be "turned into hell" (Hebrew: sheol, the grave; 9:17), because God will not forget the needy and the expectations of the poor will not perish forever (9:18).

David closes the psalm by asking God to arise, not to let man prevail, to let them be judged (9:19), and to put them in fear so "that the nations may know themselves to be but men" (9:20).

Summary: When praying about your problems, begin by praising God for His just judgments in the past.

A point to ponder: Those who know the Lord's faithfulness trust Him (9:10).

Psalm 10: When the Wicked Seem to be Winning

Psalm 10 is an individual lament psalm probably written by David. In the Hebrew text, Psalms 9 and 10 are an alphabetic acrostic (almost every verse begins with the succeeding letter of the Hebrew alphabet). The Greek translation of the Old Testament (the Septuagint) combines them, but the Hebrew text and the English translations make them two separate psalms. In Psalm 10, David sees the wicked winning (10:5).

The Problem: The Wicked (10:1-11) David asks why the Lord is standing off and hiding in a time of trouble (10:1) when, in pride, the wicked persecute the poor (Hebrew: "weak;" 10:2). He asks that the wicked be caught in the plot he devises (10:2; see 7:15-16, 9:15-16). Even though the psalmist doesn't understand why, he prays and puts his request before the Lord.

The wicked man boasts of his desires, blesses the greedy, and renounces the Lord (10:3). In his pride, the wicked does not seek God; God is in none of his thoughts (10:4; Hebrew: "purposes"). The wicked man prospers, but God's judgments are out of his sight and he sneers at his enemies (10:5). The wicked man says, "I shall not be moved; I shall never be in adversity" (10:6). The mouth of the wicked is full of cursing, deceit, and opposition and under his tongue is trouble and iniquity (10:7).

In other words, the wicked man is proud, boastful, greedy, self-sufficient, and a rejecter of God, out of whose mouth comes cursing, deceit, oppression, trouble, and iniquity.

The wicked lurks in secret places to murder the innocent and fixes his eyes on the helpless (10:8). Like a lion, the wicked secretly waits to catch the poor and like a fisherman, he draws the poor in his net (10:9), so that the helpless may fall by his strength (10:10). The wicked says in his heart, "God has forgotten; He hides His face and will never see (10:11). The reason the wicked practice their wickedness is they do not believe that God will hold them accountable (see 10:13).

Prayer for Destruction (10:12-15) The psalmist asks the Lord to arise, lift up his hand, and not forget the humble (10:12). He also asks why wicked people renounce God and why the wicked man says God will not hold him accountable (10:13).

Pointing out that the Lord observes the trouble, the psalmist requests God to repay it because the helpless commit themselves to Him and the Lord is the helper of the fatherless (10:14). The problem is not that the Lord is unaware of what the wicked are doing or that He does not care.

So the psalmist asks that the Lord to break the arm of the wicked, seeking out his wickedness until there is none to be found (10:15). The expression "break the arm" means "break his power."

Praise of God (10:16-18) The psalmist proclaims that the Lord is King forever and, gazing into the future, declares that the nations have perished out of His land (10:16). The Lord is in control! The Lord has heard the desire of the humble, prepared their hearts, and listened to their prayer to do justice to the fatherless and oppressed that the "man of the earth" may oppress no more (10:17-18).

Summary: When you see the wicked prosper and persecute others, pray for their destruction, and praise the Lord for His sovereignty, answered prayer, and justice.

A point to ponder: When you do not understand why God allows wickedness (see "why" in verses 1 and 13), plead your case before the Lord and praise Him for His sovereignty, justice, and answer prayer.

Psalm 11: When Your Very Foundation is Shaken

Psalm 11 is a psalm of trust written by David. In it, David feels that his very foundation is shaken (11:3).

Counsel to Flee (11:1-3) David begins by saying he will trust the Lord (11:1a). His advisors are telling him that he should flee as a bird to the mountain (11:1b), because the wicked bend their bow and load it with an arrow that they may shoot the upright (11:2). Because David's life is in danger, he is being told to flee. Those giving him this advice view him as a helpless bird flying to a mountain for protection. These advisors add, "If the foundations are destroyed, what can the righteous do?" (11:3). The foundations are the foundations of society, law and order, justice and righteousness.

David is saying he will flee to the Lord for protection. This may be during the time that Saul sought to slay David (1 Sam. 18:11, 19:10). Fleeing the physical danger may be a wise move, but trusting flight for protection is not wise. The real protection is in the Lord. The nation's foundation may be crumbling, but the believer's foundation is the Lord. So, when facing physical danger, even the destruction of society, trust the Lord.

Confidence in the Lord (11:4-7) At this point, David turns his attention to the Lord.

The Lord is in His Temple, sitting on His throne, watching the sons of men (11:4). The Lord is in control and is aware of the plight of His people.

The Lord tests the righteous and hates the wicked, who practice violence (11:5). The Lord is not idle; He tests the righteous to see if they will trust Him. In the meantime, He hates the wicked, who would harm the righteous.

The Lord will rain coals, fire, brimstone, and a burning wind on the wicked (11:6). The Lord hates what the wicked are doing and will judge them like He did Sodom and Gomorrah (Gen. 19:24).

The Lord will judge the wicked because He is righteous, loves righteousness, and sees the upright (11:7). The Lord seeing the upright indicates the Lord views them with affection and favor.

Summary: When your foundation is shaken, trust the Lord to judge your enemies and protect you.

A point to ponder: When society is crumbling and the prophets of doom advise us to take drastic measures to protect ourselves, remember that the Lord is in control and will judge the wicked and care for those who trust Him.

Psalm 12: When You Live Amid Vile Speech

Psalm 12 is an individual lament psalm written by David. In it, David is living amid vile speech (12:2).

A Plea for Deliverance (12:1-4) David begins with the cry, "Help, Lord, for the godly man ceases! For the faithful disappear from among the sons of men" (12:1). Because of the actions of the wicked, it seems to David as if the godly and the faithful will disappear from the earth. That is hyperbole, but it is the way David felt.

With "flattering lips" and a "double heart," the wicked speak "idly" (12:2). The Hebrew word translated "idly" means "emptiness, vanity, worthless" and is used here for "falsehood, lies" (see "falsehood" in the NASB and "lies" in the NIV). What they say is flattering, but they are speaking falsehood. David asks for help (12:1) because he lives amidst vile speech.

David also pleads with the Lord to "cut off all flattering lips" and "the tongue that speaks proud things" (12:3). He describes the wicked as saying, "With our tongues, we will prevail; our lips are our own. Who is lord over us?" (12:4). Because they do not submit to any authority, including God, the wicked think they can say anything they want. They imagine they can flatter, lie, and deceive with impunity. David pleads with the Lord to put an end to these arrogant men. Their root problem is pride.

A Promise of Deliverance (12:5) The Lord says that "the oppression of the poor" and "the sighing of the needy" will cause Him to "arise" and set them in the safety for which they yearn (12:5).

A Proclamation of God's Power (12:6-8) Having just recorded what the Lord says (12:5), David proclaims, "The words of the Lord are pure, like silver tried in a furnace of earth, purified seven times" (12:6). Unlike the words of the wicked, the words of the Lord are pure, that is, they are not mixed with lies and falsehood.

Psalm 12:7 says, "You will keep them, O Lord, You shall preserve them from this generation forever." In the Hebrew text, the word "them" in the phrase "preserve them" is in the singular and should be translated "he." Therefore, this verse is a reference to the poor and needy (12:5) rather than the Word of God (12:6). God says He will preserve the needy and the poor and His words are not mixed with falsehood, not only in David's day but in every day forever.

David concludes, "The wicked prowl on every side when vileness is exalted among the sons of men" (12:8). The Hebrew word translated "vileness" means "worthlessness." When vileness and worthlessness are exalted, the wicked prowl to see what harm they can do. The problem in this psalm is not just lies against an individual; it is an environment permeated with falsehood, lies, and deception.

Summary: When you live amid vile speech (an environment where lies and liars abound), remember that the Word of God is pure, and the God of the Word preserves the godly.

A point to ponder: If you live in an atmosphere of worthless words of lies, deceptions, false flattery, and cursing, think about things that are true, pure, and praiseworthy (Phil. 4:8) and seek God's help (12:1) to be preserved (12:7) from the world of worthless words.

Psalm 13: When You Feel Forsaken by God

Psalm 13 is an individual lament psalm written by David. From the psalm itself, it is apparent that David had a severe problem; he prayed, and God did nothing. The nature of the problem is not known, but David felt as if God had forsaken Him (13:1).

David Lamented (13:1-2) In the first two verses, David asks "how long" four times. He says, "How long, O LORD? Will You forget me forever? How long will You hide Your face from me?" (13:1). The figure of forgetfulness indicates a lack of help. The expression "to hide the face" means "to withhold favor." David felt like God had withheld His favor, forgotten him, forsaken him, and that this experience would last forever.

David continues, "How long shall I take counsel in my soul, having sorrow in my heart daily?" (13:2a). When God did nothing, David turned to his own counsel and asked how long he would have to do that. The Hebrew word rendered "sorrow" means "grief." He says he experienced grief daily. Repeated failure produced repeated grief.

David concludes, "How long will my enemy be exalted over me?" (13:2b). As if all that was not enough, his enemy was winning!

David Prayed (13:3-4) David asks God to consider him (the opposite of hiding His face) and hear him (the opposite of "forget me in verse 1), lest he die (13:3a). He asks God to "lighten my eyes" (13:3b). "Lighten my eyes" is not a reference to enlightenment. It refers to the dimness of the eyes produced by extreme weakness or approaching death (see 1 Sam 14:27, 29, where Jonathan, after being reduced to extreme faintness, partook of food and is said to have had his eyes enlightened). So, the prayer is for renewed strength. David is saying, "If you do not hear and heed my plea, I will die." In his case, that was probably literally true.

The second reason David wants God to answer is, "Lest my enemy says, 'I have prevailed against him;' lest those who trouble me rejoice when I am moved" (13:4). David is saying, "If you don't answer, they will compose comedies out of my tragedies."

David Trusted (13:5-6) Abruptly, David exclaims, "But I have trusted in Your mercy" (13:5a). The Hebrew word translated "mercy" means "goodness, kindness, lovingkindness." No matter what happens or what appears to be happening, David says, "I will trust the Lord. He is kind and merciful; He will do what is best for me."

This complete confidence is further expressed in the phrase, "My heart shall rejoice in Your salvation" (13:5b). This is a deliberate, conscious choice. Then David clears his throat for a song: "I will sing to the LORD because He has dealt bountifully with me" (13:6). This does not mean the problem has been solved. Although at the moment it appeared God had forgotten and had forsaken him, David knew that God had abundantly blessed him in the past. So, even though he is sobbing with sorrow at the moment, he is confident that he will sing again because God will bless him again. Notice he says he will sing *to* the Lord. He will praise God in song.

Summary: When you feel forsaken by God, keep praying, trusting, and praising.

A point to ponder: Someone has said, "Resolve never to be dumb while God is deaf." Remember His past blessings. If you trust God in the dark, He will change your "midnight" into music.

Psalm 14: When You Are People Watching

Psalm 14 is a wisdom psalm written by David. Except for slight changes in verses 5 and 6, Psalm 14 is identical to Psalm 53. In it, David is people-watching (14:1-3).

The Sinfulness of the Human Race (14:1-3) "The fool said in his heart, 'There is no God,' they are corrupt, they have done abominable works, there is none who does good" (14:1; see also 53:1). Although the psalm begins by speaking about the fool, it becomes obvious that it is about the whole human race (see "none," in verse 1 and "the children of men" in verse 2, etc.). Because sinners do not believe there is a God (or they do not seek Him, 14:2) and because they are morally corrupt, they do abominable works, such as devouring God's people (14:4). None do the good that is acceptable by God.

The Lord looks down from heaven to see if He can find any who understand His truth or seek Him (14:2). He discovers that all have turned aside from His will and ways and become corrupt: "there is none who does good, no, not one" (14:3). Not even God can find an exception to the sinfulness of the human race! Paul cites these verses in Romans 3:10-12 to demonstrate the universal sinfulness of people.

To sum up, people on this planet are not good, are morally corrupt, do abominable works, do not understand God's truth or seek Him, and have turned aside from His will. The fool says, "There is no God;" the rest live as if there is no God.

The Judgment of Sinners (14:4-6) God asks, "Have all the workers of iniquity no knowledge, who eat my people as they eat bread, and do not call on the Lord?" (14:4). Those who do not call on the Lord are workers of iniquity who devour God's people like eating bread.

Psalm 14:5 says, "There, they are in great fear, for God is with the generation of the righteous." The word "there" is a reference to the judgment. Because sinners have not called on the Lord (14:4) and because God is with the righteous, not the sinners (14:5), they will have great fear when they stand before God.

Psalm 14:6 says, "You shame the counsel of the poor, but the Lord is his refuge." Those who disregard God have no regard for the poor. The Lord is their refuge.

The Longing for the Kingdom (14:7) David concludes, "Oh, that the salvation of Israel would come out of Zion! When the Lord brings back the captivity of His people, let Jacob rejoice in Israel be glad" (14:7). David longs for the "salvation of Israel," that is, the deliverance of Israel from sinners. He longs for God to "bring back the captivity of his people," which is a longing for the establishment of the messianic kingdom on the earth. Zion, another name for Jerusalem, will be the capital of the kingdom. When the kingdom comes, God will judge sinners who devour His people (14:4) and Israel will rejoice (14:7). God is their refuge now (14:6) and will completely deliver them later (14:7).

Summary: When you are people watching, it is obvious that they do not know God, they are sinners, and they do abominable things, but God will judge them and be a refuge for His people now and completely deliver them later.

A point to ponder: When you see (or experience) sinners harming others (or you), remember that God will judge them and be a refuge to His people now, as well as completely deliver them from the very presence of sinners when He establishes His kingdom.

Psalm 15: When You Seek God's Fellowship

Psalm 15 is a wisdom psalm written by David. In it, David is seeking God's fellowship (15:1).

The Questions (15:1) David asks, "LORD, who may abide in Your tabernacle? Who may dwell in Your holy hill?" These two questions are two ways of asking the same thing (this type of construction is called synonymous parallelism). The Tabernacle sat on the holy hill of Zion, a part of Jerusalem (see 2:6, 3:4). It was a tent where the glory of God dwelt. David asks who may abide (dwell) with God in His tent. No one actually "lived" in the Tabernacle, but David asks, "Who may come live with You in Your tent? Who may fellowship with You?"

The Answer (15:2-5) The answer lists eleven characteristics of the person who can have intimate fellowship with the Lord.

1. The person who walks uprightly (15:2a). "Walk" refers to how a person lives. The Hebrew word translated "uprightly" means "integrity."

2. The person who works righteousness (15:2b). Those who "work righteousness" do what is right.

3. The person who speaks the truth in their heart (15:2c). To speak the truth in the heart means to speak sincerely. Such a person does not think one thing and say another.

4. The person who does not backbite with their tongue (15:3a). The Hebrew word translated "backbite" means "slander."

5. The person who does not do evil to their neighbor (15:3b). Doing evil to others is bad; doing evil to someone close, such as a neighbor, is worse.

6. The person who does not take up a reproach against his friend (15:3c). This refers to those who criticize their friends.

7. The person whose eyes despise a vile person (15:4a). The Hebrew word translated "vile" means "rejected." This person rejects those God rejects.

8. The person who honors those who fear the LORD (15:4b). Fearing the Lord involves trust, reverence, and, yes, fear. Those who fear the Lord are to be honored.

9. The person who swears to their own hurt and does not change (15:4c). This is about those who take an oath and keep it, even if it costs them.

10. The person who does not put out their money at usury (15:5a). Charging interest on a loan to a brother was forbidden in the Mosaic Law (Lev. 25:35-37).

11. The person who does not take a bribe against the innocent (15:5b). The Mosaic Law pronounced a curse on anyone taking a bribe to harm an innocent person (Deut. 27:25).

The people who do these things shall never be moved (15:5c). They will be stable.

Summary: When you seek God's fellowship, know that those who live lives of integrity and righteousness in deeds, speech, attitude, and finances will be stable and fit to sit in God's tent, fellowshipping with Him.

In short, obedient people are "at home" with the Lord. In the words of Jesus, "If anyone loves Me, he will keep My word; and My Father will love him, and We will come to him and make Our home with him" (Jn. 14:23). Anyone can come to the Lord anytime for cleansing, mercy, etc., but the Lord is looking for obedient believers with whom He can have fellowship.

A point to ponder: Are you sitting in God's tent fellowshipping with Him, or do you occasionally poke your head in the tent?

Psalm 16: When You Are Facing Death

Psalm 16 is a psalm of trust written by David referencing the Messiah. In this psalm, David faces death (16:1), but the details of the situation are unknown.

Trust for Present Preservation (16:1-8). David asks God to preserve him because he has put his trust in Him (16:1). The Hebrew word translated "trust" means to "seek refuge." David asks the Lord to preserve him because he seeks refuge in Him. Verse 1 is the sum of the whole Psalm. When facing death, David trusted the Lord. He adds that he has told the Lord, "You are my Lord, my goodness is nothing apart from You" (16:2). At this point, David reviews his life as evidence that he is trusting the Lord and his goodness is from the Lord (16:2-8).

David delights in the saints, the "excellent ones," on the earth (16:3).

David dislikes idolaters (16:4). He says he would not drink their offering of blood nor take up the names on his lips of those who hasten after other gods, whose sorrows will be multiplied (16:4).

David declares that the Lord is his inheritance, the Lord has maintained his lot in life (16:5), and lines have fallen to him in pleasant places (a figure of speech taken from the allotment of the land after the conquest), so that he has a good inheritance (16:6). David says he will bless the Lord who has given him counsel (16:7a). Having received the counsel of the Lord, his heart instructs him in the night season (16:7b). In addition, David says he has set the Lord always before him and because the Lord is at his right hand he will not be moved (16:8). He is stable (see 15:5).

Although facing death, David trusts the Lord (16:1). The Lord is his inheritance (16:5-6). He blesses the Lord who has given him counsel (16:7). He has set the Lord before him (16:8).

Joy for Future Preservation (16:9-11) David concludes (see "therefore" in verse 9) that because he has trusted the Lord in this life (16:1-8), he can rejoice and have hope that God will preserve him in the next life (16:9). As he explains (see "for" in verse 10a), the Lord will not leave his soul in the grave (16:10a).

The second half of verse 10 says, "Nor will you allow your holy one to see corruption." David cannot refer to himself because his body saw corruption (in the grave after his death). Furthermore, for a person to die and his body not experience corruption means he was resurrected. Therefore, the expression "Your Holy One" refers to the Messiah. The Midrash, a compilation of Jewish interpretations of the Scripture, indicates this is a reference to the Messiah. In Acts 2:25-28, Peter quotes Psalm 16:8-11, saying it refers to the Messiah (Acts 2:30). In Acts 2:31, Peter quotes Psalm 16:10 and says it was fulfilled in the resurrection of Jesus. In Acts 13:35, Paul quotes Psalm 16:10 and says that David saw corruption (Acts 13:36), "but He whom God has raised up saw no corruption" (Acts 13:37). Psalm 16:10 is a prophecy of the resurrection of Jesus Christ!

David concludes, "You will show me the path of life; in Your presence *is* fullness of joy; at Your right hand *are* pleasures forevermore" (16:11). David is confident that the Lord will preserve him from death now (see "path of life") and when he is in God's presence there will be the fullness of joy and pleasure forever.

Summary: When you are facing death, trust the Lord to preserve you now and rejoice that the Lord will preserve you in death and that the Lord will resurrect His Holy One.

A point to ponder: We need to learn to trust the Lord in this life, delighting in the saints, detesting idolatry, and blessing the Lord for His benefits so that when we face death, we will have learned how to rejoice in the Lord.

Psalm 17: When You Face Vicious Enemies

Psalm 17 is a lament psalm written by David. Although many psalms are prayers, only five are designated as prayers (17, 86, 90, 102, 142). In Psalm 17, David faces vicious enemies (17:9-12).

Plea for Vindication (17:1-5) David begins by asking God to hear his prayer (see "hear," "attend," and "give ear" in verse 1). He claims he has a just cause, not from deceitful lips (17:1). Therefore, he asks God to look on that which is upright and vindicate him (17:2).

David tells the Lord that He has tested him and found nothing because he had purposed that his mouth would not transgress (17:3). By God's Word, David says he has been kept from the path of the destroyer (17:4), his steps have held to God's path, and he has not slipped (17:5; NASB). David is not claiming he is sinless; he is claiming that in his present conflict with evil people, he has done nothing worthy of their opposition, and, therefore, he asks God to vindicate him.

Plea for Protection (17:6-12) Again, David pleads with the Lord to hear his prayer ("hear me," "incline your ear," and "hear my speech" in verse 6). David asks the Lord to show His lovingkindness as He does when He saves those who trust in Him from those who rise up against them (17:7). He asks the Lord to keep him as the apple (pupil) of His eye and under the shadow of His wings (17:8). Because his enemy has set their eyes on him (17:11), David asks the Lord to keep His eye on him and protect him like a bird protects its young under its wings.

At this point in the psalm, David describes the wicked people who oppose him. He says they are vicious enemies (17:9); they have closed up their fat (insensitive, callous) hearts (17:10), and speak proudly (17:10). They have surrounded David and set their eyes against him, determined to kill him (17:11). They are like a lion lurking in a secret place, eager to tear his prey (17:12).

Plea for Deliverance (17:13-15) David asks the Lord to arise, confront, and cast down his enemies so that he might be delivered from them (17:13). The Lord may use humans to do this (17:14), but it will be by His sword (17:13).

Again, David describes the wicked. They live only for this life, to fill their bellies with hidden treasure, that is, treasure hidden from others, and they have a lot of it because they can leave their possessions to their children (17:14).

David concludes, "As for me, I will see your face and righteousness; I should be satisfied when I awake in your likeness" (17:15). In contrast to his wicked enemies who live only for this world, David will be satisfied with his relationship with the Lord. "Awake" has been interpreted to refer to the next day in David's life (God will protect him) and as a reference to the resurrection. Instead of the transitory treasure of the wicked, David anticipates an eternal reward of being resurrected to spend eternity in God's presence and be like Him.

Summary: When you face vicious enemies who want to kill you, plead your case before the Lord and ask the Lord to vindicate and deliver you.

A point to ponder: When you have a just cause, do not hesitate to argue your righteous behavior before the Lord.

Psalm 18: When God Delivers You

Psalm 18 is a victory song written by David. With slight variations, it is recorded in 2 Samuel 22. The variations are probably due to changes made when it was adapted for use in Israel's public worship. It is the fourth longest psalm in the Psalter. In it, David speaks of the Lord delivering Him from all his enemies and from Saul (see the superscription; 18:4; 17; 19).

The Lord's Person (18:1-3) David says the Lord is his strength (18:1), his rock, fortress, deliverer, shield, horn (power) of salvation, and stronghold (18:2). Therefore, David says he will love the Lord (18:1), trust the Lord (18:2), and call on the Lord, who is worthy to be praised (18:3). He concludes, "So shall I be saved from my enemies" (18:3).

The Lord's Deliverance (18:4-19) When David was facing death, he was afraid (18:4). He felt like a wall of water was coming at him (see "floods" in 18:4) and animal traps were set in the field where he was walking (see "snares" in 18:5), but he called upon the Lord (18:6).

The Lord was angry (18:7). He shook the earth (18:7). Devouring fire came out of His mouth (18:8). He descended from heaven (18:9) with high winds (18:10), torrential rain (18:11), hailstones (18:12), thunder (18:13), and lightning (18:14). He rescued David like a lifeguard snatching a drowning man from the water (18:16). The point of this poetic language is that the Lord will move heaven and earth to deliver His servant. David proclaims, "He delivered me from my strong enemy, from those who hate me, for they were too strong for me" (18:17) and "He delivered me because He delighted in me" (18:19). The Lord delights in those who serve Him (David is called "the servant of the Lord" in the superscription).

The Lord's Blessing (18:20-50) David declares that because he faithfully followed the Lord (18:20-23), the Lord, faithful to His word (18:30), blessed him (18:24-27). The Lord shows mercy to the merciful (18:25). He saves (delivers) the humble (18:27; Constable says, "He saves the humble and humbles those who think they can save themselves"). He is a shield to all who trust in Him (18:30).

David extols the Lord, who is his rock (18:31), strength (18:32-33), and teacher (18:34). Because the Lord enabled him (18:35-36), David pursued his enemies, overtook them, and destroyed them (18:37). They fell under his feet (18:38) because God gave him strength (18:39-40). When they prayed, the Lord did not answer them (18:41). David was able to cast them out like dirt in the streets (18:42). David was even able to conquer surrounding nations (18:43-45; 2 Sam. 8). Thus David proclaims, "The Lord lives! Blessed be my rock! Let the God of my salvation be exalted" (18:46).

Because the Lord has delivered him from his enemies (18:47-48), David says, "Therefore I will give thanks to you, O Lord, among the Gentiles and sing praises to your name." David concludes, "Great deliverance He gives to His king, and shows mercy to His anointed, to David and his descendants forever" (18:50).

Psalm 18:43-50 has messianic implications. While these verses are about David, they picture what the Messiah will do. Psalm 18 ends, declaring that God will show mercy to His anointed, David, and his descendants forever. In Romans 15:9, Paul quotes Psalm 18:49 to show that because of the work of Christ, Gentiles would glorify God for His mercy.

Summary: When God delivers you, praise Him for what He is to you (strength, rock, fortress, etc.) and what He has done for you.

A point to ponder: Don't just generally say, "Praise the Lord for His blessings." *Be specific. Specifically,* name what He means to you and *specifically* describe what He has done for you.

Psalm 19: When You See God's Revelation

Psalm 19 is a wisdom psalm written by David. In it, David sees God's revelation of His glory in the world (19:1) and His will in His Word (19:7-9).

The Revelation of God in the World (1:1-6) David declares, "The heavens declare the glory of God and the firmament shows his handiwork" (19:1). The moon, the sun, and the stars declare God's glory. The firmament (the sky) shows God's work. The revelation of God in creation is continuous. Day after day, night after night, it reveals the knowledge of God (19:2). It is also universal. There is no language where its voice is not heard (19:3). It extends "to the end of the world" (19:4a).

Focusing on the sun as a specific illustration, David uses figures of speech to describe it. It is a traveler. It does not stay in one place; it lives in a tent (see "tabernacle" in 19:4b). It is like a bridegroom coming out of his chamber for his wedding (19:5a). The sun appears every morning full of joy. It is like a long-distance runner (19:5b-6). It runs from one end of the heaven to the other so that nothing is hidden from its heat. God's revelation is continuous and universal.

The Revelation of God in the Word (19:7-11) In verses 1-6, the psalmist uses the word "God," but in verses 7-11, he uses the word "Lord" (Yahweh), the personal name of God. The world reveals God's work; the Word reveals who He is.

In Psalm 19:7-9, David uses six terms for the Word (the law of the Lord, the statutes of the Lord, the commandment of the Lord, the fear of the Lord, and the judgments of the Lord) and gives six descriptions of it (perfect, sure, right, pure, clean, true and righteous). The Word is a perfect law, a sure testimony, right statutes, pure commandments, clean fear of the Lord, and true and righteous judgments. In other words, the Word is pure and sure.

In Psalm 19:7-9, David also indicates what the Word does. It converts the soul, makes wise the simple, rejoices the heart, enlightens the eyes, and endures forever. Note the progression: conversion, wisdom (growth), joy, maturity (enlightens the eyes).

Therefore, the Word is more desirable than gold (19:10a) and sweeter than honey (19:10b). It is valuable and delightful because it warns the servant of God and obeying it results in great reward (19:11). It is profitable and pleasurable. The progression includes conversion, wisdom (growth), joy, maturity, preservation, and reward.

The heavens reveal the work of God; the Word reveals the will of God.

The Response to God's Revelation (1:12-14) Having seen the glory of God in the world and the will of the Lord in the Word, David asks for three things: to be cleansed from errors (sins of ignorance) and secret (hidden) faults (19:12), to persevere from presumptuous (willful) sins (19:13; note the progression of the sins), and that his words and thoughts be acceptable to the Lord, who is his strength and redeemer (19:12).

Summary: When you see God's revelation of His glory in the world and His will in His Word, your response should be to ask God to cleanse you, keep you from sin, and give you strength for your words and thoughts to be acceptable in the sight of the One who redeemed you.

A point to ponder: What we see activates our appetite. We should contemplate the revelation of God in the world and in His Word to activate our appetite to know Him and please Him.

Psalm 20: When You Are Facing a Battle

Psalm 20 is a royal psalm written by David. In this psalm, David is facing a battle (20:1).

The Desire of the People (20:1-5) In the first five verses, the people (see "we" in verse 5) express their desire for the king ("you" throughout the five verses refers to the king). The king is about to enter battle ("the day of trouble" in verse 1 refers to the day of battle).

The people say, "May the Lord answer you" (20:1a), "May God defend you" (20:1b), "May He send you help and strength" (20:2), "May He remember and accept your offerings" (20:3), "May He grant your heart's desire and fulfill all your purpose" (20:4), and "May the Lord fulfill all your petitions" (20:5). The people pledge that they will rejoice in the king's salvation (deliverance) and will set up banners (20:5). Anticipating victory, the people say they will rejoice and set up banners in celebration.

The Declaration of the King (20:6-8) At this point in the psalm, instead of the people speaking (see "we" in verse 5), the king speaks (see "I" in verse 6). The king responds to the people, saying, "I know the Lord saves His anointed; He will answer from His holy heaven with the saving stre ngth of His right hand" (20:6). As is usually the case in the Psalms, salvation is a reference to deliverance. David is confident the Lord will deliver him and give him victory in battle.

Psalm 20:7-8 continues the theme of confidence that the Lord will deliver. The question is, "Who is speaking?" Some commentators claim that the king is still speaking (see NKJV Study Bible), while others contend that the people are speaking again (see Ryrie Study Bible). Some say it is a choir of the king and the people (Barnes). The continuation of the theme of confidence suggests that the speaker is David. He is expressing his confidence and the confidence of the people.

At any rate, the point is that some people trust in chariots and horses, the ancient weapons of war (20:7a), but the faithful will "remember the name of the Lord our God" (20:7b), meaning that they will remember to trust the Lord. Those who trust in human means for victory will bow down and fall (20:8a), but those who trust the Lord will arise and stand upright (20:8b).

The Prayer of the People (20:9) The psalm ends with, "Save, Lord! May the King answer us when we call" (20:9). In this verse, the "King" is a reference to the Lord. The people are asking the Lord to answer their prayer and deliver David.

Summary: When facing a battle, have other people pray for you and trust the Lord, rather than human means, for victory.

A point to ponder: Our battles are not military battles but battles nonetheless. When we face battles, we tend to trust our ingenuity; if we pray, we pray alone. In those situations, we should enlist other people's prayers and personally pray and trust the Lord. Matthew Henry said, "The prayer of others for us must be desired, not to supersede, but to second our own for ourselves."

Psalm 21: When Your Battle is Won

Psalm 21 is a royal psalm written by David. Psalm 20 was written *before* the battle; Psalm 21 was composed *after* the battle. In Psalm 20, the people spoke first. Then the king spoke. In Psalm 21, the king speaks first. Then, the people respond. In Psalm 21, David has won the battle (21:1).

The Praise of the King (21:1-7) Having been victorious in battle, David says he will have joy in the Lord's strength and greatly rejoice in the Lord's salvation (deliverance from his enemies) (21:1). He goes on to say that the Lord has given him his heart's desire and has not withheld from him the request of his lips (21:2). In Psalm 20, the people desired that God would grant to David his heart's desire (20:4). David now acknowledges that the Lord has done that.

David lists the blessings of God, which include goodness and a crown of gold, that is, his kingship (21:3), life, that is, length of days (21:4), deliverance, honor, and majesty (21:5), being blessed and exceedingly glad (21:6), lovingkindness (see "mercy"), and stability (21:7). David says that he received these blessings because he trusted in the Lord, who was merciful (21:7).

The Proclamation of the People (21:8-12) Anticipating the king's future blessings, the people proclaim the ultimate defeat of the king's enemies (the enemies of the king are the enemies of the Lord). They tell the king his right hand (a figure for power) will find his enemies, that is, those that hate him (21:8). In His wrath, the Lord will swallow them up and fire will devour them (21:9). Their descendants will be destroyed from the earth (21:10). The reason (see "for" in verse 11) that they will be destroyed is because they intended evil against the king and devised a plot which they were not able to perform (21:11). The king will make them turn their back (retreat) and string his bow with arrows toward their faces, that is, he will defeat them (21:12). Psalm 21:8-12 is primarily about David, but prefigures the ultimate victory of the Messiah, the son of David.

The Praise of the People (21:13) The psalm concludes with the people saying, "Be exalted, O Lord, in your own strength! We will sing and praise your power" (21:13). Realizing that it was the Lord's strength that gave victory this time, they anticipate praising the Lord for future victories because of His power.

Summary: When your battle is won, you should acknowledge that your strength, victory, and blessings come from the Lord, and you should anticipate future victories and praise God's power.

A point to ponder: When we are victorious spiritually, it is because we have trusted the Lord, not because we are smart or powerful, but because the Lord is powerful and gracious. Also, past victories should make us anticipate future victories. After all, we should have learned to trust the Lord for strength and victory.

Psalm 22: When You Feel Abandoned by God

Psalm 22 is a lament psalm written by David. David describes his experience, but no recorded incident in his life fits all the details of this psalm. The New Testament says at least some of the details were fulfilled in the experience of Jesus (Mt. 27:35; Heb. 2:12). It is one of the most quoted psalms in the New Testament. In it, David feels abandoned by God (22:1).

David's Perplexity (22:1-10) David feels abandoned by God (22:1-2). He cries, "My God, My God, why have You forsaken Me? *Why are You so* far from helping Me, *and from* the words of My groaning?" (22:1). On the cross, Jesus quotes the first half of this verse (Mt. 27:46; Mk. 15:34). Three things compound David's perplexity: 1) God is silent, even though he prayed day and night (22:2), 2) God is sovereign (22:3), and 3) God answered others (22:4-5).

David is mocked (22:6-8). David felt worthless (see "worm" in verse 6). People reproached him and despised him (22:6) and ridiculed him (22:7), saying, "He trusted in the Lord, let Him rescue him" (22:8; see the experience of Jesus in Mt. 27:39-44; 27:27-31).

David trusts the Lord (22:9-10). He has trusted the Lord all of his life (22:9-10).

David's Plea (22:11-21) David pleads with the Lord not to be far away because trouble is near and there is none to help (22:11). In vivid figurative language, David describes his plight (22:12-18). His enemies are like vicious bulls that surround him (22:12), like hungry lions poised to attack (22:13). His strength is gone (22:14-15). He was at death's door (22:15). His enemies pierced his hands and his feet (22:16), which may be figurative here but describes the literal experience of the Messiah (Zech. 12:10), Jesus (Lk. 24:39-40; Jn. 20:27). People stared at his protruding bones (22:17). Seeing that he was about to die, they divided his clothes among themselves by casting lots (22:18; see Mt. 27:35; see also Mk. 15:24; Lk. 23:34; Jn. 19:24). David pleads with the Lord not to be far from him, to help him (22:19), to deliver him (22:20) and to save him (22:21). God answered David's prayer (22:21).

David's Praise (22:22-31) In response to the answered prayer, David declares that he will publicly praise the Lord to his brethren in the assembly (22:22). The book of Hebrews says Jesus spoke these words (Heb. 2:11-12). David invites all who know the Lord and all of Israel to praise the Lord (22:23), because He answers prayer (22:24). Again, David declares that he will praise God in the assembly (22:25). Then he turns his attention to the people in the congregation, encouraging them not to lose heart (22:26). There will come a day when people from all over the world will turn to the Lord (22:27), which will take place in the Kingdom when the Lord rules all nations (22:28-29). In the meantime, posterity will serve the Lord by telling the next generation about Him (22:30) and that generation will tell the next generation (22:30) what the Lord has done (22:31). The Lord answers prayer and rescues people. Therefore, He can be trusted.

Summary: When you feel abandoned by God and are being pursued almost to death, plead with God and publically praise Him when He answers your prayer. David's own experience foreshadowed the experience of Christ.

A point to ponder: When you are facing death's door and feel that God has abandoned you, plead with Him and trust Him to draw near and deliver you, and when He does, publicly praise Him.

Psalm 23: When the Lord is Your Shepherd

Psalm 23 is a psalm of trust written by David. The point of the psalm is stated in the first verse and is developed in the remainder of the psalm. In it, David declares that the Lord is his Shepherd (23:1).

The Person of the Shepherd (23:1) This well-known psalm begins with the famous words, "The Lord is my shepherd, I shall not want" (23:1). The figure of the shepherd was, no doubt, suggested by David's experience as a shepherd (1 Sam. 16:19). In this poem, he reverses roles, saying that the Lord is his Shepherd and he is a lamb. As his shepherd, the Lord meets all of David's needs so well that he can say, "I shall not want." This is the point of the entire psalm.

The Provisions of the Shepherd (23:2-6) The Shepherd meets various needs.

1. The Shepherd meets the physical need of the sheep (23:2): "He makes me to lie down in green pastures. He leads me beside the still waters" (23:2). The reference to "green pastures" suggests that David is speaking of God meeting his physical need for food. Lying down in a green pasture is a picture of abundant supply. The sheep is not only fed; he is full. Furthermore, the lamb lies in green pastures (plural), indicating that this abundant supply is not an isolated incident but a recurring event. Some say this is not a reference to the food supply but to peace, but the next statement about water supports the idea that physical needs were in David's mind (see Mt. 6:31-34; Phil. 4:20).

2. The Shepherd meets the spiritual need of the sheep (23:3): "He restores my soul. He leads me in the paths of righteousness for His name's sake" (23:3). Like sheep, believers tend to wander away. The shepherd leaves the ninety-nine to find and restore the wandering one. Once restored, the Shepherd guides the sheep in a path of righteousness for His namesake.

3. The Shepherd meets the emotional need of the sheep (23:4): "Yea, though I walk through the valley of the shadow of death, I will fear no evil, for You *are* with me; Your rod and Your staff, they comfort me" (23:4). The Hebrew word translated "shadow of death" means "deep shadow" and is used figuratively of distress or extreme danger. When faced with dangerous situations, the sheep have no fear because the Shepherd is with them. His rod and staff, instruments of protection, comfort them. David adds, "You prepare a table before me in the presence of my enemies. You anoint my head with oil; my cup runs over" (23:5). The Shepherd prepares a table, a place of peace and fellowship, in the very presence of the sheep's enemies. The Shepherd anoints the head of the sheep with oil, which was used to prevent rodents from harming the sheep.

4. The Shepherd meets the eternal need of the sheep (23:4): "Surely goodness and mercy shall follow me all the days of my life and I will dwell in the house of the LORD forever" (23:6). God's goodness and mercy shall follow the sheep in this life and provide a home with Him in the next. The Shepherd does this by dying for the sheep (Jn. 10:11). In the Old Testament, the sheep died for the shepherd, but in the New Testament, the Shepherd died for the sheep.

Summary: When the Lord is your shepherd, He meets your physical, spiritual, emotional, and eternal needs.

A point to ponder: David says, "The Lord is *my* shepherd." For this to work, the Lord must be *your* shepherd. Make Him your shepherd; take all your needs to Him (1 Pet. 5:7).

Psalm 24: When You Seek to Approach God

Psalm 24 is a royal psalm written by David. Psalm 15 asks, "Who may *abide* in your tabernacle? Who may dwell in your holy Hill?" (15:1, italics added). Psalm 24 asks, "Who may *ascend* into the hill of the Lord? Or who may stand in His holy place?" (24:3, italics added). The answer in Psalm 15 is a righteous person; the answer in Psalm 24 is a righteous person, but Psalm 24 adds that the King of Glory is coming. The occasion of Psalm 24 is unknown, but the content suggests that David composed this psalm when he brought the Ark of the Covenant to Jerusalem. At any rate, in this Psalm, the issue is approaching God (24:3).

The Affirmation of God's Ownership (24:1-2) David announces that the earth, all its fullness, and those who dwell in it belong to the Lord (24:1) because He established it upon the seas (24:2; Gen. 1:10). God owns everything because He made everything. He is the sovereign Lord.

The Answer Concerning Ascent (24:3-6) If God is Lord over all, who may approach Him? "Who may ascend unto the hill of the Lord? Or who may stand in His holy place? (24:3). The answer is, he who has clean hands, a pure heart, has not lifted up his soul to idols, nor sworn deceitfully (24:4). In other words, people who have right actions ("clean hands"), right motives ("a pure heart" and "has not lifted up his soul to idols"), and right speech ("nor sworn deceitfully"). Those approaching the Creator God require the right thoughts, words, and deeds. Idolatry disqualifies people for admission to God's presence.

Such people shall receive blessing from the Lord and righteousness from the God of their salvation (24:5). These are like Jacob; they are the ones who seek God (24:6). The chronological order is seeking God, obtaining the righteousness of God by faith (Gen. 15:6; Phil 3:9), and being blessed by God.

An Anthem to the King of Glory (24:7-10) The gates of Jerusalem are personified; their heads are bowed down. David tells them to lift up their heads and the doors are told to be lifted up because the King of Glory is coming in (24:7). In David's day, the presence of God (the King of Glory) was represented by the ark being carried into the Tabernacle. The King is coming, the King of Glory! This prefigures the coming of Christ to reign as King on the earth.

At this point, the psalmist asks, "Who is the King of glory?" (24:8a). The answer is He is "the Lord strong and mighty, the Lord mighty in battle" (24:8b). The coming King is the Lord Himself, that is, God. Jesus, of course, is both Lord (God) and coming King. Just before He comes, He will be victorious in battle (the Tribulation).

Again, the gates of Jerusalem are told to lift up their heads and the doors are told to be lifted up because the King of Glory is coming in (24:9). The repetition is for emphasis.

Again, David asks, "Who is the King of glory?" (24:10a). This time, the answer is, "The Lord of hosts, He is the King of Glory" (24:10b). The Lord of hosts (with an army) is the coming King of Glory.

Summary: When you seek to approach God, the Creator, the sovereign Lord, remember that the ones qualified to approach the King are the ones who have the right actions, attitudes, and speech.

A point to ponder: We should cleanse our hands and purify our hearts so that we may approach God now and be ready for the coming King.

Psalm 25: When You Need Forgiveness

Psalm 25 is a unique psalm written by David. It contains elements of a lament and penitential psalm, making it unique. With a few exceptions, it is an acrostic; each verse begins with successive Hebrew alphabet letters. In it, David needs forgiveness.

The Prayer of David (25:1-7) In the first part of this Psalm, David prays for three things.

David prays for protection (25:1-3). He lifts his soul to the Lord (25:1) and trusts the Lord to let him not be ashamed (disappointed) before his enemies, that is, that they not be allowed to triumph over him (25:2). Let those be ashamed who deal treacherously without cause (25:3).

David prays for guidance (25:4-5). He asks the Lord to show him His ways, to teach him His paths (25:4), and to lead him in His truth because the Lord is the God of his salvation and on Him, David waits (25:5). Guidance comes from the Word of God. So this is like praying for God to give him an understanding of His word (Ps. 119:18).

David prays for forgiveness (25:6-7). He asks God to remember His tender mercies and lovingkindness (25:6), not to remember the sins of his youth, and to remember him according to His mercy for his goodness' sake (25:7).

The Attributes of God (25:8-14) In this portion of the psalm, David repeats some of his requests in the first part of the psalm, only this time, he focuses more on the character of God.

The Lord guides. Because the Lord is good and upright, He teaches sinners in the way (25:8), guides the humble in justice, and teaches the humble His way (25:9). The Lord's paths are mercy and truth to those who keep His Word (25:10).

The Lord forgives. This time, David again asks the Lord to forgive his iniquities because the Lord's name is great (25:11).

The Lord blesses. Those who fear the Lord are taught His ways (25:12), dwell in prosperity, their descendants inherit the earth (25:13), and the Lord reveals His secrets to them (25:14).

The Lord protects. "My eyes *are* ever toward the LORD, for He shall pluck my feet out of the net" (25:15).

The Plea of David (25:16-20) David pleads, "Turn Yourself to me, and have mercy on me, for I *am* desolate and afflicted" (25:16), "Bring me out of my distress" (25:17), "Look on my affliction and my pain" and "Forgive all my sins" (25:18). The mixture of asking for deliverance from trouble and forgiveness of sins suggests that perhaps David's trouble was due, at least to some degree, to his sin. David also pleads that the Lord will consider his many enemies, who hate him (25:19), deliver him and let him not be ashamed because he puts his trust in the Lord (25:20).

David concludes this psalm with a plea for Israel. He says, "Redeem Israel, O God, Out of all their troubles!" (25:21). This verse does not follow the acrostic of the rest of the Psalm.

Summary: When you need forgiveness, deliverance, and guidance, ask the Lord for them, emphasizing His character, and pray for others.

A point to ponder: God provides forgiveness of sins, deliverance from trouble, and guidance by His Word because of who He is. We need humility, faith, and prayer.

Psalm 26: When You Are Falsely Accused

Psalm 26 is a lament psalm written by David. In it, David has been falsely accused (26:1).

A Prayer for Examination (26:1a) David prays, "Vindicate me, O Lord, for I have walked in my integrity" (26:1b). The Hebrew word translated "vindicate" means "judge" and the one rendered "integrity" means "integrity, innocence." David is not claiming he is sinless. He asks the Lord to judge that he is innocent of the charges against him. He adds, "I have also trusted in the Lord; I shall not slip" (26:1b). Because he trusted in the Lord, he had lived an innocent life of these false charges.

To prove his innocence, David invites the Lord to examine him, prove him, and try his mind and heart (26:2) because God's lovingkindness was before his eyes and he walked in God's truth (26:3). David is inviting the Lord to examine him to demonstrate that he is innocent of the charges brought against him.

To further establish his innocence, David declares that he had not sat with idolaters, hypocrites, or wicked people; instead, he has hated the assembly of evildoers (26:4-5).

On top of all of that, David says he will wash his hands in innocence so that he can go to the altar of the Lord (26:6) to proclaim his thanks and tell of God's wondrous works (26:7). David asserts that he has loved God's house, the place where God's glory dwells (26:8). David prefers the assembly of the saints (26:6-8) rather than the assembly of evildoers (26:4-6). He is confident that God will find him not guilty of the charges against him.

A Petition for Divine Discrimination (26:9-10) David asks the Lord not to gather his soul with sinners, nor his life with bloodthirsty men, that is, murderers (26:9). Their hands are full of sinister schemes and bribes (26:10). David is asking God to distinguish him from sinners. In other words, David anticipates the Lord judging the wicked and he wants to be separated from them so that he will not be judged with them.

A Promise of Praise (26:11-12) Turning his attention to himself, David says, "But as for me, I will walk in my integrity." So he asks God to redeem him from this problem and be merciful to him (26:11). David concludes with the promise, "My foot stands in an even place; in the congregations, I will bless the Lord" (26:12). As in other psalms, David promises public praise. The point is that David is promising that he will continue to walk in innocence and wait for the Lord to save him from his accusers, and when that happens, he will publicly praise the Lord.

Summary: When falsely accused, ask God to examine you to demonstrate your innocence, to deliver you from your accusers, and promise to publicly praise God when He does.

A point to ponder: When you are falsely accused, your *first response* should be to take your case to the Lord. Ask Him to judge your innocence. That is not to say that you should not defend yourself. It is to say, "Get the Lord on your side first." Ask Him to vindicate you.

Psalm 27: When You Are Facing a Fearful Danger

Psalm 27 is a lament psalm written by David. In it, David faces fearful danger.

Confidence in the Face of Danger (27:1-6) David begins by saying, "The Lord is my light and my salvation; whom shall I fear? The Lord is the strength of my life; shall I be afraid?" (27:1). Evidently, David was facing a fearful danger, but since the Lord is his light (understanding) during dark dangers, deliverance from dangers, and strength in the midst of dangers, he will not fear. In the past, when his enemies came against him to eat his flesh, like a wild beast pouncing on it prey, they stumbled and fell (27:2). So now, even if an army pitched their tents near him to attack him, he will not fear; he will be confident (27:3).

David can have such confidence in the Lord because he desires to dwell in the house of the Lord all the days of his life (27:4), to behold the beauty of the Lord, and to inquire in His Temple (27:4).

David explains ("for"), "For in the time of trouble He shall hide me in His provision; in the secret place of His Tabernacle He shall hide me; He shall set me high on a rock" (27:5). In this "time of trouble" David is confident the Lord will deliver him. So when the Lord lifts David's head above all of his enemies, he will offer sacrifices of joy in the Tabernacle and sing praises to the Lord (27:6).

A Cry for God's Help (27:7-13) Turning from speaking *about* the Lord (27:1-6), David speaks *to* the Lord, saying, "Hear O Lord, when I cry with my voice! Have mercy upon me and answer me" (27:7). He reminds the Lord that when He said, "Seek My face," he did just that (27:8). So he asked the Lord, "Do not hide Your face from me; do not turn your servant away in anger" (27:9a). The Lord has been his help in the past, so he asks that the Lord not forsake him now; the Lord is the God of his salvation (deliverance) (27:9b). David is not expressing doubt that the Lord may deliver him. In fact, he says, "When my father and my mother forsake me, then the Lord will take care of me" (27:10).

After crying to the Lord for the Lord to hear him and have mercy on him (27:7-10), David entreats the Lord to "Teach me your ways, and lead me in a smooth path, because of my enemies" (27:11). He asks the Lord to deliver him from his adversaries, false witnesses (slander), and those who breathe out violence against him (27:12). Again, he is not expressing doubt or discouragement. He says, "I would have lost heart unless I had believed that I would see the goodness of the Lord in the land of the living" (27:13).

Counsel to Others (27:14). David concludes by counseling others, "Wait on the Lord; be of good courage, and He will strengthen your heart; wait I say on the Lord!" (27:14).

Summary: When facing danger, be confident that the Lord will deliver you in your present fearful danger, cry to the Lord for deliverance, and with courage and strength, wait on the Lord to work.

A point to ponder: When facing a fearful danger, such as people forsaking you, wanting to do you harm, or even desiring to devour you, reflect on the Lord's past deliverance in your life, seek Him, trust Him, and wait on Him. Do not fear; be of good courage. The Lord is your strength.

Psalm 28: When You Deal with Wicked Enemies

Psalm 28 is a lament praise psalm written by David. In it, David is dealing with wicked enemies (28:3-5).

A Plea to be Heard (28:1-2) David pleads with the Lord, "To you, I will cry, O Lord my Rock; do not be silent to me. Lest, if you are silent to me, I become like those who go down to the pit" (28:1). The pit is a reference to the grave. David is pleading with the Lord to hear him lest he die. In the next verse, he continues his plea, "Hear the voice of my supplication when I cry to You when I lift my hands toward Your holy sanctuary" (28:2). The sanctuary is a reference to the holy of holies, where God dwelt. Again, the plea is to be heard. There is urgency in David's voice, probably because the danger from his wicked enemy was imminent.

A Petition to Judge the Wicked (28:3-5) At this point, David talks to the Lord about his wicked enemies. Concerning his enemies, David requests two things. First, he requests that he not be taken away with the wicked, who speak peace but have evil in their hearts (28:3). This is a prayer for deliverance from death. Second, he requests that God judge the wicked (*according* to their deeds, *according* to their wickedness, and *according* to the work of their hands); "render to them what they deserve" (28:4). David makes this request "because they do not regard the works of the Lord, nor the operation of His hands" (28:5a). David declares God will destroy them (28:5b).

Praise to the Lord (28:6-9) David praises the Lord "because He has heard the voice of my supplication" (28:6) and because the Lord, who is his strength and shield and in whom he trusts, has helped him (28:7). In verse 7, David talks about his personal relationship with the Lord. He speaks of "*my* strength," "*my* shield," "*my* heart trusts in him," "*my* heart greatly rejoices, and with *my* song I will praise Him."

Prayer for God's People (28:8-9) In verses 8 and 9, David talks about God's people. He says, "The Lord is *their* strength and He is the saving refuge of His anointed," that is, their king (28:8). He asks God to save His people, bless His inheritance, shepherd them, and bear them up forever (28:9).

Summary: When you deal with a wicked enemy, ask the Lord to give them what they deserve, trust the Lord, praise the Lord for His strength and protection, and pray that He will save and shepherd His people.

A point to ponder: When dealing with a wicked enemy, it is easy to pray that God will give them what they deserve and that He will protect us, but what we often fail to do is pray for others who are also affected by this enemy.

Psalm 29: When You Are Watching a Thunderstorm

Psalm 29 is a royal psalm written by David. It has been suggested that it was sung at state events, like "God Save the Queen" or "Hail to the Chief" today. The word "Lord" (Yahweh), the personal name of God, appears 18 times in these 11 verses. In this psalm, David watches a thunderstorm (29:3-9).

Invitation to Praise the Power of the Lord (29:1-2) Three times in these two verses, David says, "Give unto the Lord." David invites "mighty ones" to give the Lord "glory and strength" (29:1), "the glory due to His name" (29:2a), and to worship Him in the beauty of holiness (29:2b; see these phrases in 96:7-9).

The mighty ones (Hebrew: "sons of the mighty;" see NASB) are either angels (the Hebrew wording is similar to Job 1:6) or the people of God (see 96:7-9; 1 Chron. 16:29, and 2 Chron. 20:21, where the same invitation here is given to the people of the earth). Verse 9 indicates this is a reference to angels. The Hebrew word translated "beauty" means "adornment, splendor." The invitation is to worship God in the splendor of holiness (see NIV; ESV). Thus, this passage calls angels to worship God in the splendor of His holiness.

Illustration of the Power of the Lord (29:3-9) The phrase "the voice of the Lord" occurs seven times in verses 3-9. It is a figure of speech for thunder (thunder is a voice from heaven). David watches a thunderstorm as it rises from the "waters" over the Mediterranean Sea (29:3). It is a powerful storm full of majesty (21:4). He watches it as it reaches landfall, splintering the sturdy cedars of Lebanon, tossing them about as if they were matchsticks (29:5), making them skip like a calf or young wild ox (29:6). The thunder is accompanied by "flames of fire," that is, lightning (29:7). The storm moves from Lebanon and Sirion (Mt. Hermon) in the north to Kadesh. It shakes the wilderness of Kadesh (29:8), makes the deer give birth prematurely, and strips the forest bare, that is, it blows the leaves off the trees (29:9a). All in God's temple (angels) say, "Glory!" at the display of God's power (29:9b).

It has been suggested that the backdrop of this psalm is the worship of Baal, the pagan god of the storm who thundered in the heavens. If so, the point is that the Lord, not Baal, is God.

The Availability of the Power of the Lord (29:10-11) After watching such a powerful storm, David declares, "The Lord sat enthroned at the Flood and the Lord sits as King forever" (29:10). The Hebrew word translated "flood" is only found here and in Genesis 6-11, where it is used of the Flood of Noah's day. The thunderstorm that David witnessed reminded him that God was sitting on His throne during the Flood and He will sit on that throne as King forever.

David concludes, "The Lord will give His strength to His people; the Lord will bless His people with peace" (29:11). Throughout this psalm, David makes references to God's strength (see "straight" in verse 1 and "powerful" in verse 4, as well as the manifestation of God's power in the storm). God's power is available to God's people. God also gives peace. He is able to raise the storm and make the storm subside (Mk. 9:37-39).

Summary: When you are watching a thunderstorm, be reminded of God's power, for which He should be praised and which is available to God's people.

A point to ponder: When storms come and it seems that things are out of control, remember that God is in control, is powerful, and gives His people, the ones who trust Him, His power.

Psalm 30: When You Are Delivered from Death's Door

Psalm 30 is a declarative praise psalm written by David. In it, David is facing death's door (30:3).

Praise for God's Deliverance (30:1-5) David extols the Lord because the Lord has lifted him up, has not let his foes rejoice over him (30:1), has healed him (30:2), has brought him up from the grave, and kept him alive (30:3). David is not saying he was resurrected; he is saying he was delivered from a fatal illness, that is, from death's door. Had the Lord not restored him, his enemies would have rejoiced over his death.

David not only praises the Lord himself but also invites the saints to praise the Lord and give thanks "in remembrance of His holy name" (30:4) because God's anger is only for a moment, and His favor is forever. "Weeping may endure for a night, but joy *comes* in the morning" (30:5). Evidently, David's illness (30:2) was God's discipline for David's sin (1 Cor. 11:30). David's praise is that God's discipline is short (only for a moment, a mere night), but His blessings are lifelong and then some (forever).

Review of Past Sins (30:6-10) David describes what led to his discipline. He says, "Now in my prosperity, I said, 'I shall never be moved'" (30:6). When he was prospering, he thought the situation would never change. Prosperity lulls us into a false sense of security. When we are prosperous, we should never think we can now coast through the rest of life without continual dependence on the Lord.

David adds, "Lord, by Your favor You have made my mountain stand strong" (30:7a; "mountain" may be a figure for David's kingdom). In other words, as he looks back, he realizes that God's grace made him strong. Then he sinned and when he did, God hid His face from David and David was troubled (30:7b). Some commentators suggest that this is referring to God's discipline on David because of his census (2 Sam. 24; 1 Chron. 21). Because of that act of David's disobedience, 70,000 people died.

David cried to the Lord (30:8), saying, "What profit *is there* in my blood when I go down to the pit? Will the dust praise You? Will it declare Your truth?" The pit is a reference to the grave. David is saying to the Lord, "What profit is there in my death ('blood')? If I die, I will not be able in this life to publicly praise You for Your deliverance, nor will I be able to declare Your truth to others." So David pleads, "Hear, O Lord, and have mercy on me; Lord, be my helper!" (30:10). In the context of this psalm, asking for mercy is asking God to save his life (30:2-3).

Praise for God's Mercy (30:11-12) God answered David's prayer for mercy, so David praises the Lord: "You have turned for me my mourning into dancing; You have put off my sackcloth and clothed me with gladness" (30:11). God took off David's sackcloth of mourning and put garments of gladness on him. In his new outfit, David danced. He was no longer sick. So he says, "To the end that *my* glory may sing praise to You and not be silent. O Lord my God, I will give thanks to You forever" (30:12). David promised to praise God for the rest of his life.

Summary: When you are delivered from death's door due to God's discipline, cry out to God for His mercy and praise Him for His merciful deliverance (restoration to health).

A point to ponder: Not all sickness is due to sin, but when it is, pray for deliverance and praise God when it comes. In short, when delivered from death's door, praise the Lord!

Also, remember: "Weeping may endure for a night, but joy *comes* in the morning" (30:5).

Psalm 31: When You Are in Agony

Psalm 31 is a lament psalm filled with expressions of trust written by David. In it, David is in agony (31:9-10)

A Plea for Deliverance (31:1-2) Because he trusts the Lord, David pleads for the Lord never to let him be ashamed, to deliver him (31:1), to listen to him, to speedily deliver him, to be his refuge and to be his fortress to save him (31:2). David is distressed.

An Expression of Trust (31:3-8) David explains ("for") that since God is his rock and fortress, He should lead him and guide him for His name's sake (31:3) and since God is his strength, he should pull him out of the net others have secretly laid for him (31:4). David declares, "In your hands, I commit my spirit; you have redeemed me, O Lord God of truth" (31:5). On the cross, Jesus quoted the first part of this verse (Lk. 23:46; see also Acts 7:59). David goes on to say that he hated idolaters, but trusts in the Lord (31:6) and that he will rejoice in God's mercy because the Lord has considered his trouble (31:7), has not shut up his hand to his enemy, and has set his feet in a wide place (31:8). Note: David is rejoicing in God's mercy *before* he is delivered. Paul and Silas sang praises to God in jail (Acts 16:25). David is distressed but still trusts the Lord.

Lament over Danger (31:9-13) David asks for mercy because of his trouble, grief (31:9), sighing, failed strength because of his iniquity, wasted bones (31:10), as well as being a reproach to his enemies and repulsive to his acquaintances (31:11), being forgotten as if he were dead, being like a broken vessel (31:12), being slandered, and being schemed against to take his life (31:13). David's agony was the result of his sin (31:10) as well as the sins of others against him (31:13). No wonder David is in agony!

Petition for Deliverance (31:14 to 18) David asks that since he trusts the Lord (31:14), the Lord deliver him (31:15), make his face shine upon him (be favorable), save him (13:16), not let him, but the wicked, be ashamed (31:17), and let lying lips be put to silence (31:18).

Praise for Deliverance (31:19-22) At this point, David begins to praise the Lord for His goodness (31:19), for His protection (31:20), and for His "marvelous kindness" (31:21). David confesses, "For I said in my haste, I am cut off from before Your eyes; nevertheless, You heard the voice of my supplication when I cried out to You" (31:22). Amid his distress, David jumped to the conclusion that he had been cut off from God's consideration.

Exhortation to Trust (31:23-24) From his experience, David offers advice to others. He says, "Oh, love the Lord all you saints! The Lord preserves the faithful and fully repays the proud person" (31:23) and "Be of good courage and He shall strengthen your heart, all you who hope in the Lord" (31:24). When those who trust the Lord and love the Lord are determined to be of good cheer, God will strengthen them, preserve them, and repay the proud who are against them. It pays to trust the Lord.

Summary: When you are in agony because of your sin and the sins of others against you, who were scheming to take your life and verbally abusing you, pour out the way you feel before the Lord, trust the Lord, praise the Lord, and tell others to do the same.

A point to ponder: When you are in agony, don't wait until you are delivered to rejoice and praise the Lord. Rejoice in the Lord amid the agony (Jas. 1:2).

Psalm 32: When You Contemplate Forgiveness

Psalm 32 is a penitential psalm written by David. A penitential psalm is a psalm of repentance (see 6; 38; 51; 102; 130; 143). After his sin with Bathsheba and his murder of her husband Uriah (2 Sam. 11), David wrote Psalm 51. Psalm 32 is the sequel to Psalm 51. In it, David contemplates forgiveness (32:1-2).

The Happiness of Forgiveness (32:1-2) David proclaims, "Blessed (Hebrew: 'happy;' see 1:1) is he whose transgression is forgiven, whose sin is covered" (32:1) and "Blessed is the man to whom the Lord does not impute iniquity, in whose spirit there is no deceit" (32:2). David uses three different words to describe what he did: transgression (Hebrew: rebellion), sin (Hebrew: missing the mark), and iniquity (Hebrew: guilt).

The Misery Caused by Sin (32:3-4) David can say that he is happy now, but he describes what it was like before he confessed. He says when he "kept silent," that is, when he did not immediately confess his sin (it took him a year; see 2 Sam. 12:13-14), his bones grew old, he groaned all day (32:3), God's hand was heavy upon him, and his vitality had turned to the drought of summer, that is, he felt drained of energy (32:4). In other words, his sin affected him physically, emotionally, and spiritually.

The Confession of Sin (32:5) Finally, David says he acknowledged his sin to the Lord; he did not hide his iniquity. When he confessed his transgressions to the Lord, the Lord forgave the iniquity of his sin (32:5). Notice that the same three words he used to describe the blessedness of forgiveness, he also uses to describe his confession (transgression, sin, and iniquity).

The Counsel to Others (32:6-11) Addressing the Lord, David says because You forgive, everyone who is godly should pray in a time when You can be found (32:6). David tells the Lord, You are my hiding place, preserver from trouble, and song of deliverance (32:7). Although addressing the Lord, David is counseling the godly and testifying to them what the Lord is to him.

The Lord speaks to David (some commentators say David is still the speaker), telling him that He will instruct him, teach him, and guide him (32:8) and that he should not be like the horse or mule, who has no understanding must be harnessed with bit and bridle (32:9). Although the Lord is speaking to David, He is counseling all who know Him, to not be like a stubborn horse that will not willingly go where the rider directs it to go. The Lord wants His people to be guided willingly by His eye (32:8; like a mother's look), which is gentle guidance rather than discipline.

David counsels others. He says that many sorrows will be to the wicked, but the Lord surrounds with mercy those who trust Him (32:10). So, "Be glad in the Lord and rejoice, you righteous; and shout for joy all you upright in heart" (13:11). Those who are forgiven should be happy (32:1); they should be glad, rejoice, and shout for joy (13:11).

Summary: When contemplating the happiness of forgiveness and the misery caused by sin, counsel the godly to confess (quickly) and not be like a stubborn horse.

A point to ponder: Use your own experience to minister to others.

Psalm 33: When You Consider God's Word and Works

Psalm 33 is a praise psalm written by an anonymous author, probably David. In it, the author considers God's Word and works (33:4).

A Command for the Righteous to Praise the Lord (33:1-7) The righteous should rejoice in the Lord because praise from the upright is beautiful (Hebrew: comely; see "fitting" in the NIV; 33:1) and they should praise the Lord with the harp, with an instrument of 10 strings, with a new song, and with a shout of joy (33:2-3). A "new song" (33:3; 40:3; 96:1; 98:1; 144:9; 149:1) is a song about His new blessings (98:1; see Lam. 3:23).

The reason they should praise the Lord ("for") is His Word is right (not wrong), His works are done in truth (not false) (33:4), He loves righteousness and justice, the earth is full of His goodness (merciful kindness; 33:5), and He made the heavens and the earth by His Word (33:6-7).

To sum up, those who know the Lord should praise the Lord because His Word is right, His works are truth, just, and kind.

A Call for the Whole World to Fear the Lord (33:8-19) The whole world should fear and stand in awe of the Lord (33:8) because He spoke and what He said was done, a reference to creation (33:9). He brings the counsel of nations and the plans of people to nothing (13:10), but His counsel and plans stand forever (33:11). So, "Blessed (Hebrew: happy) is the nation whose God is the Lord, the people he has chosen as his own inheritance" (33:12). The people God chose as His inheritance was Israel.

Furthermore, the Lord sees all the inhabitants of the earth (33:13-14), fashions each heart, and considers all their works (33:15). Thus, He knows that no king is saved by his army (33:16-17; "a horse is a vain hope for safety"). He sees those who fear Him and hope in His mercy (Hebrew: lovingkindness) to deliver them from death and keep them alive in famine (33:18-19).

The sum of this subsection is that the whole world should fear the Lord because His Word is reliable, His people are happy, His knowledge is complete (He knows who trusts Him), and His deliverance is sure.

A Commitment to Trust the Lord (33:20-22) The psalmist concludes, "Our soul waits for the Lord; He is our help or shield. Our hearts shall rejoice in Him because we have trusted in His holy name. Let your mercy (Hebrew: lovingkindness), O Lord, be upon us, just as we hope in you" (33:20-22). Those who know what the Lord is like wait on Him for help and protection, rejoice in Him, trust Him, pray to Him, and hope in Him.

Summary: When you consider God's Word and works, command the righteous to praise the Lord because of His Word and works, call all to fear the Lord because of His Word and works, and not only praise Him but also trust Him.

The structure of this psalm revolves around the commands to praise the Lord and fear the Lord, but the emphasis within that structure is on the Lord's Word (33:4, 6, 9, 11) and works (33:4, 5, 6, 7, 10, 12, 13, 15, 18, 19).

A point to ponder: If we contemplated God's works as revealed in His Word more, we would praise and trust Him more. We are so busy thinking about other things we don't have time to read, much less contemplate, the Word we have from God.

Psalm 34: When You Saved from a Fearful Situation

Psalm 34 is a praise psalm written by David. It is an acrostic. Except for one letter, each verse begins with a successive letter of the Hebrew alphabet (there is no verse for the Hebrew letter *waw,* which should be after verse 5). The superscription says that David wrote this psalm when he pretended madness to escape from Abimelech, king of Gath (1 Sam. 21:10–15; Achish is the personal name for Abimelech, which is his throne name; see Ps. 56). In this Psalm, David has been saved from a fearful situation (34:4).

A Call to Praise the Lord (34:1-10) David fled from Saul to Abimelech, king of the Philistine city of Gath, but once there, he feared for his life (34:4; 1 Sam. 21:10-15, esp. verse 12). He opens this psalm saying he will praise God continually (34:1-2) and invites others to join him in exalting the name of the Lord (13:3). David explains that he sought the Lord and the Lord heard him and delivered him from his fears (34:4). This applies to others. Those who look to the Lord will be radiant (34:5; like Moses in Ex. 34:29) and those who fear the Lord will be delivered (34:7). David is the example of a "poor man," that is, one who could not save himself, who cried out to the Lord and had the Lord hear him and save him out of all of his troubles (34:6).

David exhorts others to taste and see that the Lord is good; the Lord blesses those who trust him (34:8). David also exhorts saints to fear the Lord (to reverence Him and have a healthy fear of Him) because there is no want to those who fear him (34:9). Young lions (kings of the beasts) may lack, but those who seek the Lord will not lack any good thing (34:10).

A Call to Fear the Lord (34:11-22) In the second section of the psalm, David invites God's people (he calls them "children") to listen to him and he will teach them the fear of the Lord (34:11). He begins his instruction with a question: Who desires life and loves many days that he may see good? (34:12). In other words, if you are interested in a long, good life, here is what you should do: 1) Do not speak evil or deceit (34:13; Peter quotes this verse in 1 Pet. 3:10). Do not just refrain from speaking evil; depart from evil (34:14a). 2) Do good and seek peace (34:14b; Peter quotes this verse in 1 Pet. 3:11).

David explains that the eyes of the Lord are on the righteous, His ears are open to their cry (13:15), and His face is against those who do evil to cut off their remembrance from the earth (34:16; Peter quotes verses 15 and 16 in 1 Pet. 3:12).

David explains what the Lord does for the righteous. He hears the cry of the righteous and delivers them out of all their troubles (34:17). He is near to those who have a broken heart and saves those who have a contrite spirit (34:18). Although the righteous have many afflictions, the Lord delivers them out of all of them (34:19). He guards their bones (34:20; see Jn. 19:36). Those who hate the righteous will be condemned; evil shall slay the wicked (34:21).

In the Hebrew text, verse 22 breaks the acrostic structure of the psalm. It does not begin with the next letter of the Hebrew alphabet. Thus, it is set apart as a summary statement. None of those who trust the Lord will be condemned; the Lord redeems his servants (34:22).

Summary: When you are saved from a fearful situation, praise the Lord, invite others to praise the Lord, and fear the Lord because He delivers the righteous.

Note the repetition of "fear" (34:4, 11, once in each section of the psalm) and "righteous" (34:15, 17, 19, 21). Those who fear the Lord and live righteously will be delivered. Praise Him!

A point to ponder: Fear the Lord, not some fearful situation.

Psalm 35: When You Are Treated Unjustly

Psalm 35 is a lament psalm (some called it an imprecatory psalm; imprecatory means "to invite a curse on someone) written by David, possibly when Saul's men were hunting David (see 1 Sam. 24:15). In it, David speaks of being treated unjustly (35:7).

Prayer for Deliverance (35:1-10) David prays that the Lord would plead his cause with those who strive against him (35:1). He asks God to take hold of the shield and buckler (35:2), to draw out the spear (35:3), and let those who seek his life be put to shame (35:4). In short, David asks the Lord to "fight against those who fight against me" (35:1). He wants the Lord to take up arms like a soldier and fight for him. He wants the Lord to say, "I am your salvation," that is, your deliverance from your enemies.

David prays that his enemies would be like chaff before the wind (35:5) and that their way would be dark and slippery (35:6). He desires that the Angel of the Lord (who some say is the pre-incarnate Christ) pursue them (35:5-6), because (see "for" in verse 7) "without cause" his enemies are seeking his destruction (35:7). So he asks that destruction come upon them unexpectedly (35:8). He wants the net they have set for him (35:7) to catch them (35:8).

David declares that he will rejoice in the Lord and in His deliverance (35:9), because the Lord delivers the poor (those who are helpless) from those who seek their harm (35:10).

Plight over Injustice (35:11-18) David laments the "fierce witnesses" who reward evil for good (35:11-12). When they were sick, David fasted and prayed for them (35:13). He was as concerned for them as one mourns the death of his own mother (35:14), but when David was facing adversity, they rejoiced, attacked (35:15), and mocked him (35:16). So David asks how long the Lord would see all of this before rescuing him from destruction (35:17) and promises to praise God in the great assembly when God does deliver him (35:18).

Petition for Vindication (35:19-28) David petitions the Lord not to allow those who hate him without a cause to rejoice (35:19; being hated without a cause was ultimately fulfilled in Jesus, Jn. 15:25), because (see "for" in verse 20) they do not seek peace, they devise deceitful schemes (35:20), and open their mouth against him (35:21).

David pleads with the Lord to not keep silent, not to be far from him (35:22), to awake to his cause (35:23; it seemed to David that the Lord was napping), and to vindicate him (35:24a). He pleads with the Lord to not let his enemies rejoice over him (35:24b), not to let them say that they have swallowed him (35:25), and to let them be clothed with shame and dishonor (25:26). David also pleads with the Lord to let those who favor his righteous cause shout for joy and to let the Lord be magnified (35:27).

David concludes that when the Lord answers his prayer, his tongue shall speak of His righteousness and praise Him all day long (35:28).

Summary: When you are treated unjustly, plead with the Lord for vindication and deliverance and when He answers your prayer, praise Him and tell others what He did so they will praise Him.

In this psalm, people who were near and dear to David (35:14) turned against him unjustly [see "without cause" in verses 7 (twice) and 19]. He addresses God as "my God" (Hebrew: Elohim) and "my Lord" (Hebrew: Adonai), indicating that he is appealing to God's power and sovereignty (35:23) to vindicate and deliver him (35:24-26).

A point to ponder: Don't retaliate; let the Lord vindicate you.

Psalm 36: When You Read God's Revelation

Psalm 36 is a wisdom psalm written by David. In the superscription, David calls himself "the servant of the Lord," which is the title the Lord gave him as King (2 Sam. 3:18, 7:5, 8). In this psalm, David speaks of God's revelation (36:1).

A Revelation Concerning the Wicked (36:1-4) The oracle (a divine utterance, that is, a prophetic revelation; translated "says the Lord" in Micah 4:6) David received within his heart concerning the transgression of the wicked was, "There is no fear of God before his eyes" (36:1). The Hebrew word translated "fear" is not the normal Hebrew word that is translated fear in the Old Testament. The one that is used here means "terror, dread." In other words, it is not just "fear;" it is great fear, alarm, and terror. The wicked sin because they are not afraid of God. In Romans 3:18, Paul quotes this verse as the climactic characteristic of sin.

David explains (see "for" in verse 2) that when the wicked look at their sin and when they hate, instead of fearing God, they flatter themselves in their own eyes (36:2). They cease to be wise and do good (36:3b). Consequently their words are wicked and deceitful (36:3a), they devise of wickedness on their bed, and do not abhor evil (36:4). When they lie down in bed at night, they plot and plan their wickedness for the next day.

A Reflection Concerning the Lord (36:5-9) In contrast to the wicked, the Lord is merciful, faithful (13:5), and righteous (36:6a). The Lord's righteousness is like a great mountain that reaches high into the heavens and His judgments are like the great depths of the sea, which are beyond comprehension (36:6b). He preserves both man and beast (36:6c).

Since God is full of lovingkindness, people trust Him, like nestlings seeking shelter under the wings of the mother bird (36:7). Since God gives His children drink from the river of His pleasures, they are "abundantly satisfied" (13:8; the wicked are never satisfied, Prov. 27:20). David goes on to explain (see "for" in verse 9), that God is the one who gives life and light (36:9). To those who trust Him (36:7) and are satisfied with His pleasures (36:8), God gives the light of wisdom which leads to a satisfying an abundant life.

A Request Concerning the Future (36:10-12) Having spoken directly to the Lord concerning His characteristics (36:5-9), David turns his attention to making a request of the Lord. He requests that the Lord continue His lovingkindness to those who know Him and His righteousness to those who are right in heart (36:10). He also requests that the foot of the proud not come against him and the hand of the wicked not drive him away (36:11).

David closes with the thought, "There the workers of iniquity have fallen; they have been cast down and are unable to rise" (36:12). In the end, the wicked will be destroyed, from which there will be no remedy.

Summary: When you read God's revelation, you learn that the wicked have no fear of God, that God is merciful and righteous, and that those who know God should trust God to continue His lovingkindness toward them.

A point to ponder: The Word of God gives us insight into the wickedness of the wicked.

Psalm 37: When You Fret Over the Wicked

Psalm 37 is a wisdom psalm written by David as an older man (37:25). It is an acrostic; every second verse begins with a successive letter of the Hebrew alphabet. In it, David speaks of fretting over the wicked (37:1, 7, 8).

A Call to Focus on the Lord (37:1-11) Three times, David says, "Do not fret" (37:1, 7, 8). The Hebrew word translated "fret" means to be "hot, angry, vexed." Do not get upset over the prosperity of evildoers because (see "for" in 37:2) they will soon be cut down like grass (37:2). Their success is temporary. Trust the Lord, do good (37:3), delight in the Lord (37:4), commit your way to the Lord (37:5), rest in the Lord, wait patiently for Him, do not fret because the wicked prosper (37:7, 8b), cease from anger, and forsake wrath (37:8a). If you trust and delight in the Lord, He will give you the desires of your heart (37:3), bring it to pass (37:5), and bring out your righteousness (37:6). The reason for not fretting and instead focusing on the Lord is repeated: "For evildoers shall be cut off; but those who wait on the Lord, they shall inherit the earth" (37:9). Evildoers will be cut off in a little while (37:10), but the meek shall inherit the earth (37:11; see Mt. 5:5). In short, fret not over evildoers; focus on the Lord. The success of evildoers is temporary; the meek, righteous people who focus on the Lord will inherit the earth.

The Conclusion of Evildoers (37:12-22) The wicked may plot against the just (37:12), but the Lord sees his day is coming (37:13). The wicked may prepare to slay the upright (37:14), but the wicked will be slain (37:15). Better to be poor and righteous than rich and wicked (37:16) because the arms of the wicked will be broken, but the Lord upholds the righteous (37:17). The wicked shall perish (37:20), but the inheritance of the upright shall be forever (37:18-19). The wicked borrow and do not repay, but the righteous give (37:21), so the wicked shall be cut off and the righteous shall inherit the earth (37:22).

The Condition of the Righteous (37:23-31) The Lord delights in a good man (37:23) and upholds him (37:24). The Lord provides for the righteous (37:25) and his descendants are blessed (37:26). So, depart from evil and do good (37:27), because the Lord preserves his saints forever and the descendants of the wicked shall be cut off (37:28). The righteous have God's Law in their heart (37:31a) and speak wisdom (37:30), so their steps shall not slide (37:31b).

The Contrast Between the Wicked and the Righteous (37:32-38) The wicked seek to slay the righteous (37:32), but the Lord takes care of the righteous (37:33). The wicked shall be cut off (37:34b-36), but the righteous who wait on the Lord and keep His way shall inherit the land (37:34a). The wicked shall be destroyed (37:38), but the future of the upright is peace (37:37).

The Conclusion for the Righteous (37:39-40) The Lord is the strength and salvation (deliverance) of the righteous (37:39). The Lord delivers the righteous from the wicked because the righteous trust Him (37:40) when the wicked prosper and oppose them.

Summary: When you are about to fret over the wicked, focus on the Lord, trust Him, and remember that in the end, evildoers will perish and the righteous will be blessed.

Three times, David says, "Do not fret" (37:1, 7, 8). Five times he refers to inheriting the earth (37:9, 11, 22, 29, 34). Notice the commands: do not fret (37:1, 7, 8), trust in the Lord (37:3, 5), do good (37:3), feed on His faithfulness (37:3), delight in the Lord (37:4), commit your way to the Lord (37:5), rest in the Lord (37:7), wait patiently for the Lord (37:7, 34), cease from anger (37:8), forsake wrath (37:8), keep His ways (37:34), and mark the blameless man (37:37).

A point to ponder: Don't fret; focus on the Lord.

Psalm 38: When You Are Dealing with the Effects of Sin

Psalm 38 is penitential (a psalm of repentance) written by David. In it, David deals with the effects of sin (38:3-5).

The Effects of Sin on the Body (38:1-8) David pleads with the Lord not to rebuke him in wrath, nor chasten him in hot displeasure (38:1). David explains ("for") the Lord's arrows have pierced him deeply and the Lord's hand has pressed him down (38:2).

David describes his bodily suffering in detail. Because of his sin and God's anger, he says there was no soundness in his flesh, nor health in his bones (38:3), his iniquities are over his head like of heavy burden that is too heavy for him (38:4), and says his wounds are foul and festering because of his foolishness (38:5). He goes on to explain that he was troubled, bowed down, and mourning all day long (38:6), because ("for") his loins were full of inflammation and there was no soundness in his flesh (38:7). Because of the turmoil in his heart, he was feeble, severely broken, and groaning (38:8).

The Effects of Sin on Relationships (38:9-14) For the second time, David addresses the Lord (38:9). This time he begins by describing his relationship to the Lord and. He tells the Lord that his desire is before Him and his sighing is not hidden from Him (38:9). He explains to the Lord that his heart pants, even though his strength fails and the light of his eyes is gone from him (38:10). Then he describes the effect of his sin on his relationships. His loved ones, his friends, and his relatives stand aloof from him as if he has the plague (38:11). The Hebrew word translated "plague" was used for leprosy. Those closest to him avoided him as if he were a leper! Those who seek his life lay a snare for him, speak of his destruction, and plan deception (38:12). His response to all of this is like a deaf man who does not hear and a mute who does not speak (38:13). In other words, in response, he is silent (38:14). He does not defend himself against the accusations of his enemies.

Dealing with the Effects of Sin (38:15-22) For the third time, David addresses the Lord (38:15). This time, he begins by describing his confidence that the Lord will hear his prayer (38:15), lest his enemies rejoice over him (38:16). He readily admits his continual sorrow and anguish over his sin (38:17-18). He reminds the Lord that his enemies are vigorous, strong, and hateful toward him (38:19), rendering evil for good because he has followed that which is good (38:20). So he asks the Lord not to forsake him or be far from him (38:21). Rather, he asks the Lord to hasten to help him, acknowledging that the Lord is his salvation (deliverance; 38:22).

Summary: When you are dealing with the effects of sin, including physical sickness, desertion of family and friends, as well as opposition from enemies, flee to the Lord, acknowledging your sin and seeking His protection from your enemies.

As a result of his sin (38:3, 4, 5, 17-18), God disciplined David (38:1). The discipline included physical weakness and sickness (38:2-8; see 1 Cor. 11: 30), broken relationships with his family and friends (32:11), and enemies who wanted to destroy him (38:12, 16, 19). Commenting on this passage, Tom Constable said, "Sometimes believers bring physical, emotional, and interpersonal suffering on ourselves by sinning. In such cases, God may discipline us with pain so we may learn not to do the same thing again. In the process, we should reaffirm our trust in God as our deliverer from all of our woes."

A point to ponder: Maybe committing (or continuing) that sin is not a good idea. What do you think?

Psalm 39: When You Are Sick Because of Sin

Psalm 39 is a wisdom psalm written by David. In it, David speaks of being sick because of sin (39:8-10).

The Practice of Silence (39:1-3) David restrained his mouth with a muzzle before the wicked, lest he sin with his tongue (39:1), but his heart was hot within him; it burned with fire (39:2). So he spoke (39:3)—to the Lord (see 39:4, 7, 12).

A Prayer for Knowledge About the Brevity of Life (39:4-6) Addressing the Lord, David prays to know the measure and the end of his days, that he may know just how frail he really is (39:4). He employs two figures of speech, the breadth of a hand (four fingers wide) and a vapor (something that passes quickly), to describe the brevity of life (39:5). Our days are nothing before God (39:5). David adds, "Surely every man walks about like a shadow; surely they busy themselves in vain; he heaps up riches and does not know who will gather them" (39:6).

It has been suggested that David was an older man when he wrote this psalm. As an older man, he realized that spending one's life accumulating wealth is in vain because one day we will die, and who knows who will end up with the wealth we accumulated? There is more to life than money.

A Petition for Deliverance (39:7-11) Again addressing the Lord, David asks a question, "What do I wait for?" (39:7a). In light of the brevity of life and the futility of gathering wealth, what should we expect out of life? David answers, "My hope is in You" (39:7b). His son Solomon learned this lesson the hard way. At the end of his life, Solomon wrote a book describing the futility of life. At the end of that book, he said, "Let us hear the conclusion of the whole matter: fear God and keep His commandments, for this is man's all" (Eccl. 12:13).

As David contemplates life before the Lord, he makes several requests. First, he prays, "Delivered me from all my transgressions" (39:8). Evidently, David had sinned (39:8), God had rebuked him (39:11), and as a result, David had experienced some form of illness (39:10). As in Psalm 38, David's suffering was due to sin (39:1-2).

Second, David prays, "Do not make me the reproach of the foolish" (39:8). When David says, "I was mute, I did not open my mouth, because it was You who did it" (39:9), he is referring to the fact that he was silent before his enemies (39:1) when God had disciplined him with some form of sickness.

Third, David requests, "Remove Your plague from me; the blow of Your hand consumes me" (39:10). As David explains when God rebukes sin, man's beauty melts away like a moth eating a garment; he is but a vapor (39:11). Having confessed his sin (39:8), David asks God to remove the discipline (39:10).

A Plea to be Heard (39:12-13) For the third time in this psalm, David addresses the Lord. This time, he asks the Lord to hear his prayer (39:12), to be as kind to him as Israel was supposed to be to a stranger and sojourner (39:12; see Deut. 10:18-19), and to remove the discipline so that he may regain his strength before he dies (39:13).

Summary: When you are sick because of sin, keep silent before the wicked, acknowledge your sin, and, realizing the brevity of life, ask the Lord to remove His discipline.

A point to ponder: Sickness, whatever the cause, makes us realize our frailty (39:4) and the brevity of life (39:5). Also, David is asking God to extend his life rather than continue His chastening.

Psalm 40: When Countless Problems Overwhelm You

Psalm 40 is a praise psalm written by David. In it, David is overwhelmed with countless problems (40:12).

Praise for Past Deliverance (40:1-10) David praised God for His past deliverance. When he patiently waited for the Lord, the Lord heard him (40:1), brought him up out of a horrible pit, out of miry clay, set his feet on a rock, and established his steps (40:2). David compares his plight to a prisoner in a pit and a traveler trapped in a quagmire of clay. Then, he praises God for delivering him, setting his feet on a rock instead of clay, and establishing his feet on a path instead of the pit. On top of that, the Lord put a new song in David's mouth, a song of praise to God, which many will see, fear, and as a result, trust in the Lord (40:3). A "new song" (33:3; 40:3; 96:1; 98:1; 144:9; 149:1) is a song about His new blessings (98:1; see Lam. 3:23).

David proclaims, "Blessed is the man who makes the Lord his trust and does not respect the proud, nor such as turn aside to lies" (40:4). This is David's new song to encourage people to trust the Lord and not himself or others who lie, perhaps a reference to idols.

Turning to the Lord, David exclaims, "Many, O Lord my God, are Your wonderful works;" all the things You have done for us cannot be counted (40:5). David explains that God opened his ears and he realized that God did not desire or require sacrifices such as burnt offerings and sin offerings (40:6). God does not want external ceremony; He wants internal trust.

Pleasure in Past Obedience David adds, "Then I said, 'Behold I come; in the scroll of the book it is written of me. I delight to do Your will, O my God, and Your law is within my heart" (40:7-8). God's Word was in David's hand and heart. Instead of an animal sacrifice (40:6), he offers himself as a living sacrifice (Rom. 12:1). Jesus spoke these words to the Father (Heb. 10:4-6). David goes on to declare that he proclaimed the good news of righteousness in the great assembly (40:9); he did not hide it within his heart (40:10a). He proclaimed God's righteousness, faithfulness, deliverance, lovingkindness, and truth (40:10b).

Prayer for Present Deliverance (40:11-17) David pleads for God's tender mercies, lovingkindness and truth to preserve him (40:11) because innumerable evils (more than the hairs of his head) have surrounded him and his own iniquities have overtaken him so that he is not able to look up, and his heart has failed him (40:12). David says, "Be pleased, O Lord, to deliver me; O Lord, make haste to help me!" (40:13). Verses 13-17 are virtually identical to Psalm 70.

With a series of requests, all beginning with the word "let," David asks the Lord to let those who seek to destroy his life be ashamed and confused (40:14a). Let those who wish him evil be driven backward and brought to dishonor (40:14b). Let those who say to him "Aha, aha" (they were taunting him) be confounded because of their shame (40:15). Let those who seek the Lord rejoice and be glad in Him (40:16a). Let those who love God's salvation (deliverance) continually say, "The Lord be magnified" (40:16b).

David concludes, "But I am poor and needy; yet the Lord thinks of me. You are my help and my deliverer; do not delay, O my God" (40:17).

Summary: When countless problems overwhelm you, praise God for past deliverance, remember past obedience, and pray for the Lord's speedy deliverance.

A point to ponder: Don't be overcome; be an overcomer by looking to the Lord.

Psalm 41: When You Are Sick, Lied about, and Betrayed

Psalm 41 is a lament psalm written by David. In it, David speaks of being sick (41:3, 7), lying about (41:5-7), and being betrayed (41:9).

The Blessings of the Merciful (41:1-3) David opens this psalm by declaring that those who consider the poor are blessed (41:1). God blesses those who take care of those who cannot take care of themselves. Then, David mentions three ways the Lord will bless the merciful (see "the Lord" in verses 1, 2, and 3). The Lord will deliver the merciful in time of trouble (41:1). The Lord will keep the merciful alive and bless them, including not delivering them to their enemies (41:2). The Lord will strengthen and sustain them on their sickbed (41:3). In short, the blessings are deliverance (in a time of trouble and from enemies) and strength (during the time of illness).

A Plea for Mercy in Healing (41:4-9) Addressing the readers (see "I said"), David says he asked the Lord for mercy to heal his soul because he had sinned (41:4). Apparently, David had sinned and God had disciplined him with sickness (see 1 Cor. 11:30). To make matters worse, his enemies took advantage of his sickness. They asked, "When will he die, and his name perish?" (41:5).

Changing from the plural ("enemies") to the singular ("he"), David says, "If he comes to see me" (41:6). The word "me" is not in the Hebrew text (in English translations, it is in italics indicating it is not in the Hebrew text). In other words, when a particular individual came to see David lying on his sickbed, he did not come to console David; he came to see David suffering (David says he came to gather iniquity). When he left, he told lies about David (41:6).

Those who hated David started a whispering campaign designed to hurt him (41:7). They spread the gossip that an "evil disease" clings to him and he will not rise up from his sickbed (41:8). This is the second reference in this psalm to David's death. In verse 5, his enemies ask, "When will he die?" Now, in verse 8, those who hate him say he is going to die.

David's "familiar friend," one he trusted, one who ate his bread, lifted up his heel against him (41:9). The figure of lifting up a heel is taken from a horse that turns and kicks the one who fed him. David's close friend betrayed him. His "familiar friend" was a false friend! Part of this verse is quoted in John 13:18-19 as being ultimately fulfilled in Judas's betrayal of Jesus. As in David's case, Jesus and Judas ate together (Mt. 26:21-25; Mk. 14:18-21; Lk. 22:21) and Jesus called Judas a "friend" (Mt. 26:50).

A Plea for Mercy in Victory Over Enemies (41:10-13) This time addressing the Lord directly (see also 4), David asks the Lord to be merciful to him to raise him so that he can repay his enemies (41:10; David's enemies were those who opposed God's appointed king). David says he will know that the Lord is well-pleased with him because his enemies do not triumph over him (41:11). David adds that God upholds him in his integrity and sets him before His face forever (41:12). David asks for a long life on earth (41:2) and is sure of eternal life later (41:12).

The psalm begins by describing blessings for the merciful. It ends by blessing the Lord (41:13). The psalms can be divided into five "books" (see 72:18-19; 89:52; 106:84; 150:1-6). Psalm 41 is the last psalm in the first book. This doxology marks the end of Book I.

Summary: When you are sick due to sin and betrayed, plead for God's mercy for healing and vindication, knowing God blesses the merciful. He shows mercy to the merciful.

A point to ponder: Jesus said, "Blessed are the merciful, for they shall obtain mercy."

Psalm 42: When You Long for God and His People

Psalm 42 is an individual lament psalm, probably written by David. The superscription before the psalm says, "To the Chief Musician. A contemplation of the sons of Korah." The psalm was written by David to them (see the first person throughout the Psalter). They were singers in the Temple choir (2 Chron. 20:19). In some Hebrew manuscripts, Psalms 42 and 43 are united as one. In this psalm, the psalmist is separated from God's house (42:4, 6), is being taunted by his enemies (42:3, 10), and is discouraged (42:56). He longs for God and His people.

A Longing for God (42:1-5) Using an illustration of thirst, the psalmist expresses a deep desire for God. He says, "As the deer pants for the water brooks, so pants my soul for you, O God" (42:1). Perhaps he is referring to a deer longing for water in the midst of a prolonged drought. Then he plainly says, "My soul thirsts for God, for the living God" (42:2a).

With the question, "When shall I come and appear before God?" the psalmist explains what he has in mind. In the Old Testament, there was only one place where a person could appear before God: the Tabernacle (see 43:3) and, later, the Temple. In other words, the psalmist is lamenting being separated from the place where he could worship God. He is far north of Palestine (42:6; see also verse 4), yearning to return to the sanctuary in Jerusalem (see 43:3-4).

His enemies were continually saying to him, "Where is your God?" causing him to shed tears day and night (42:3). He adds, "When I remember these things, I pour out my soul within me. For I used to go with the multitude; I went with them to the house of God, with the voice of joy and praise, with a multitude that kept a pilgrim feast" (42:4). He longs to praise God with God's people. The author asks himself, "Why are you cast down, O my soul? And why are you disquieted within me? (42:5a; this is repeated in 42:11 and 43:5). Then he preaches to himself, saying, "Hope in God, for I shall yet praise Him" (42:5b), meaning he will praise God again in the sanctuary in Jerusalem with God's people (see "go with the multitude" in verse 4).

A Lament over Enemies (42:6-11) Turning his attention to God, the psalmist says, "O my God, my soul is cast down within me; therefore I will remember you from the land of Jordan, from the heights of Hebron, from the Hill Myzar" (42:6). The author is determined to remember the Lord, but in the meantime, he is overwhelmed. He views his troubles like a torrent of water pouring over him as if he were standing under a waterfall and on top of that is the noise of the waterfall (42:7). Even in the midst of his trouble, the Lord pours out His lovingkindness to him in the daytime, and he praises God at night (42:8).

Yet the author says, "I will say to God my Rock, 'Why have you forgotten me? Why do I go morning because of the oppression of the enemy?' As with the breaking of my bones, my enemies reproach me while they say to me all day long, 'Where is your God?'" (42:9-10). He is praising God (42:8) and, at the same time, he is asking God why He has not delivered him from his enemies (42:9-10). He calls God "my Rock" and, at the same time, asked God, "Why have you forgotten me?" (42:9).

The psalmist closes this lament by reminding himself that he will praise God again in Jerusalem. He says, "Why are you cast down, O my soul? And why are you disquieted within me? Hope in God; for I shall yet praise Him, the help of my countenance and my God" (43:11).

Summary: When you long for God and His people because you are separated from them, constantly remind yourself to trust the Lord for reunion.

A point to ponder: It is okay to talk to yourself, provided you say the right things to yourself.

Psalm 43: When Attacked by a Deceitful Enemy

Psalm 43 is a lament psalm, probably written by David. In some Hebrew manuscripts, Psalms 42 and 43 are united as one psalm. If that is the case, Psalm 43 is a continuation of Psalm 42. Psalm 42:5, 42:11, and 43:5 are exactly alike ("Why are you cast down, O my soul? And why are you disquieted within me? Hope in God; for I shall yet praise Him, the help of my countenance and my God"). In Psalm 43, the author speaks of being attacked by a deceitful enemy (43:1).

A Prayer for Vindication (43:1-2) The psalmist prays, "Vindicate me, O God, and plead my cause against an ungodly nation; Oh, deliver me from the deceitful and unjust man!" (43:1). A whole host of people were against him and one ungodly, unjust, and deceitful man had attacked him (see 42:10). The adversary had been deceitful, meaning he lied about him, making it even more difficult to defend himself. So he prays for God to vindicate him.

The psalmist explains ("for"), "For you are the God of my strength; why do you cast me off? Why do I go mourning because of the oppression of the enemy?" (43:2). The reason for asking God to vindicate him is that God is his strength, but he is perplexed as to why God has not intervened. The psalmist felt abandoned by God.

A Plea for Reunion (43:3) The psalmist pleads with the Lord, "Oh, send out your light in Your truth! Let them lead me; but them bring me to your holy hill and your tabernacle" (43:3). The psalmist is pleading for the Lord to deliver him from the false accusations of his enemy. Only God's light and truth could deliver him from the lies of his enemy. Furthermore, the psalmist pleads with the Lord to bring him to God's holy hill (Mount Zion in Jerusalem) where he can be reunited with God's people worshiping God in God's Tabernacle.

A Promise of Praise (43:4-5) The psalmist adds, "Then I will go to the altar of God, to God my exceeding joy; and on the harp, I will praise you, O God, my God" (43:4). The psalmist makes a promise that when he is delivered and allowed to go back to Jerusalem, he will publicly praise God at the altar of the Tabernacle.

Psalm 43 concludes with the same refrain mentioned twice in Psalm 42 (see 42:5, 11): "Why are you cast down, O my soul? And why are you disquieted within me? Hope in God; for I shall yet praise him, the help of my countenance and my God" (43:5). This is an expression of confidence and trust in the Lord that God will answer his prayer to be allowed to return to Jerusalem.

Summary: When a deceitful enemy attacks you, pray for God to vindicate you, plead your case with the Lord, trust Him to answer you, and praise Him when He does.

An adversary may falsely accuse you, but you can be confident that God will ultimately vindicate you and bring you into His presence, where you can praise Him.

The refrain that is repeated three times in these two psalms ("Why are you cast down, O my soul? And why are you disquieted within me? Hope in God; for I shall yet praise him, the help of my countenance and my God" in 42:5, 11, and 43:5) indicates that the author talked to himself.

A point to ponder: Use self-talk to remind yourself not to be discouraged and to encourage yourself to trust the Lord.

Psalm 44: When You Are Innocent and Suffer Defeat

Psalm 44 is a national lament psalm probably written by David. For an explanation of the sons of Korah, see the note at the beginning of Psalm 42. In this psalm, the author is innocent and suffers defeat (44:17-19).

Praise for Past Victory (44:1-8) The psalmist begins by telling God that they have heard from their fathers what He had done in the past (44:1). It was God who conquered the land under Joshua (44:2); it was not their hands, but God's hand that gave them possession of the land (44:3). Therefore, God is to be praised (44:8) for giving the victory (44:4; this singular "my" is used collectively of the nation of Israel; see "our" in verse 5). Through the Lord, Israel will be victorious over their enemies (44:5, 7) because they do not trust their bow or sword to save them (44:6). God is to be trusted and praised. In the present defeat (44:9-16), people need to be reminded of what God has done for them in the past.

Lament for the Present Defeat (44:9-16) In the present situation, the Lord did not go with the army (44:9). Consequently, they had to retreat and the enemy took spoils (44:10). The nation was like sheep slaughtered for food (44:11); God sold them for next to nothing (44:12). Israel was a reproach, scorn, and derision among their neighbors (44:13). They were made a byword (a proverbial saying) among the nations, who shook their heads (44:14). In other words, Israel was being laughed at and ridiculed. They were experiencing dishonor and shame (44:15), because of the reproach of their enemy and avenger (44:16).

Protest of Their Innocence (44:17-22) Throughout their ordeal, Israel remained faithful. Even though "all of this has come upon us" (ridicule, dishonor, shame, and reproach), "we have not forgotten You, nor have we dealt falsely with Your covenant" (44:17; they had not forsaken the Mosaic Covenant), but You have "broken us and covered us with the shadow of death" (44:19).

The psalmist says, "If we had forgotten the name of our God, or stretched out our hands to a foreign God, would not God search this out? For he knows the secrets of the heart" (44:20-21). Verses 17-21 are a protest of their innocence. They have been loyal to the Lord. They would have deserved their defeat if they had deserted the Lord, but even in the face of a disastrous defeat and abandonment (temporarily) by the Lord, they continued to obey Him.

The psalmist adds, "Yet for your sake, we have been killed all the day long; we are counted as sheep for the slaughter" (44:22). Even though they had been loyal to the Lord, they were being killed for His sake. The world is at war with the Lord. Paul quoted this verse in Romans 8:36 as proof that God does not forsake them even though God's people suffer.

Plea for God's Intervention (44:23-26) The psalmist concludes the psalm with a passionate plea for the Lord to intervene. He cries, "Awake! Why do you sleep, O Lord? Arise! Do not cast us off forever" (44:23). He asks, "Why do you hide your face and forget our affliction and our oppression? (44:24). He explains, "For our soul is bowed down to the dust; our body clings to the ground" (44:25). They were about to die. So, the psalmist pleads, "Arise for our help, and redeem us for your mercy's sake" (44:26). The Lord had sold them (44:12) and now he asked the Lord to buy them back ("redeem us"). The psalmist pleads God's mercy, not their faithfulness.

Summary: When you are innocent and suffer defeat, praise God for past victories, pour out your heart in the present defeat, and plead for intervention, reminding God of your innocence.

A point to ponder: If you are innocent when suffering, plead your innocence before God.

Psalm 45: When You Contemplate a Royal Wedding

Psalm 45 is a royal psalm, probably written by David. For an explanation of the sons of Korah, see the note at the beginning of Psalm 42. It is about the wedding of a king in Israel (perhaps Solomon), but ultimately refers to the Messiah, who will fulfill all of it (45:6-7, 14).

Praise for the Groom (45:1-9) With his heart "overflowing with a good theme," the psalmist recites his composition concerning the King. He says, "My tongue is the pen of a ready writer" (45:1). He speaks out of a heart full of joy. Describing the groom, the psalmist says, "You are fairer than the sons of men; grace is poured upon your lips; therefore, God has blessed You forever" (45:2). The King is the greatest, as is evident by His gracious speech which God has blessed forever. Addressing the King as "Mighty one" (a messianic title), the psalmist tells Him to gird His sword on his thigh (45:3) and to ride "prosperously because of truth, humility, and righteousness" (45:4). The enemies of injustice will fall under Him (45:5).

The King is addressed as God (45:6); His throne is forever, and, yet, He is distinguished from God, in that God has anointed Him with the oil of gladness more than His companions (45:7). The New Testament book of Hebrews applies verses 6 and 7 to Jesus (Heb. 1:8-9). The house of David was promised an eternal throne (2 Sam. 7:16). Jesus will be the eternal occupant of it (Lk. 1:32-22). The ancient Davidic kings of Israel foreshadowed the coming of King Jesus.

As the King comes "out of the ivory palaces," His wedding garments are scented with myrrh, aloes, and cassia, that is, perfumes (45:8). The daughters of the King (His attendants) were among the most honorable women and the queen, arrayed in gold, stands at His right hand (45:9).

Advice for the Bride (45:10-15) The queen is advised to forget family and people (45:10). Her husband is to be the primary object of her affection (Gen. 2:24). She is reminded that the King will desire her beauty and "because He is your Lord, worship Him" (45:11). The daughter of Tyre will bring a gift (a gift from Tyre was a most desirable gift) and the rich will seek her favor (45:12). As queen she will have the love and respect of other powerful people.

The bride is a "royal daughter," the daughter of a king. She is clothed in glorious apparel of wool laced with gold (45:13). She is brought to the King "in robes of many colors" followed by bridesmaids (45:14). "With gladness and rejoicing," they enter the king's palace (45:15).

A Benediction for the Couple (45:16-17) The psalmist pronounces a benediction of great prosperity on the King. His sons (descendants) shall outnumber the fathers (ancestors) and the sons shall be princes in all the earth (45:16). His name will be remembered for all generations and the people will praise Him forever (45:17).

Summary: When contemplating a royal wedding (or any wedding), remember that Jesus is a coming King who will marry His bride.

Psalm 45 describes a royal wedding between an ancient king of Israel and his bride, but it is evident that the psalm goes beyond a royal wedding of two humans (see "forever" in verses 2, 6, 17 and "worship Him" in verse 11, as well as the fact that the King is called God in verse 6). King Jesus will return to be married to His bride (Rev. 19:7-9, 11-16). In the meantime, we should tell people of the coming King (45:1), make Him the primary object of our affection (45:10), and worship Him (45:11).

A point to ponder: The Bible uses ordinary things to remind us of spiritual things. Think about that when you see such ordinary things as a wedding or a traffic light (stop, caution, go).

Psalm 46: When You Are in Physical Danger

Psalm 46 is a trust psalm written by an unknown author. For an explanation of the sons of Korah, see the note at the beginning of Psalm 42. This psalm may have been written during the siege of Jerusalem by Sennacherib (2 Kings 18:13-19:37). In it, the psalmist is in physical danger (see "refuge" in 46:1, 7, 11 and see 146:9).

God's Protection (46:1-3) The psalmist proclaims, "God is our refuge and strength, a very present help in trouble" (46:1). In the ancient world, a city's defense was that it was built on a high hill surrounded by a high wall. The psalmist declares that God, not the city or the wall, is our defense. God is also our strength and is present to help in times of trouble. The figure of a refuge suggests that the trouble is a physical danger.

The psalmist concludes, "Therefore we will not fear even though the earth be moved, and the mountains be carried into the midst of the sea; the waters roar and be troubled, though the mountains shake with its swelling" (46:2-3). The psalmist will not fear no matter what happens. Even if the mountains and the sea fall apart, the psalmist will not fear because he will trust the Lord as his shelter and strength in every actual and imagined situation.

God's Presence (46:4-7) The psalmist turns his attention to Jerusalem. He says, "There is a river whose streams shall make glad the city of God, the holy place of the tabernacle of the most high" (46:4). The stream that makes the city of Jerusalem glad may be a reference to the tunnel that king Hezekiah had built at the siege by Sennacherib to carry water from the Gihon spring outside the city to a cistern inside the city (2 Chron. 32:30). Likewise since God is in the midst of His people, He will help them at the break of dawn when military attacks often occurred and they shall not be moved (46:5). Even though the nations may rage and kingdoms are moved when God uttered His voice the earth melted; this is an indication of His mighty power (46:6). So, God's people can say, "The Lord of hosts is with us; the God of Jacob is our refuge. Selah" (46:7). The God who preserved Jacob is with His people and is their refuge. New Testament believers can say that the Lord is with us; He is in us.

God's Exaltation (46:8-11) The psalmist invites the people of God to "Come, behold the works of the Lord." He has made desolations in the earth (46:8), makes wars to cease to the end of the earth, breaks the bow and cuts the spear in two, and burns the chariot in the fire (46:9). God's people are to view in their mind's eye the Lord's past deliverances of His people. Ultimately, the Messiah will do such things during His reign on the earth (Isa. 2:2-4; 11:6-9).

God invites His people to "Be still, and know that I am God; I will be exalted among the nations, I will be exalted in the earth" (46:10). The command to be still has been used as an exhortation to prepare for worship, but in the context of this psalm, it is a call for stillness before the Lord for impending judgment (see Hab. 2:20; Zeph. 1:7; Zech. 2:13). He will be victorious. He will be exalted. All the earth will bow before Him.

The psalmist repeats the refrain given in verse 7, "The Lord of hosts is with us; the God of Jacob is our refuge. Selah" (46:11). The psalm begins and ends with God being a refuge.

Summary: When you are in physical danger, do not fear; remember that the Lord is with you, the Lord is a refuge, and the Lord is present to help and strengthen.

Psalm 46 was the basis for Martin Luther's hymn "A Mighty Fortress Is Our God."

A point to ponder: Seek the Lord for His strength, whether in danger or not.

Psalm 47: When You Are Called to Praise the King

Psalm 47 is an enthronement psalm (47:1-9, 93, 95-99) written by an unknown author. For an explanation of the sons of Korah, see the note at the beginning of Psalm 42. In Psalm 47, people are called to praise the King (47:1-2, 6-7).

A Call to Praise the Coming King (47:1-4) All peoples (nations) are called to clap their hands and shout to God with the voice of triumph (47:1). The clapping of the hands is an indication of joy and, in this case, adoration. The reason ("for") is the Lord is awesome; "He is a great King over all the earth" (47:2). The Hebrew word translated "awesome" means "fear, to stand in awe, reverence." The Lord is the great Sovereign of the universe. Everyone on the earth should applaud Him with joy.

The Lord is sitting on the throne now, but in the future, "He will subdue the peoples under us, and the nations under our feet. He will choose our inheritance for us, the excellence of Jacob whom He loves. Selah" (47:3-4). The "us" in these verses is a reference to Israel ("Jacob"). As the Sovereign King of the universe, the Lord will one day subdue all nations and, at that time, give Israel her inheritance, the land of Canaan. When Jesus Christ returns, He will subdue all nations and exalt Israel. The inheritance of New Testament believers is their reward for service at the Judgment Seat of Christ (Col. 3:22-24).

A Call to Praise the Enthroned King (47:5-7) The coming King is now pictured as an enthroned King. Thus, the psalmist says, "God has gone up with a shout, the Lord with the sound of the trumpet" (47:5). Hence the call, "Sing praises to God, sing praises! Sing praises to our King, sing praises! (47:6). The reason ("for") for singing praises is "God is the King of all the earth; sing praises with understanding" (47:7). By this point in the psalm, He is enthroned as the King of all the earth.

A Call to Praise the Reign of the King (47:8-9) Having been enthroned, the King now reigns. "God reigns over the nations; God sits on His holy throne" (47:8). Jesus Christ is the One who will rule over all the nations of the earth (Rev. 19:15).

The psalmist concludes, "The princes of the people have gathered together, the people of the God of Abraham. For the shields of the earth belong to God; He is greatly exalted" (47:9). Shields are symbols of authority. When the King is enthroned, the shields of the earth belong to Him.

Summary: When you are called to sing praises to the King, which all the people of the earth are called to do, praise Him for His present and future reign with joy, adoration, and reverence.

All the people of the earth (see "all you peoples" in verse 1 and "all the earth" in verse 2) are to praise the God of Israel (see "Jacob who He loves" in verse 6 and "the God of Abraham" in verse 9) who will one day rule over them.

A point to ponder: When the Lord taught the disciples how to pray, He instructed them to say, "Your kingdom come" (Mt. 6:10), a reference to the future kingdom the Lord will set up when He comes. We should think about the coming kingdom more often, especially in our prayer life.

Psalm 48: When God Has Protected You

Psalm 48 is a praise psalm written by an unknown author. For an explanation of the sons of Korah, see the note at the beginning of Psalm 42. In Psalm 48, God protects Jerusalem (48:4-6).

The Greatness of Jerusalem (48:1-3) The psalmist begins by declaring, "Great is the Lord and greatly to be praised," but quickly turning his attention to Jerusalem, he adds, "in the city of our God, in His holy mountain" (48:1). The city of God is Jerusalem, which is on top of a hill. The psalmist says that Mount Zion on the sides of the north is beautiful, the joy of the whole earth, and the city of the great King (48:2). Mount Zion is another name for Jerusalem. It is said to be on the sides of the north because the Canaanites thought the gods resided in some remote northern location. Jesus called Jerusalem "the city of the great King" (Mt. 5:35). The psalmist declares that the true God resides in Jerusalem. The Ark of the Covenant was there. God was even in the palaces of Jerusalem and was known as her refuge (48:3). Jerusalem is great because it is the city of the great King.

The Security of Jerusalem (48:3-8) In the next subsection of the psalm, the psalmist describes the kings of the world approaching and retreating from Jerusalem. He says they assembled, passed by (48:4), saw it, marveled, were troubled, and hastened away (48:5). Fear and pain gripped them, pain as of a woman in birth pangs (48:6) and as when God breaks the ships of Tarshish with an east wind (48:7). As the east wind, which could destroy the mighty ships on the Mediterranean, caused the sailors to fear, so the kings who assembled against Jerusalem were afraid and hastened away. The Lord delivered Jerusalem. The psalmist himself heard and saw the Lord deliver Jerusalem; he declares God will establish it forever (48:8).

The Rejoicing over Jerusalem (48:9-14) As a result of the victory described in verses 4-8, the psalmist says they thought about God's lovingkindness (48:9) and righteousness (48:10b). God is to be praised to the ends of the earth (48:10a). Let Mount Zion (Jerusalem) rejoice (48:11a). Let the daughters of Judah (the cities of Judea) be glad (48:11b).

The psalmist invites people to walk around Zion (Jerusalem), count her towers (48:12), mark her bulwarks, and consider her palaces so they may tell what happened to following generations (48:13). The psalmist concludes, "This is God, our God forever and ever; He will be our guide even to death" (48:14).

Summary: When God has protected you, rejoice, praise Him, and proclaim to others, including the next generation, His lovingkindness and righteousness.

A point to ponder: When God delivers us, we usually thank Him for His deliverance but often forget to go to the next level and praise Him for His lovingkindness.

Psalm 49: When You Are Intimidated by the Wealthy

Psalm 49 is a wisdom psalm written by an unknown author. For an explanation of the sons of Korah, see the note at the beginning of Psalm 42. In Psalm 49, the wicked wealthy intimidates the psalmist (49:5-6).

A Plea to Hear Wisdom (49:1-4) All the peoples of the earth (49:1-2) are called to hear wisdom (49:3). The psalmist says he will listen (49:4a) and once he has learned, he will disclose his dark saying on his harp (49:4b). The Hebrew word translated "dark saying" means "riddle, enigma, perplexing question." As the rest of the psalm reveals, the perplexing question has to do with being intimidated (perhaps oppressed) by the wicked wealthy (see "fear" in verse 5 and "afraid" in verse 16).

A Pronouncement on the Worthlessness of Wealth (49:5-12) Seeing sin all around him, the psalmist asks why *he* should fear (49:5). As the next verse indicates, he is talking about the sin of those who trust in their wealth (49:6). He declares that none of those who trust in their wealth can redeem his brother nor give God a ransom for him (49:7). He explains ("for") that redemption is costly (49:8) and that wealth will not prevent death (49:9). The words "ransom" and "redemption" are not references to spiritual salvation. We cannot buy our way out of dying (see verses 10-11). When it comes to death, wealth is worthless. Both the wise and the fool die, leaving their wealth to others (49:10). They think they will live forever. They called their lands by their own name to perpetuate it (49:11), but like animals, they die (49:12). Wealth may get a building or a street named after you, but it cannot prevent death.

A Proclamation to Trust God (49:13-20) Those who are foolish (49:13) are like sheep who die, and their beauty is consumed in the grave (49:14). Death is like a shepherd leading them to the grave. When the psalmist says, "The upright shall have dominion over them in the morning" (49:14), he means the upright will have the upper hand over the wicked in the next life. Thus, the psalmist can confidently proclaim, "But God will redeem my soul from the power of the grave, for He shall receive me" (49:15). God will receive him on the other side of the grave. (Some interpret "morning" to be the dawning of a new day, that is, cessation of the evil days mentioned in verse 5, but the expressions "the power of the grave" and "He shall receive me" in verse 15 support the idea the psalmist is talking about living with the Lord forever.)

In verse 5, the psalmist said he would not fear. Now, he tells others not to be afraid. He says, "Do not be afraid when one becomes rich when the glory of his house is increased" (49:16) "for when he dies he shall carry nothing away; his glory shall not descend after him" (49:17). Do not be intimidated by the wicked wealthy. As the saying goes, "You can't take it with you." The psalmist goes on to say that while the wicked wealthy live, they bless themselves (49:18), but they shall die just like their fathers before them (49:19). The psalm ends with the same basic refrain in verse 12, namely, like the animals the wicked wealthy will die (49:20). The difference is their lack of endurance in verse 12 and their lack of understanding in verse 20.

Summary: When intimidated by the wicked wealthy, listen to the wisdom that reminds us that the wicked die and cannot take their wealth with them, but those who know the Lord will be received by Him when they die.

A point to ponder: From an eternal perspective, life looks different.

Psalm 50: When God Judges You

Psalm 50 is a wisdom psalm written by Asaph. In it, God judges His people (50:4).

An Introduction of the Judge (50:1-6) In the first six verses, a number of things are said about God, but the main point is that He is a Judge (50:6). The "Mighty One, God the Lord" calls the earth to stand before Him (50:1). Out of Zion (Jerusalem; 50:2), the perfection of beauty, God shines forth. When He comes, devouring fire and tempestuous storm will be before Him (50:3). He is coming to judge His people (50:4). So, He says, "Gather my saints together to Me" (50:5) and the psalmist adds, "Let the heavens declare His righteousness, for God Himself is Judge" (50:6).

The First Indictment by the Judge (50:7-15) God invites His people to hear their God who will testify against them (50:7). He will rebuke them for their sacrifices (50:8) and not take sacrifices from them (50:9). He doesn't need their sacrifices, because all the beasts of the field, the cattle on a thousand hills, birds of the mountain, and wild beast of the field are His (50:9-11). He says, "If I were hungry, I would not tell you; for all the world is Mine and all its fullness" (50:12), adding, "Will I eat the flesh of bulls, or drink the blood of goats?" (50:13). The point is, God does not need their sacrifices.

Why is God rebuking them for bringing sacrifices? Did He not command them to do that? The psalmist explains their problem when he says, "Offer to God thanksgiving and pay your vows to the most high" (50:14). God adds, "Call upon Me in the day of trouble; I will deliver you and you shall glorify Me" (50:15). They were offering sacrifices, but they were not doing it with thanksgiving, nor were they calling on the Lord to deliver them out of their trouble.

Second Indictment by the Judge (50:16-23) God indicts them because they talk about His covenant (50:16), but they hate instruction which is obvious from the fact that they do not obey Him (50:17). God accuses them of consenting with a thief, being partakers with adulterers (50:18), using their mouths to speak evil and deceit (50:19), and slandering their own brother (50:20). They give lip service to God's Word (15:16), but they disobey it (50:17-20). They were hypocrites! Furthermore, apparently, they thought God was like them (50:21)! God says He has been silent, but now He will rebuke them (50:21).

In light of the judgment to come, God gives His people this counsel: "Now consider this, you who forget God, lest I tear you in pieces, and there be none to deliver: whoever offers praise glorifies me; and to him who orders his conduct aright I will show the salvation (deliverance) of God" (50:22-23). God wants His people to praise Him and practice righteousness. When they look to Him instead of forgetting Him, He will deliver them from their troubles.

Summary: When God judges you, He judges you for your sins against Him and your sins against others.

God's people had sinned against Him, a violation of the first part of the Ten Commandments, and against others, a violation of the second part of the Ten Commandments. God does not want just the externals of religion; He wants people who have an internal attitude of gratitude, trust and obey Him, and treat others according to His Word.

A point to ponder: Going through the motions of the externals of religion (attending church, reading the Bible, etc.) and even talking about God's Word does not please God. God wants gratitude, dependence upon Him, and a loving relationship with others.

Psalm 51: When You Commit Serious Sins

Psalm 51 is a penitential psalm written by David. In it, David is confessing his serious sin with Bathsheba (see the superscription; 2 Sam. 11-12).

A Prayer for Forgiveness (51:1-6) Having committed adultery with Bathsheba and the murder of Uriah, her husband, and having been exposed by Nathan the prophet, David prays for God to blot out the record of his transgression (51:1b), washing him from his iniquity, and cleansing him from his sin (51:2) based on His mercy (Hebrew: grace), lovingkindness, and tender mercies (Hebrew: compassion) (51:1). The reason ("for") for cleansing is confession. David confesses that he has transgressed God's law, that his sin is ever before him (15:3), and that his sin is against God, who is justice and blameless when He judges (51:4). About a year had lapsed between David's sin and his confession. For a year, his sin had been constantly in his thoughts (for more details, see 32:3-4).

David not only confesses his sin, he confesses that he is a sinner by nature—from the moment of conception (51:5). He was a sinner when he came out of the womb! In other words, the real problem is not just David's act of sin but his nature. Thus, David says, "Behold, You desire truth in the inward parts, and in the hidden part You will make me to know wisdom" (51:6). The problem is internal, and therefore the solution is internal.

A Prayer for Restoration (51:7-12) With a series of requests, one right after the other, David requests restoration. He pleads: purge me with hyssop (the hyssop branch was used in ceremonial cleansing), wash me (51:7), make me to hear joy (51:8; the reference to broken bones is a figurative way of saying that his sin had crushed him), blot out my iniquities from the record so that You do not see it anymore (51:9), create a clean heart in me (51:10), renew a steadfast spirit within me (51:10), do not take Your Holy Spirit from me (51:11), restore the joy of my salvation and uphold me by Your generous Spirit (51:12). In the Old Testament, the Holy Spirit was given for service. When David asks that the Holy Spirit not be taken from him, he asks that God not take away his service as the king. David is not saying anything about the loss of his salvation. He is concerned about the loss of the *joy* of his salvation.

A Promise of Service (51:13-19) Dave promises God that if He delivers him from the "guilt of bloodshed" (a reference to his murder of Uriah, Bathsheba's husband), he will teach others God's ways (51:13) and sing of God's righteousness (51:14); he will praise God (51:15). David explains ("for") that if God desired an animal sacrifice, he would give it, but God does not delight in burnt offerings (15:16). "The sacrifices of God are a broken spirit, a broken and a contrite heart" which God will not despise (15:17). David closes by praying for Jerusalem. He asks that God build the walls of Jerusalem (51:18), so that He will be pleased (the same Hebrew word translated "delight" in verse 16) with the sacrifices of righteousness as well as the animal sacrifices they will offer (15:19).

Summary: When you commit serious sins, ask God for forgiveness and restoration and promise to serve Him after you are forgiven.

A point to ponder: This psalm illustrates how sin affects the sinner (51:3, 8), others (51:14), and God (51:4). It also indicates that forgiveness affects the sinner (51:13), others (51:13), and God (51: 14, 15, 19). David's service consisted of teaching, singing, and praying for others.

Psalm 52: When Someone Lies About You

Psalm 52 is a didactic psalm written by David. In it, David is thinking of Doeg the Edomite telling Saul David had fled to Ahimelech, the priest at Nob, for provisions (see the superscription; 1 Sam. 21:7, 22:9-10). Angered by that, Saul had Doeg destroy the priest and his family (1 Sam. 22:11-19).

A Description of the Wicked (52:1-4) The psalm opens with a question, "Why do you boast in evil, O mighty man?" (52:1a). The mighty man is Doeg, who not only did something evil (he killed Ahimelech, his family, and others; see 1 Sam. 22:18-19.), he boasted about it! David asked this question in light of the fact that "the goodness of God endures continually" (51:1b). The Hebrew word translated "goodness" is the one that is often translated "lovingkindness." The boasting of the wicked, which is temporary (52:5), is in striking contrast to the lovingkindness of God, which endures.

David describes Doeg by talking about his tongue and his heart. Doeg speaks deceitfully, which makes his tongue destructive like a sharp razor (52:2). Words are deceitful when they misrepresent the truth. The problem, however, is not just his speech; it is his heart. He *loves* evil more than good and, thus, would rather speak lies than righteousness (52:3). He loves devouring words; David calls him a "deceitful tongue" (52:4). To speak deceiving words that destroy people is bad, but to *love* to do it is worse.

The Destruction of the Wicked (52:5-7) After saying that God will destroy Doeg, David describes the destruction more specifically. God will take him away, pluck him out of his dwelling place, and uproot him from the land of the living (52:5). He will die. David adds that the righteous shall see, fear (stand in awe before God), and laugh at the one who is destroyed (52:6), saying, "Here is the man who did not make God his strength, but trusted in the abundance of his riches and strengthened himself in his wickedness" (52:7).

The Declaration of the Righteousness (52:8-9) In contrast to the wicked, who trust their riches and end up with nothing, David says he is like a green olive tree in the house of God (52:8a). The green olive tree is a figure of both prosperity and longevity. Olive trees can live hundreds of years. In contrast to his uprooted enemy (2:5), David is a stable, flourishing green olive tree (see 1:2-3). David then makes three declarations.

David declares, "I trust in the mercy of God forever and ever" (52:8b). The Hebrew word translated "mercy" is the same one that is translated "goodness" in verse 1 and, as in verse 1, it means lovingkindness. Rather than trust in riches (52:7), David declares he will trust in the grace of God.

David declares, "I will praise You forever because You have done it" (52:9a). David will praise God because it is God by His grace (52:8b) who, in contrast to the wicked, has made him stable and prosperous with the prospect of living a long life (52:8a).

David declares, "In the presence of Your saints I will wait on Your name, for it is good" (52:9). David will wait on the Lord to deal with his enemy, confident in the character of God.

Summary: When someone lies about you, remember that God will judge the wicked, trust the Lord, praise the Lord, and wait on the Lord to deal with the wicked person in your life.

A point to ponder: When hurt and harmed by the deceitful, destructive lies of someone, don't despair; trust the Lord to deal with them and, in the meantime, praise the Lord for His goodness.

Psalm 53: When You Observe People

Psalm 53 is a wisdom psalm written by David. Except for using "God" instead of "Lord" (53:4, 6) and a few changes in verses 5 and 6, Psalm 53 is identical to Psalm 14. In Psalm 53, David observes people (53:2).

The Sinfulness of the Human Race (53:1-3) Like Psalm 14, Psalm 53 begins by saying, "The fool has said in his heart, 'There is no God.' They are corrupt, and have done abominable iniquity; there is none who does good" (53:1). Although the psalm begins by speaking about the fool, it becomes obvious that it is about the whole human race (see "none," in verse 1 and "the children of men" in verse 2, etc.). Because sinners do not believe there is a God (or they do not seek Him, 53:2) and because they are morally corrupt, they do abominable iniquity, such as devouring God's people (53:4). None do the good that is acceptable by God.

The Lord looks down from heaven to see if He can find any who understand His truth or seek Him (53:2). He discovers that all have turned aside from His will and ways and become corrupt: "There is none who does good, no, not one" (53:3). Not even God can find an exception to the sinfulness of the human race! Paul cites these verses in Romans 3:10-12 to demonstrate the universal sinfulness of people.

To sum up, people on this planet do not do the good that is acceptable to God, are morally corrupt, do abominable iniquity, do not understand God's truth or seek Him, and have turned aside from His will. The fool says, "There is no God;" the rest live as if there is no God.

The Judgment of Sinners (53:4-6) God asks, "Have all the workers of iniquity no knowledge, who eat up my people as they eat bread, and do not call on God?" (53:4). Those who do not call on the Lord are workers of iniquity who devour God's people like eating bread.

Psalm 53:5 says, "There they are in great fear, where no fear was, for God has scattered the bones of him who encamps against you; you have put them to shame because God has despised them" (53:5). The word "there" is a reference to the judgment. Because sinners have not called on the Lord (53:4), they will have great fear when they stand before God. In the meantime, God has delivered Israel. He has "scattered the bones of him who encamps against you" and "despised them." Thus, Israel has been able to put them to shame (53:5). This verse differs from Psalm 14:5, which suggests that perhaps Psalm 14 is being applied to a specific deliverance of Israel.

The Longing for the Kingdom (53:6) David concludes, "Oh, that the salvation of Israel would come out of Zion! When God brings back the captivity of His people, let Jacob rejoice, let Israel be glad" (53:6). David longs for the "salvation of Israel," that is, the deliverance of Israel from sinners. He longs for God to "bring back the captivity of his people," which is a longing to establish the messianic kingdom on the earth. Zion, another name for Jerusalem, will be the capital of the kingdom. When the kingdom comes, God will judge sinners who devour His people (53:4), and Israel will rejoice (53:6).

Summary: When you observe people, especially those who harm God's people, note that they do not know God, are sinners, and do abominable iniquity, but God will judge them.

A point to ponder: When you see (or experience) sinners harming others (or you), remember that God will judge them.

Psalm 54: When Your Enemies Do Evil

Psalm 54 is a lament psalm written by David. David is dealing with the Ziphites, revealing to Saul that David was hiding among them (see the superscription; 1 Sam. 22; 23:19-23; 26:1-3).

A Prayer for Deliverance (54:1-3) David begins this psalm by making four requests (54:1-2). "Save me, O God, by Your name, and vindicate me by Your strength" (54:1). God's name and God's strength are virtual synonyms (this is called a synonymous parallelism, that is, the second half of verse means the same thing as the first half). By asking God to vindicate him, David is protesting his innocence. David adds, "Hear my prayer, O God; give ear to the words of my mouth" (54:2). In short, hear my prayer to deliver me and vindicate me.

David gives the reason for his request ("for"). He says, "For strangers have risen up against me, and oppressors have sought after my life; they have not set God before them. Selah" (54:3). The strangers are the people of Ziph and the oppressors are the soldiers of Saul. In this case, David is asking for God's assistance because the hostility of his enemies was contrary to God's will.

A Proclamation of God's Help (54:4-5) Suddenly, David proclaims, "Behold, God is my helper; the Lord is with those who uphold my life" (54:4). It is possible that at this point in the Psalm, David received a message that God had indeed delivered him (54:7). At any rate, David is confident that God will help him and deliver him from the threat of death.

David continues, "He will repay my enemies for their evil. Cut them off in Your truth" (54:5). The key word here is "truth." David is talking about justice, repaying his enemies for their evil. The issue is not that David hates his enemies. It is that they have done evil.

A Promise to Praise (54:6-7) David says, "I will freely sacrifice to You; I will praise Your name, O Lord, for it is good" (54:6). The free sacrifice of which David speaks is the free will (peace) offering mentioned by Moses (Lev. 3, 7). God's name is good (see 52:9), that is, God is good. God is good and just to deliver David and punish his enemies, who are God's enemies as well (54:3).

David gives the reason for his praise ("for"). He says, "For He has delivered me out of all trouble; and my eye has seen its desire upon my enemies" (54:7). David will praise the Lord because his prayer has been answered. He has been delivered and his enemies have been punished.

Summary: When your enemies do evil (they are acting contrary to God's will), pray for the Lord to deliver you based on His justice and praise Him when He answers your prayer.

A point to ponder: When faced with an evil enemy, it is proper to pray for justice. In this case, God may deliver you and punish your enemies sooner than you think, but God will punish evil one way or another (in time or at the judgment).

Psalm 55: When a Friend Turns Against You

Psalm 55 is a lament psalm written by David. In it, David is dealing with an intimate friend (55:12-13) turning against him. Many commentators have suggested that the friend was Ahithophel (2 Sam. 15:31).

A Plea for Himself (55:1-8) David pleads with the Lord to hear his prayer (55:1-2) because of the oppression of his enemy (55:3a). He explains ("for") that they (his enemy and his cohorts) hate him, bring trouble upon him (55:3b), he is severely pained (55:4), and the horror of their threats has overwhelmed him (55:5). So he says, "Oh that I might have wings like a dove! I would fly away and be at rest" (55:6). If he could, he would wander into the wilderness (55:7) to escape "from the windy storm and tempest" (55:8). He felt like running away!

A Petition Concerning His Enemy (55:9-15) Turning his attention to his enemies, David petitions the Lord to destroy and divide their tongues (cause confusion as He did at Babel), because of the violence and strife they have caused in the city (55:9). They are constantly causing trouble (55:10). Because of these terrorists, destruction, oppression, and deceit do not depart from the streets (55:11). Note, these people caused violence, strife, iniquity, trouble, destruction, oppression, and deceit.

David explains that his opponent is not an enemy who hates him. If that were the case, he could bear it or hide from him (55:12). His antagonist was his companion, his confidant, his close friend with whom he had worshiped the Lord. He and his intimate friend shared "sweet counsel" (55:13-14). Now, his good friend has become his adversary who has stabbed him in the back. So his petition is that death would seize his former friend and his allies because of their wickedness (55:15). Letting them "go alive" into the grave describes a violent rather than peaceful death. Those who live by the sword die by the sword. Sin leads to death (Rom. 6:23).

A Proclamation of Confidence in God (55:16-23) David declares that he will call upon God and the Lord will save him (55:16). He is determined to call on the Lord morning, noon, and night (55:17). God will deliver him from the many who are against him (55:18). God will hear him and afflict them because they do not fear God (55:19). His enemy has broken the peace they had between them (55:20). Their words were smoother than butter, but war was in their hearts; their words were softer than oil, but they drew their swords (55:21). They were full of deceit.

David invites others to cast their burden on the Lord, who will sustain them and never permit the righteous to be moved (55:22; see 1 Pet. 5:7).

David concludes by proclaiming that God will bring these bloodthirsty and deceitful men down to destruction and that he will trust in the Lord (55:23).

Summary: When a friend turns against you, pour out your pain to the Lord, ask Him to destroy your adversary (ask for justice), and trust Him to do it.

A point to ponder: When stabbed in the back by a close friend, do not take out your own knife; drop to your knees, pour out your pain to the Lord, and trust Him for justice.

Psalm 56: When You Fear for Your Life

Psalm 56 is a lament psalm David wrote when the Philistines captured him in Gath and he feigned insanity (see 1 Sam. 21:10-15). In it, David feared for his life (56:3, 6).

A Plea for Deliverance (56:1-7) David pleads with the Lord, "Be merciful to me, O God" (56:1a). Then he explains why he needs God's mercy ("for"). He speaks of a man fighting him all day and swallowing him up (56:1b). He explains that it is not just a single man; many fight against him and hound him all day (56:2).

David declares, "Whenever I am afraid, I will trust in you" (56:3). He is determined to praise God's Word, trust in God's mercy, and not fear (56:4). Thus, he asks, "What can flesh do to me?" (56:4; see Rom. 8:31). The implied answer to his question is that no one can do anything to him unless God permits it.

David describes his enemies. He says all day they twist his words and all of their thoughts are of evil against him (56:5a). They gather together, hide, mark his steps and lie in wait for his life (56:6b). They plot his death and attempt to carry out their plan. David asks, "Shall they escape by iniquity?" (56:7) and pleads, "In anger cast down the peoples, O God!" (56:7). They are planning iniquity (his death) and since God hates such sin, David pleads for the Lord to deliver him by destroying his enemies.

A Proclamation of Trust (56:8-11) David is confident of God's deliverance because God is for him and he trusts the Lord. David proclaims, "You number my wanderings." He asks God to "put my tears in Your bottle; are they not in Your book?" (56:8). The Lord is attentive to every detail of David's life, every step, every tear. David is asking the Lord to collect his tears in a bottle, perhaps, with the idea that the volume of the tears will move the Lord to action. David declares, "When I cry out to You, then my enemies will turn back; this I know because God is for me" (56:9).

Psalm 56:10-11 rephrases the refrain of Psalm 56:4. Again, David is determined to praise God's Word, trust in God's mercy, and not fear (56:10-11a). Thus, he asks again, "What can man ("flesh" in verse 4) do to me?" (56:11b). Again, the implied answer to his question is that no one can do anything to him unless God permits it.

A Promise of Praise (56:12-13) David reminds God that the vows he made to Him are binding; he will praise God (56:12). David explains ("for"), "You have delivered my soul from death." David closes with the question, "Have You not kept My feet from falling, that I may walk before God in the light of the living?" (56:13). David speaks of his future deliverance as though God had already delivered him.

Summary: When you are fearful for your life, plead for deliverance, trust the Lord, and praise Him when He delivers you.

A point to ponder: In a fearful situation, even when fearing for your very life, remember that nothing can happen to one of God's children without His permission (56:4, 11). As Paul says, "If God is for us, who can be against us?" (Rom. 8:31).

Psalm 57: When People Try to Trap You Like an Animal

Psalm 57 is a trust psalm written by David. In it, David is hiding in a cave from Saul (see the superscription; see also Ps. 142). David hid in caves twice, once in Adullam (1 Sam. 22:1–2) and once in En Gedi (1 Sam. 24:1–7).

A Plea for Mercy (57:1-3) David pleads for mercy, saying, "Be merciful to me, O God, be merciful to me!" (57:1a). His reason ("for") for asking for mercy is that he is trusting in the Lord. As David pens this passage, he is sitting in a cave, having fled from Saul, but he says that the shadow of God's wings is his refuge "until these calamities have passed by" (57:1).

David continues, "I will cry out to God Most High, to God who performs all things for me" (57:2) and expresses the confidence that God will save him and reproach the one that would swallow him up; "God will send forth His mercy and His truth" (57:3).

A Description of His Plight (57:4-6) David describes his life as being among voracious lions prowling for prey, as being "among the sons of men who are set on fire, who have teeth that are spears and arrows, and their tongue a sharp sword" (57:4). In the midst of his trouble, David not only desires God's mercy, he also desires God's glory. He says, "Be exalted, O God, above the heavens; let Your glory be above all the earth" (57:5). Again, David turns his attention to his plight, saying, "They have prepared a net for my steps; my soul is bowed down; they have dug a pit before me; into the midst of it they have fallen." (57:6). His enemies have prepared a net to catch him like a bird, but like a bird hiding under the wing of its mother for protection, David has taken refuge in the Lord (57:1). They have dug a hole to trap him like an animal, but they fall into the hold that they have dug.

In this psalm, David describes his plight as being like an animal people are trying to trap. They prepared a net to catch him like a bird. They dug a pit to trap him like an animal. They are like lions with sharp teeth about to pounce on their prey. Life is like a jungle with hostile hunters trying to trap us and wild beasts threatening to devour us.

Praise for Deliverance (57:7-11) David assures the Lord that his heart is steadfast; he will sing and give praise to God (57:7). He invites the lute and the harp to wake up and join him (57:8). He declares he will praise the Lord among the nations of the world (57:9) because ("for") God's mercy reaches into the heavens and His truth into the clouds (57:10). David wants God to be glorified, especially God's mercy and truth (57:3, 10). So he concludes, "Be exalted over God above the heavens; let Your glory be above all the earth" (57:11). Psalm 57:11 is a repetition of the refrain in verse 5 for God's glory.

Summary: When people try to trap you like an animal, plead for God's mercy, flee to Him as a refuge, trust Him to deliver you, and be concerned, not just for your own safety, but for His glory.

A point to ponder: When we are in trouble, we tend to think of our deliverance, and even when we plead with the Lord for deliverance, we are often still absorbed in our deliverance. In those situations, we should also be concerned that God be glorified in our lives (Phil. 1:20).

Psalm 58: When You Deal With an Unjust Judge

Psalm 58 is an imprecatory psalm (imprecatory means "to invite a curse on someone") written by David. In it, David deals with an unjust judge (58:1-2).

A Portrayal of Violent Judges (58:1-5) David opens with questions. Addressing unjust, violent judges, David asks, "Do you indeed speak righteousness, you silent ones? Do you judge uprightly, you sons of men?" He is asking the judges if they judge righteously. Then David answers his own question, saying, "No, in heart you work wickedness; you weigh out the violence of your hands in the earth" (58:2). The wickedness of their hearts results in violence at their hands.

David describes these violent, unjust judges as being estranged from the womb, going astray as soon as they are born, speaking lies (58:3), and being like a poisonous serpent (58:4a). He likens them to a deaf cobra that stops its ears refusing to obey a snake charmer (58:4b-5). Like all men, these judges were born sinners; they lie, hurt, and harm others and are deaf to all appeals and authority.

A Prayer for Vengeance (58:6-8) David prays, "Break their teeth in their mouth, O God! Break out the fangs of the young lions, O Lord!" (15:6). These unjust, violent judges are pictured as having teeth that are eating the righteous alive and fangs that poison people. David is asking that their teeth and fangs be broken, that is, that their ability to hurt and harm people be destroyed.

David asks God to let them flow away as a flood of water when they bend their bow, to let their arrows be cut into pieces (58:7), and to let them be like a snail that melts away and a stillborn child that doesn't see the sun (58:8). David is asking for their destruction so that they cannot hurt people with their arrows.

A Promise of Vindication (58:9-11) David promises the wicked that before their pots can feel the burning thorns, in his wrath, God shall take them away like a whirlwind (58:9). It takes time for a pot of water to boil. Thorns burn quickly. David asks that God's judgment be sudden like water boiling in a pot before the pot can feel it, swift, quick-burning thorns, and sure, like a destructive whirlwind.

David promises the righteous will rejoice when they see God's vindication and that God will wash their feet in the blood of the wicked (58:10), so that men will say, "Surely there is a reward for the righteous; surely He is God who judges the earth" (58:11). These judges thought they had all power, but the righteous know that there is an all-powerful One in the earth.

Summary: When dealing with an unjust judge, pray for vengeance and rest assured the wicked will be judged, and the righteous shall be rewarded.

A point to ponder: The wicked are sometimes in high places with the power to harm the righteous, but God is the righteous, all-powerful Judge. The just Judge will punish unjust judges and their injustice.

Psalm 59: When You Need a Bodyguard

Psalm 59 is an imprecatory (imprecatory means "to invite a curse on someone") psalm written by David. In it, David deals with Saul sending soldiers to Michal's house where David was hiding, and the soldiers watched to kill him (see the superscription; 1 Sam. 11-17). David needed a bodyguard (see the word "defense" in 59:1, 9, 16, 17).

A Plea for Deliverance (59:1-5) David pleads with the Lord to deliver him, to defend him (59:1), and save him from bloodthirsty men (59:2). He explains ("for") that they lie in wait for his life, but that's not because he has sinned (59:3-4a). Sometimes, David's suffering was because of his sin; on other occasions, such as this one, it was not. Therefore, David pleads with the Lord to awaken and punish, without mercy, the nations who are threatening Israel (59:4b-5). Notice that he goes beyond his problem to address the national threat.

A Proclamation of Confidence (59:6-10) Even though David's enemies growl like wild dogs (which in the ancient world were not pets; 59:6) and belch with swords in their lips (they use words as weapons; 59:7), David is confident that the Lord will laugh at them (59:8). So David will wait on the Lord, who is his strength and defense (59:9), his bodyguard. He is confident that God will let him see his desire for his enemies (59:10).

A Prayer for Judgment (59:11-15) David's desire for his enemies is not that God slays them, but that God would scatter them so that they are no longer a threat and so that God's people do not forget the seriousness of sin (59:11). Here David addresses God as "our shield" (bodyguard). The reason ("for") David prays for this punishment of his enemies is their pride, their cursing, and their lying (59:12). He also desires that God would ultimately consume them that they may not be—to let them know that God rules in Israel to the ends of the earth (59:13).

Psalm 59:14 is a repetition of Psalm 59:6, only this time, instead of being followed by a reference to the destructive speech of his enemies (59:7), the refrain is followed by pointing out that they are not satisfied (59:15). David is reminding the Lord of the evil of his enemies, which is why the Lord should judge them.

A Promise of Praise (59:16-17) David promises to sing the praises of God's power and mercy because God has been his defense and refuge in the day of his trouble (59:16). He concludes, "To You, O my Strength, I will sing praises; for God is my defense, my God of mercy" (59:17). God is his strength (59:9, 17) and his defense (59:1, 9, 16, 17; see "shield" in verse 11).

Summary: When you need a bodyguard because your life is being threatened, plead for God to be your defense and strength, pray for judgment on your enemies, and praise God when He protects you.

There are repeated references in this psalm to David's enemies using words as weapons (59:6, 7, 12, 14).

A point to ponder: When your life is being threatened either by words or weapons, remember that there is a merciful God who is a bodyguard (see "defense" in verses 1, 9, 16, 17; "shield" in verse 11, "refuge" in verse 16) and avenger on those who do evil to His children.

Psalm 60: When a Setback Causes You to be Confused

Psalm 60 is a didactic ("teaching") psalm written by David. In it, David is fighting against nations in the north, and Joab is victorious in the south (see the superscription; 2 Sam. 8:13; 1 Chron. 18:12). Psalm 60:5-12 is identical to Psalm 108:6-13. In Psalm 60, David's setback (defeat) caused confusion (60:3).

The Agony of Defeat (60:1-5) David opens with a lament that because God has been displeased, He has cast them off and broken them down; that is, they have suffered defeat in a battle against Aram of Zobah and Mesopotamian allies (60:1a; see 2 Sam. 8). He prays, "Oh restore us again" (60:1b). Since God had allowed this temporary defeat, He could restore them to victory. Continuing his lament, David says, "You have made the earth tremble; you have broken it" (60:2). He prays, "Heal its breaches, for it is shaking" (60:2b). To that, David adds that God has shown His people hard times and made them drink the wine of confusion (60:3). David was confused because God had given them given a banner to summon those who fear Him to fight, but they suffered defeat (60:4). God had allowed the defeat to teach Israel a lesson. So David asks, "That Your beloved may be delivered, save with Your right hand and hear me" (60:5).

The Assurance of Victory (60:6-8) Assured of victory, David declares, "God has spoken in His holiness: I will rejoice" (60:6a). God will divide Shechem and measure out the Valley of Succoth (60:6b). Shechem and the Valley of Succoth are places of past victories in fulfillment of God's promises concerning the land. God says Gilead, Manasseh, Ephraim are Mine, Judah is My lawgiver (6:7) and Moab is My wash pot (60:8). God will cast His shoe over Edom and Philistia will shout in triumph (60:8). Moab is like a pot of water in which God will wash His feet; Edom is the servant to whom He throws His shoes; Philistia will provide the victory song. In other words, the entire land of Israel belongs to God and He will give it to whoever He wills. David is assured of victory because God said so.

Adoration to God (16:9-12) David asked, "Who will bring me to the strong city? Who will lead me to Edom?" (60:9). David answers his own question, "Is it not You, O God, who cast us off? And You, O God, who did not go out with our army?" (60:10). The One who cast them off in a temporary defeat (60:1) will be the One who will lead them to ultimate victory.

David requests, "Give us help from trouble, for the help of man is useless" (60:11). In the final analysis, man's help without God's help is no help at all. David concludes, "Through God, we will do valiantly, for it is He who shall tread down our enemies" (60:12). As promised, they did do valiantly; they won the battle.

Summary: When a setback causes you to be confused, remember that God is in control and He will ultimately give you the victory.

A point to ponder: God sometimes allows a temporary defeat to teach us that man's help is useless, that He is the One who is in control, and He is the One who will give us victory.

Psalm 61: When You Feel Overwhelmed

Psalm 61 is a royal psalm written by David. In it, David is overwhelmed (61:2).

A Petition for Deliverance (61:1-2) David begins, "Hear my cry, O God; attend to my prayer." (61:1). He goes on to say, "From the ends of the earth I will cry to You when my heart is overwhelmed; lead me to the rock that is higher than I." (61:2). David felt as if he was at the ends of the earth, alone, separated from his people. He also felt overwhelmed. So, he pleads for God to lead him to a rock for protection and security. The rock may be Masada or a figure of God Himself. Verse 3 suggests the rock is God.

A Proclamation of Confidence (61:3-7) David uses four figures of speech to refer to God as his protection and security: shelter (61:3 a), a strong tower (61:3b), tabernacle (61:4a), wings of a bird, as though David were a small chick hiding under its mother's wing. (61:4b). Since God has protected him in the past (see the past tense in verse 3), David will trust Him for protection in the future (see the future tense in verse 4).

David explains ("for") that God has heard his vow and given him the heritage of those who fear God's name (see 61:1). This is an appeal to God's covenant, either God's covenant with Moses or God's covenant with David (2 Sam. 7:16). So David is confident the God will prolong his life (61:6) and he will abide before God forever (61:7a). Hence he proclaims, "Oh prepare mercy and truth, which may preserve him!" (61:7b).

A Promise of Praise (61:8) David concludes, "I will sing praise to your name forever, that I may daily perform my vows" (61:8; see 61:5).

Summary: When you feel overwhelmed, flee to the Lord for protection, confident that based on His former faithfulness, He will protect you and praise Him when He does.

A point to ponder: The saints of God are not always "on top of it all;" they can feel emotionally overwhelmed.

Psalm 62: When You Are Verbally Attacked

Psalm 62 is a trust psalm written by David. In it, David is verbally attacked (62:3-4).

An Expression of Trust (62:1-7) David says, "Truly my soul silently waits for God; from Him comes my salvation" (62:1). The expression "silently waits" is a reference to his dependence on the Lord. "Salvation" in this case, is not spiritual salvation; it is deliverance from danger. David is expressing his dependence on the Lord to be delivered from danger. Since God alone is his rock, deliverance, and defense, David declares that he will not be greatly moved (62:2).

David asks, "How long will you attack a man?" (62:3a). This question indicates why David needs to be delivered. He is being attacked. Nevertheless, because of his trust in the Lord, he is confident that he will be delivered. Hence, he says to his attackers, "You shall be slain, all of you, like a leaning wall and tottering fence" (62:3b). Some commentators (and translations) apply "leaning wall and tottering fence" to David as if his enemies thought of him as the weak wall and the falling fence, but other commentators say the leaning wall and flimsy fence are referring to David's attackers (Calvin; Barnes; Lange). The context supports the later translation.

David explains, "They only consult to cast him down from his high position; they delight in lies; they bless with their mouth, but they curse inwardly" (62:4). Evidently, the attack includes verbal attacks. On the one hand, his attackers blessed him. Yet, they lied about him and cursed him, consulting each other about how they might bring him down. They spoke; David silently trusted the Lord (62:1).

Again, David expresses his trust in the Lord. Psalm 62:5-6 is a virtual repetition of Psalm 62:1-2. This time, David says, "My soul, wait silently for God alone, for my expectation is from Him" (62:5; see "only" in 62:2). Instead of saying "salvation" (62:1), David says "expectation" (62:5). Psalm 62:6 is a restatement of Psalm 62:2, except verse 6 drops the word "greatly," making "I shall not be moved" even stronger. This time, David adds, "God is my salvation and my glory; the rock of my strength, and my refuge is in God" (62:7).

An Exhortation to Trust (62:8-10) Having expressed his trust in the Lord, David exhorts others to "trust in Him at all times" and "pour out your heart before Him" because God is a refuge for you too (62:8). David warns against trusting people, saying, "Surely men of low degree are a vapor, men of high degree are a lie; if they are weighed on the scales, they are altogether lighter than vapor" (62:9). Humans, whether they are in a low position or a high position, are not sufficient objects of trust. They would not weigh as much as a vapor if placed on a balance scale. To be more specific, do not trust in oppressing people. Do not put your hope in stealing from them and, if riches do increase, do not set your heart on them (62:10). People, whether their actions are good or bad, are poor objects of trust.

Exaltation of God (62:11-12) David exalts God, who has spoken not just once but twice, indicating that power (62:11) and mercy (62:1a) belong to Him. David concludes, "For You render to each one according to his works" (16:12b). Trust God, who is powerful and merciful and is the one who will judge people according to their works.

Summary: When verbally attacked, trust God to deliver you and remind others to do the same because people and their actions are untrustworthy, but God is powerful and merciful.

A point to ponder: Don't trust a vapor (63:9); rest on a rock (62:2).

Psalm 63: When You Cannot Sleep

Psalm 63 is a royal psalm written by David. In it, David is in the wilderness away from the Ark of the Covenant, fleeing for his life from Saul, and cannot sleep (see superscription; 63:6, 9).

David's Desire (63:1-2) David says, "O God, you are my God; early will I seek You; my soul thirsts for You; my flesh longs for You in a dry and thirsty land where there is no water" (63:1). David uses his thirst for water in the wilderness as an illustration of his thirst for the Lord. Like seeking a drink of water when he first wakes up, David declares he will seek God in the morning. David reminds the Lord that he looked for Him in the sanctuary, that is, the Tabernacle so that he might see God's power and glory (63:2). From God's presence in the Tabernacle, David had learned about God's power and glory, which taught him that he needed to seek the Lord early every day. He is seeking fellowship with God and dependence on Him.

David's Declaration (63:3-8) David's desire for the Lord results in his declaration that he will praise the Lord. He says, "Because your lovingkindness is better than life, my lips shall praise You" (63:3). To David, God's love, kindness, and grace are better than life itself. So he says, "Thus will I praise You while I live; I will lift up my hands in Your name" (63:4). David is determined not just to praise the Lord in the morning but for the rest of his life. Believers are to lift holy hands to the Lord in prayer (1 Tim. 2:8). David declares, "My soul shall be satisfied as with the marrow and fatness, and my mouth shall praise You with joyful lips" (63:5). His spiritual thirst (63:1) shall be satisfied (63:5) like the body is satisfied after a meal of rich food.

David adds, "When I remember You on my bed, I meditate on You in the night watches" (63:6). The Israelites divided the night into three watches. When David was having difficulty sleeping, he meditated on the Lord. As David thinks about the Lord, he rejoices because God has been his help and protection, like a bird hiding under a parent's wing. (63:7) and as he stays close to the Lord, the Lord upholds him now (63:8).

David's Defense (63:9-11) Because God has protected him in the past and upholds him in the present, David is confident that those who seek to destroy his life shall die (63:9). They shall fall by the sword and their bodies will be a portion for wild animals who are scavengers (63:10).

David concludes, "But the king shall rejoice in God; everyone who swears by him shall glory; but the mouth of those who speak lies shall be stopped" (63:11). The king is David, who declares that in the future, he will continue to rejoice in the Lord and, for that matter, so will everyone who sides with Him; but instead of using their mouth for praise, the mouth of those who speak lies shall be stopped.

Summary: When you cannot sleep, seek the Lord like a thirsty soul seeks water, praise the Lord, meditate on the Lord, rejoice in the Lord, and trust Him to protect you.

A point to point: The soul needs to be satisfied with the Lord like the body needs to be satisfied with food and drink.

Psalm 64: When You Deal With a Secret Plot

Psalm 64 is a trust psalm written by David. In it, David is dealing with a secret plot against him (64:2).

A Plea for Protection (64:1-2) David pleads with the Lord, "Hear my voice, O God, in my meditation" (64:1a). As David contemplates ("meditation") his situation, he begins to pray. His first request is simply that the Lord would hear his prayer. More specifically, he asks, "Preserve my life from the fear of the enemy" (64:1) and "hide me from the secret plots of the wicked, from the rebellion of the workers of iniquity" (64:2). Wicked workers of iniquity are secretly plotting to harm David. They are hiding their plots (see "secret plots") from David; David asks the Lord to hide him from them. In short, "Protect me."

The Plot of Enemies (64:3-6) The plot of David's enemies primarily involves words. David uses two figures of speech to describe their words. He says they "sharpen their tongue like a sword and bend their bow to shoot their arrows—bitter words" (64:3). Their words are like a sharp sword and a bent bow. They are bitter words designed to cut and kill.

David explains that they have prepared these words "that they may shoot in secret at the blameless; suddenly they shoot at him and do not fear" (64:4). Again, David mentions secrecy. They devised their plan in secret (see "secret plots" in verse 2) and carried out their plan in secret (see "shoot in secret" in verse 4). Because all of this is done in secret, when they do perform their plan, it will suddenly come upon the blameless and these wicked iniquity workers (64:2) will not fear detection. They fear neither God nor man.

David emphasizes the plot of his enemies, saying, "They encourage themselves in an evil matter; they talk of laying snares secretly; they say, 'Who will see them?'" (64:5). In other words, their plot is evil, will be done secretly, and they do not fear detection. For the third time in this Psalm, David mentions that all of this is done in secret (see 64:2, 4, 5). Furthermore, they think they have developed the perfect plan. David observes, "They devise iniquities: 'We have perfected a shrewd scheme'" (64:6a). They are so sure and proud of themselves that they congratulate themselves. While contemplating the situation, David remarks, "Both the inward thought and the heart of man are deep" (64:6b). Deep thought is profound. The plot of David's enemies indicates just how profoundly evil people can be.

The Prediction of Punishment (64:7-10) Because he has asked God for protection (64:1), David predicts, "But God shall shoot at them with an arrow: suddenly they shall be wounded" (64:7). David's enemies were planning on shooting arrows of bitter words at him (64:3) that would suddenly wound him (64:4). David predicts that God will shoot arrows of judgment at them and they will be suddenly wounded (64:7). They will stumble over their own words (64:8).

Those who see God's judgment will "flee away" (64:8b) and all men will fear and declare the work of God when they wisely consider God's judgment (64:9). The righteous shall be glad, trust the Lord, and praise God (64:10).

Summary: When dealing with a secret plot against you, ask the Lord for protection, knowing that when God judges the wicked, the righteous shall be glad and praise Him.

A point to ponder: When you become the target of malicious gossip, commit your case to the Lord and rest assured that God will turn the wickedness of the wicked on themselves.

Psalm 65: When You See God's Power in the World

Psalm 65 is a praise psalm written by David. In it, David sees God's power in the world (65:6-8).

God's Praise (65:1-4) Praise awaits God (65:1) because He hears the prayers of all who come to Him (65:2) because He provides atonement for our transgressions (65:3), and because He blesses the people He chooses (65:4a). The people who approach God and dwell with Him are not only blessed, they are satisfied with His goodness (64:4b). The progression here is prayer, forgiveness, dwelling with the Lord, blessing, and satisfaction with God's goodness.

God's Power (65:5-8) God answers prayer by His awesome deeds (65:5) and by His strength, the same strength He uses to establish mountains (65:6). By God's power, He delivers His people (65:5), and stills the turmoil of people, like He stills the noise of the sea and the waves (65:7). God's power can be seen by people who dwell in the farthest parts of the earth (65:8a). They stand in awe (are afraid) when they see God's signs in creations, such as lightning and thunder, storms and earthquakes (65:8b). They rejoice when they see God's work in the morning and the evening, that is, the sunrise and the sunset (65:8c). In short, God's power can be seen in creation (Ps. 19; Rom. 1:20).

God's Provision (65:9-13) God's power can be seen in how He provides for the earth. With rain provided by God, the earth is enriched, rivers are full, and grains grow (65:9). With rain provided by God, crops are abundantly blessed with growth (65:10). God gives the increase (1 Cor. 3:6). David pictures the year as a person with a crown of goodness and a path filled with abundance (65:11). In other words, as God strolls through the earth during the year, everywhere He goes, there is abundant growth of flowers and fruit. When David says, "They drop on the pastures of the wilderness" (65:12a), he means abundance comes to uninhabited, uncultivated regions ("wilderness"), making them pastures for flocks. Little hills rejoice (65:12b). David concludes, "The pastures are clothed with flocks; the valleys also are covered with grain; they shout for joy, they also sing" (65:13). The fields filled with flocks and the valleys covered with an abundance of growing grain shout for joy and sing praises to God.

Summary: When you see God's power in the world and His provision by making it rain, praise Him.

A point to ponder: When we look at the beauty of nature, we should not only be reminded that God is great (He is powerful), but we should remember that He is also good (He provides).

Count your blessings in this psalm. God hears prayer (65:2). God forgives sin. (65:3). God blesses us (65:4). God answers prayer (65:5). God supplies our food (65:13).

Psalm 66: When You Have Been Tested

Psalm 66 is a praise psalm written by an anonymous author. In it, the author speaks of being tested (66:10).

The Nations' Praise (66:1-12) After calling all the people on the earth to shout a joyful noise to God (66:1), to sing honor to His name, and to speak His praise (66:2), the psalmist tells them what to say to God, namely that His works are awesome and through the greatness of His power His enemies will submit themselves to Him (66:3). Then addressing God, the psalmist says, "All the earth shall worship You and sing praises to You" (66:4). This will happen in the future ("shall;" see Phil. 2:9-11).

After calling all the people on the earth to "come and see the works of God," which are "awesome" (66:5), the psalmist lists some of them, namely that He turned the sea into dry land and they (the Israelites) went through the river on foot (a reference to the Exodus; 66:6). The psalmist adds that God "rules by His power forever; His eyes observe the nations; do not let the rebellious exalt themselves" (66:7).

After calling all the people on the earth to bless God (66:8), the psalmist again lists things God has done, namely keeping us alive and not allowing our feet to be moved (66:9) because God has tested us and has refined us as silver is refined (66:10). More specifically, God brought us into the net (being trapped by enemies), laid afflictions on our backs (66:11), caused men to ride over heads (being conquered by enemies), caused us to go through fire and water, but brought us out to rich fulfillment (66:12). The nations are called to bless God because He has preserved Israel.

The Psalmist's Praise (66:13-20) Beginning with verse 13, the psalmist speaks about himself instead of to the people of the earth (note the change from "you" to "I"). He says that he will go to God's house (the Temple in Jerusalem) with a burnt offering to pay his vows (66:13), which he made when he was in trouble (66:14). The vows were probably to publicly acknowledge God's deliverance. He says he will offer animal sacrifices to the Lord (66:15), which was part of Israel's worship system.

The psalmist invites all who fear the Lord to come hear what God has done for him (66:16). He testifies that he cried to the Lord and he praised the Lord (66:17). He explains, "If I regard iniquity in my heart, the Lord will not hear" (66:18), "But certainly God has heard me; He has attended to the voice of my prayer" (66:19), which indicates that the trouble he was experiencing was not a result of his sin. He concludes, "Blessed be God, who has not turned away my prayer, nor His mercy from me!" (66:20).

Summary: When tested, praise God and invite others to do the same.

A point to ponder: Trouble is not necessarily a sign of sin (*cf* 66:14 with 66:18); it may be God's test to refine us (66:10).

Psalm 67: When You Want to See People Converted

Psalm 67 is a praise psalm written by an anonymous author. In it, the author wants to see people converted (67:1-2).

A Prayer for God's Blessings (67:1-2) The poet prays for God to be merciful to us, bless us, make His face to shine upon us (67:1), that His way may be known on the earth and His salvation among all nations (67:2). The "us" is a reference to Israel. For God to smile on His people is reminiscent of Numbers 6:24-26. For one to smile on another is for that person to show favor and approval. The prayer is for God to bless His people, Israel so that His way and salvation can become known among all nations. God's way is to bless people so they can bless others. He specifically chose to bless Israel so that they would bring salvation to the families of the earth (Gen. 12:1-3).

The First Plea for Praise (67:3-4) With evangelistic enthusiasm, the poet pleads, "Let the peoples praise You, O God; let all the people praise You" (67:3). The prayer is that the peoples of the earth would so understand God's way and God's salvation that they would praise Him. The poet continues, "Oh, let the nations be glad and sing for joy! For You shall judge the people righteously and govern the nations on earth" (67:4). Again, the prayer is that the peoples of the earth would so understand God's way and salvation that they would be glad and sing for joy. Understanding God's way and salvation results in gladness, joyful singing, and praise to God. The reason ("for") the joy and praise is, "For you will judge the people righteously and govern the nations on the earth" (67:4). The Hebrew word translated "govern" means "to lead, guide" (the same Hebrew word is translated "lead" in 23:3). The peoples of the earth should be glad and praise God now because in the future ("will"), God will exercise just judgment and guide the nations of the world. This looks forward to the kingdom of God.

The Second Plea for Praise (67:5-7) The poet repeats his plea. Psalm 67:5 is identical to Psalm 67:3, only this time, there is a different result. The poet says, "Then shall the earth yield her increase; God, our own God, shall bless us" (67:6). When the peoples of the earth learn God's way and salvation to the point that they are praising Him, He shall bless them as He has blessed Israel.

The poet concludes, "God shall bless us, and all the ends of the earth will fear Him" (67:7). This psalm began with a prayer for God to bless Israel (67:1) so that the peoples of the earth would know God's way and salvation (67:2). It ends with the same thought. When God blesses His people, others stand in awe of Him.

Summary: When you want to see people converted, pray for God's blessing on you so they will understand God's way and salvation and, thus, praise Him.

The prayer of this psalm is that God would bless Israel so the peoples of the earth would experience God's salvation, way, justice, and blessing and, as a result, praise Him.

A point to ponder: God blesses us so we can be a blessing to others. As the songwriter said, God wants us to be channels of blessing.

Psalm 68: When You are Dealing With God's Enemies

Psalm 68 is a victory psalm written by David. In it, David is dealing with God's enemies (68:1).

Prayer for God to Scatter His Enemies (68:1-6) Let God's enemies, who have become Israel's enemies, be scattered and flee (68:1), as smoke is driven away and wax is melted (68:2). When the enemies flee, the righteous will be glad (16:3) and will sing praises to God, who is pictured as riding in a chariot across the sky (16:4), who defends the helpless (68:5), and leads the Israelites to prosperity in the land. At the same time, those who rebelled died in the wilderness (16:6).

Praise for God's Past Blessings (68:7-18) David reviews God's dealings with Israel. He led them in the wilderness (68:7), shook the earth at Sinai (68:8), provided rain (68:9-10; Judges 5:4), gave them His word, which was celebrated by women (68:11; Ex. 15:20), gave them victory (68:12) and the spoils of war (68:13), and scattered their enemies like driven snow (68:14). Other mountains are jealous of Mount Zion (Jerusalem), which God chose for His dwelling (68:15-16). With an angelic army, God led the Israelites from Sinai to Jerusalem (68:17), ascended back to heaven, and received gifts from men (68:18; 2 Sam. 5:6-8). In Ephesians 4:8, Paul quotes Psalm 68:18 and changes receiving gifts to giving gifts. In ancient times, the victor shared the spoils of war with those on his side. Thus, God, the conquering King, can be said to give gifts to men. Although not stated, Psalm 68:7-18 praises God (see 68:19).

Praise for God's Present Benefits (68:19-31) Bless God for His daily benefits (68:19), His deliverance from death (68:20), and His victory over enemies (68:21), none of whom shall escape whether near (Bashan) or far (the depths of the sea; 68:22); they will be crushed like grapes (68:23). Israel has seen God proceed to His sanctuary (68:24), like an ancient King who had singers going before him and instrumentalists following him (68:25).

Bless God who has made Israel a fountain of blessing (68:26), all of Israel from the smallest tribe (Benjamin) to the largest (Judah) from the south (Zebulun) to the north (Naphtali; 68:27). Strengthen Israel, O God (68:28). When kings see the Temple in Jerusalem, they will bring presents to You (68:29; 1 Kings 10:1-13). Rebuke (subdue) the beasts of the reeds (Egypt), bulls (Assyria), and caves (Canaan) until everyone brings tribute, and scatter the people who delight in war (68:30). Envoys will come from Egypt and Ethiopia (68:31).

Praise from Everyone (68:32-35) All the kingdoms of the earth are invited to sing praises to the Lord (68:32), the One who reigns in the heavens (see 69:4), the One who sends out His voice (69:33), the One who with His strength, strengthens Israel (69:34), the One who is awesome (68:35a). David concludes, "The God of Israel is He who gives strength and power to His people. Blessed be God!" (68:35). Everyone should praise the Lord.

Summary: When you are dealing with God's enemies, who have become your enemies, pray for God to scatter them, praise God for His past blessings and present benefits, and invite others to praise our awesome God.

Scattering is mentioned three times in this Psalm (68:1, 14, 30). It begins with a prayer for God to scatter His enemies (68:1), reviews God's past scattering of His enemies (68:14), and, toward the end, it again mentions God scattering His enemies (68:30).

A point of view: When dealing with God's enemies who have become your enemies, remember God's past victories and reflect on God's awesome power.

Psalm 69: When You Suffer for Your Zeal for the Lord

Psalm 69 is a lament psalm written by David. In it, David laments that he is suffering for his zeal for the Lord (69:8-9).

David's Despair (69:1-12) David asked God to save him. He is up to his neck in water (69:1) and mire (69:2) and he is weary from crying in prayer (69:3). Those who hate him without a cause (cited in Jn. 15:25) and want to destroy him are more than the hairs on his head (69:4).

David is not sinless (69:5) and he does not want those who wait on the Lord to be discouraged (69:6) because of his reproach for the Lord's sake (69:7). His closest relatives have deserted him (69:8) because his zeal for God's house (to build the Temple) has eaten him up (16:9; cited in Jn. 2:17). His fasting has become a reproach (69:10) and his sackcloth a byword, that is a jest; a subject of derision (69:11). The leaders (those who sit at the gate) and the lowly (drunkards) are against him (69:12). This is David's despair in persecution.

David's Desire (69:13-28) David asks God (69:13) to deliver him out of deep water (69:14-15). He asks for mercy (69:16) to come quickly (69:17) so that he might be delivered from his enemies (69:18). His reproach and shame (69:19) have broken his heart and there is no one to comfort him (69:20). Instead of sustaining him with good food, they gave him poison to eat and vinegar to drink (69:21; cited in Mt. 27:34, Jn. 19:28-29).

So David asks that their table become a snare (69:22; cited in Rom. 11:9), their eyes be darkened, their loins shake continually (69:23; cited in Rom. 11:10), their experience be of God's anger (69:24), their dwelling place be desolate so that no one lives in their tents (69:25; cited in Acts 1:20) because ("for") they persecuted the ones God has wounded (69:26). David asks that God let their iniquity increase (so that it will be punished when it matures; Rom. 1:24-28), that they not be counted as righteous (69:27), and that their life be cut short (69:28). This is not a prayer for personal vengeance; instead, it is a prayer for God's punishment on those who oppose God's anointed.

David's Declaration (69:29-36) David declares that although he is poor and sorrowful at the moment when God delivers him (69:29), he will praise the name of God with a song and magnify Him with thanksgiving (69:30), which is more pleasing to the Lord than animal sacrifices (69:31). When the humble see this, they will be glad and be encouraged (69:32) because ("for") the Lord hears the poor (69:33). So let everything that moves in heaven, earth, and sea praise the Lord (69:34), because ("for") God will save Zion (Jerusalem), and rebuild the cities of Judah that the Israelites may possess it (69:35), that the descendants of His servants shall inherit it, and those who love His name shall dwell in it (69:36). David is looking forward to the fulfillment of these conditions during the Millennium.

Summary: When you suffer for your zeal for the Lord, ask God to deliver you, judge those approaching you, and promise to praise Him when He does.

Some of these verses are said to be *fulfilled* in the life of the Lord (verses 4 and 21; see also verses 9, 22, 23, 24), but the psalm is about David. What happened to David is an experience filled to the full in Jesus Christ.

A point to ponder: Do not let spiritual opposition drive you away from the Lord; use it to drive you to the Lord.

Psalm 70: When You Need Immediate Help

Psalm 70 is a lament psalm written by David. It is virtually identical to Psalm 40:13-17. In it, David needs immediate help (70:1).

A Plea for Deliverance (70:1-3) David pleads, "Make haste, O God, to deliver me! Make haste to help me, O Lord!" (70:1). David needs help to be delivered and He needs it immediately. Then, David makes a series of requests, all beginning with the word "let."

"Let them be ashamed and confounded who seek my life" (70:2a). The reason David needed immediate help is that there were people who were seeking to kill him. He prays that they might be ashamed and confounded. David is asking to be immediately delivered from being killed.

"Let them be turned back and [be] confused who desire my hurt" (70:2b). This statement is virtually an echo of the previous one. David needs immediate help because these people are trying to hurt him. He prays that they will be turned back and confused. David is asking to be immediately delivered from being hurt.

"Let them be turned back because of their shame, who say, 'Aha, aha!'" (70:3). In other words, they were taunting him and he is asking that because of their shameful behavior, they be turned back, no longer able to taunt him. David is asking to be immediately delivered from being taunted. David is asking for deliverance from being taunted, hurt, and killed.

A Prayer for God's Glory (70:4-5) At this point in the Psalm, David turns his attention from his enemies to those who love and seek the Lord. Again, he makes requests beginning with "let."

"Let all those who seek You rejoice and be glad in You" (70:4a). The result of God's deliverance of David is God's people will rejoice and be glad in the Lord. This is like the whole congregation rejoicing because one in their midst received an answer to prayer.

"Let those who love Your salvation say continually, 'Let God be magnified!'" (70:4b). The salvation spoken of here is not spiritual salvation; it is physical deliverance (see verse 1). David is asking to let those who love God's deliverance say continually, "To God be the glory." David is pleading for God's deliverance so that God's people will be glad and God will be glorified.

David concludes, "But I am poor and needy; make haste to me, O God! You are my help and my deliverer; O Lord, do not delay" (70:5). Acknowledging that this situation is beyond his strength (he is poor and needy), David ends this psalm with the same plea with which it began (compare "Make haste God to deliver me" in verse 1 with "Make haste to me, O God! You are my help and my deliverer" in verse 5). The psalm also ends as it began, with a request for speedy relief (compare "make haste to help me, O Lord!" in verse 1 with "O Lord, do not delay" in verse 5). David desperately needs the Lord to intervene—immediately.

Summary: When you need immediate help from the Lord to be delivered from harm, ask Him to immediately respond for the shame of God's enemies, the joy of God's people, and the glory of God's name.

A point to ponder: If you need immediate help from the Lord, do not hesitate to ask for it. To say to God, "Make haste" and "Do not delay," is not issuing God a command; it simply expresses your urgent need.

Psalm 71: When You Are Elderly and in Trouble

Psalm 71 is a lament psalm written by an anonymous author. In it, an elderly author is in trouble (71:4, 10, 18).

A Prayer for Deliverance (71:1-3) Saying he trusts the Lord, the psalmist asks not to be put to shame (17:1) and to be delivered (17:2). He asks the Lord to be his strong refuge because the Lord is his rock and fortress (71:3). The prayer is for deliverance because God is his refuge, rock, and fortress.

A Plea for Deliverance (71:4 to 13) The author asks the Lord to deliver him from the cruel hand of the wicked (71:4) because the Lord is his hope and has been his trust from his youth (71:5). He reviews his relationship to the Lord from birth to the present. He says the Lord has upheld him from birth, so he will continually praise the Lord, implying he has done this all his life (71:6). The psalmist says he has become a wonder (Hebrew: "sign," perhaps, an omen of things to come), but God is his strong refuge (71:7). He asks that his mouth be filled with God's praise and glory all day (71:8). The plea is for deliverance because God is his hope and because he has trusted in God all of his life.

Having walked with the Lord all of his life, he asks: 1) "Do not cast me off in the time of old age" (71:9a). 2) "Do not forsake me when my strength fails" (71:9b), for my enemies speak against me and plan to take my life (71:10), "saying, 'God has forsaken him; pursue and take him, for there is none to deliver him'" (71:11). 3) "Do not be far from me;" make haste to help me (71:12) and let my adversaries (those who seek my hurt) be confounded, consumed, and covered with reproach and dishonor (71:13).

A Promise of Praise (71:14-24) The psalmist emphatically declares, "But I will hope continually and will praise You yet more and more (71:14). "My mouth shall tell of Your righteousness and Your salvation all the day, for I do not know their limits (Hebrew: "numbers") (71:15). The Lord had delivered ("salvation") him so many times he lost count. So he declares that he will go in the strength of the Lord and will mention His righteousness (71:16).

In fact, God has taught him from his youth, and to this day, he has declared God's wondrous works (71:17). So now that he's old and gray-headed, he asks God not to forsake him until he can declare God's strength to this generation and God's power to those who are to come (71:18). This is another form of promising to praise God.

There is none like the Lord, whose righteousness is great and who has done great things (71:19). So the author is confident that this great God who has shown him great and severe troubles will revive (Hebrew: preserve) him and bring him up from the depths of the earth, that is, the deep pit into which he has fallen (71:20). This great God will increase his greatness and comfort him on every side (71:21). Therefore, the psalmist tells the Lord that he will praise Him and His faithfulness with the flute, sing to the Holy One of Israel with his harp (71:22), and use his lips to express the joy he feels because he has been redeemed (71:23). He concludes, "My tongue shall talk of your righteousness all the day long; for they are confounded, for they are brought to shame who seek my hurt" (71:24). When delivered, he will praise the Lord.

Summary: When you are elderly and in trouble, remember that the God who has delivered you all your life will deliver you again, and praise Him when He does.

A point to ponder: We should learn to trust the Lord now to prepare for old age, like saving money for retirement and storing up spiritual victories now to remember later.

Psalm 72: When You Pray for the Government

Psalm 72 is a royal psalm written by Solomon. It pertains to Solomon's rule, but the fact that the Son is introduced in verse 1 and the psalm speaks of universal rule leaves no doubt that the psalm is ultimately about the Son (Messiah) Who will reign in His kingdom. In Psalm 72, Solomon prays for the government (72:1).

The Characteristics of the Rule (72:1-7) Solomon prays for the ability to execute God's judgments (72:1a). Then he mentions the righteousness of the rule of the King's Son (notice the capital "S;" 72:1b). Solomon says the Son will judge God's people with righteousness and justice (72:2). The mountains (a figure of speech for government) will bring peace (72:3). Again, mentioning justice for the poor, Solomon says the Son will save the children of the needy and break in pieces the oppressor (72:4). The oppressors shall stand in awe ("fear") of the Son "as long as the sun and moon endure throughout all generations" (72:5). God shall come down like a refreshing rain on the earth (72:6). In the days of the Son's reign, "righteousness shall flourish and the abundance of peace (will be) until the moon is no more" (72:7). The nature of the Son's rule will be righteousness and peace.

The Coverage of the Rule (72:8-11) "He (the Son) shall have dominion from sea to sea, and from the River (the Euphrates) to the ends of the earth" (72:8). The ungovernable nomads of the wilderness will bow before Him and His enemies will lick the dust, that is, be defeated and brought into subjection (72:9). The Kings of Tarsus (Spain) will bring presents and the Kings of Sheba (Yemen) and Seba (Sudan) will offer gifts (72:10). All the Kings will fall down before Him and all nations will serve Him (17:11).

The Compassion of the Rule (72:12-14) He will deliver the needy, the poor, and those who have no helper (72:12). He will spare and save them (72:13). He will redeem them from oppression and violence (17:14).

The Consequences of the Rule (72:15-17) The gold of Sheba will be given to Him, the prayers of the people will be continually made for Him, and daily praise of the people will be offered to Him (72:15). There will be abundance in the earth (72:16). His name shall endure forever; it shall endure as long as the sun. All men shall bless Him and all nations will call Him blessed (72:17).

The Conclusion of the Rule (72:18-19) Solomon concludes, "Blessed be the Lord God, the God of Israel, who does wondrous things!" (17:18) "And blessed be His glorious name forever! And let the whole earth be filled with His glory. Amen and Amen" (72:19). God is to be praised for doing wonderful and beneficial things. The earth is to be filled with His glory and praise.

Psalm 72:20 indicates that Book II of the Psalms is concluded. David is the chief but not the sole author of these prayers (psalms).

Summary: When you pray for the government, remember the characteristics of what government should be now and what the government will be in the universal reign of the Messiah: justice, peace, and compassion (Mt. 6:10; 1 Thess. 2:1-4).

A point to ponder: The governed, as well as the government, should seek justice, peace, and compassion.

Psalm 73: When You See the Prosperity of the Wicked

Psalm 73 is a wisdom psalm written by Asaph. In it, Asaph is perplexed by the prosperity of the wicked (73:3).

The Prosperity of the Wicked (73:1-14) The psalmist begins with a personal, perplexing problem, namely that God is good to the pure in heart in Israel (73:1), but he (the psalmist) almost spiritually stumbled (73:2), because he was envious of the prosperity of the wicked (73:3). He then describes their prosperity. There are no pangs in their death and their strength is firm (73:4). They do not seem to experience trouble and plagues like other men (73:5).

Therefore, they display pride and violence like jewelry (73:6). Their eyes bulge with abundance, having more than their heart could wish (73:7). When they speak, they scoff, boast of their wicked accomplishments (73:8), and even set their mouth against the heavens (73:9).

Therefore, "His people" follow his wickedness and drink until the bottle is empty (17:10). They say God doesn't know about their sin, as if to say He doesn't care how they live (17:11).

The psalmist complains that the ungodly have it easy and increase in riches (17:12), but he lives a godly life ("cleansed my heart") in vain (73:13) because ("for") he is plagued and chastened every day all day (73:14). Without a care, the ungodly prosper, while the godly, who care about godliness, are plagued. The prosperity of the ungodly is aggravated by the plight of the godly. Instead of prosperity, all the godly get are more problems. It seems as if God prospers the proud and punishes the pure in heart.

The Destiny of the Wicked and the Righteous (73:15-28) In the final analysis, Asaph concludes that those arguments are inaccurate. In fact, he says if he had said such things, he would have misled God's people (73:15). He then explains what happened to change his mind. He says pondering the prosperity of the wicked was painful for him (73:16) "until I went into the sanctuary of God; then I understood their end" (17:17). In the sanctuary of God, he understood from the Word of God that God had set the wicked on a slippery slope to their destruction (73:18). As in a moment, they are utterly consumed with terrors (73:19). It may appear that God is sleeping now, but when He wakes up, He will despise their image (73:20). The wicked are only a step away from disaster. In a moment, their wealth could be worthless.

Thus, the psalmist confesses that his heart was grieved, his mind was vexed (73:21), and, like a dumb animal, he was foolish and ignorant before God (73:22), but he was faithful to the Lord who has sustained him (73:23), guided him, and will receive him into glory (17:24). The end of the ungodly is hell; the end of the godly is heaven. In the meantime, the psalmist says he has a God in heaven and what he desires on earth is fellowship with Him (73:25). He admits that his flesh and his heart may fail, but God is his strength and portion now and forever (73:26).

In conclusion, the psalmist draws a contrast between the ungodly and himself. He says those who are far from God will perish. God will destroy all who desert Him for harlotry (73:27), but as for him, it's good to draw near to God, to put his trust in the Lord, that he may declare all God's works (73:28).

Summary: When you see (and are perplexed by) the prosperity of the wicked, instead of comparing their present experience with your present experience, compare your present experience and future end with their future end.

A point to ponder: It is only when we view life from the perspective gained from the Word of God that we gain a proper perspective. Before jumping to conclusions, get all the facts.

Psalm 74: When You See Divine Discipline

Psalm 74 is a lament psalm written by Asaph. In it, Asaph laments the destruction of the Temple in Jerusalem (586 BC; see Ps. 79), which was God's discipline on Israel (74:1).

A Complaint over the Destruction (74:1-8) The congregation of God's people asks Him why He is so angry with them that He has cast them off (74:1). They ask Him to remember the congregation He purchased as an inheritance, which He redeemed, and Mount Zion (Jerusalem) where He dwelt (74:2). They ask Him to inspect the damage ("lift up your feet"); God's enemies have destroyed everything in His sanctuary (74:3) and roar, as well as set up banners amid His meeting place (74:4). They have broken down the carved work with axes and hammers (74:5-6). They have defiled and destroyed God's sanctuary with fire (74:7-8). This is a description of the destruction of the Temple in Jerusalem (see 2 Kings 25:9-10).

A Cry for Divine Intervention (74:9-17) The congregation also complains that they have no sign, prophet (Ezekiel had been taken to Babylon, Jeremiah to Egypt), or anyone else who knows how long the reproach of the adversary will last (74:9-10a). They ask God if this blasphemy of His name will last forever (74:10b). They ask Him why He has withdrawn His hand and suggest that He take His hand out of His bosom and destroy His enemies (74:11). In other words, this is a cry to God for His intervention.

The reason for their request ("for") is that God has been their King, who has delivered them for many years (74:12). God delivered them from Egyptian bondage by parting the Red Sea with His power (74:13a). His destruction of the "sea serpents" (74:13b) and the "Leviathan" (74:14a) is a poetic description of His destruction of the Egyptians in the Red Sea. God gave them food in the wilderness (74:14b). God dried up the Jordan so they could cross it (74:15). God created the earth. He made the sun for the day and for light (74:16). He made summer and winter (74:17). Asaph asks God to intervene because God has delivered Israel in the past and is obviously in control of creation.

A Call for Deliverance (74:18-23) Asaph adds a number of arguments for God to deliver His people. He asks the Lord to remember that the enemy has reproached Him and blasphemed His name (74:18). He asks the Lord not to deliver the defenseless turtledove (Israel) to the wild beast (Israel's enemy) and not forget the poor (74:19). He asks God to respect the covenant He made with Israel (either the Abrahamic or the Mosaic covenant) because cruelty has come from dark places (74:20). He asks God to let the oppressors be ashamed and the poor and needy praise His name (74:21). He asks the Lord to arise to plead His own cause, remembering that the foolish reproach Him daily (74:22). This is the third time Asaph has asked the Lord to remember (see verses 2 and 18). He asks the Lord not to forget the voice of His enemies; the tumult against Him increases continually (74:23). God needs to defend His reputation (see "Your name" in verse 18, "the covenant" in verse 20, "Your own cause" in verse 22, and "Your enemies" in verse 23).

Summary: When you see divine discipline, ask the Lord to remember His people and defeat their enemies for His glory as He has done in the past.

A point to ponder: When God disciplines us because we are guilty of sin, we can ask for forgiveness and deliverance based on God's character and covenant.

Psalm 75: When You Contemplate God's Judgment

Psalm 75 is a thanksgiving psalm written by Asaph. In it, Asaph contemplates God's judgment (75:2-3).

The Thanksgiving to God (75:1) Asaph says, "We give thanks to You O God, for Your wondrous works declare that Your name is near" (75:1). The wondrous works God had done for Israel declare that He is nearby and ready to work on their behalf. So they thanked God for what He has done because His works indicate He is personally nearby.

The Judgment of God (75:2-8) God says that when He chooses the proper time, He will judge uprightly (75:2). God judges when He decides the time is right, and when He judges, He judges righteously (Gen. 18:25). God could easily devastate the earth and all of its inhabitants, but He sustains it (75:3).

God tells the boastful not to deal boastfully and He tells the wicked not to lift up their horn (75:4) or speak with a stiff neck (75:5). Animals defiantly lift up their horn, a sign of strength against a foe. Oxen refuse to bow their neck to the yoke. Using these figures from the animal kingdom, God is warning the wicked about prideful boasting of their strength and stubborn resistance to His will.

Asaph explains ("for") that exaltation does not come from the east, west, or south (75:6). The North is conspicuous by its absence. It is not mentioned because no one would look to the North, that is, Assyria, for help. God is the judge who puts one down and exalts another (75:7). In the hand of the Lord, there is a cup full of red, mixed wine of His wrath that He shall pour out and all the wicked of the earth shall drink it (75:8a).

The Vow of Praise (75:9-10) Asaph vows that he will declare and sing praises to the God of Jacob forever (75:9) and God declares that He will cut off all the horns of the wicked and exalt the horns of the righteous (75:10). The wicked proudly lifted up their horn (75:4), but God will take away the very strength about which they boasted. The wicked will lose their strength, but God's people will gain strength.

Summary: When you contemplate God's judgment, thank Him and vow to praise Him for judging at the right time and judging righteously.

A point to ponder: Exaltation comes from the Lord; He exalts one and puts down another. So look to him for promotion and beware of proudly boasting about your strength.

Psalm 76: When God Gives You the Victory

Psalm 76 is a thanksgiving psalm written by Asaph. In it, God has given Israel a victory (76:3).

The Victory of God (76:1-6) God's name is great in Israel (76:1). God's dwelling is in Jerusalem (Salem and Zion are other names for Jerusalem; 76:2). It was there that He broke the arrows of the bow, the shield, and the sword of battle (76:3). God's name was great in Israel after He gave them victory over an enemy who attacked Jerusalem.

Addressing God, Asaph says, "You are more glorious and excellent than the mountains of prey" (76:4). "Mountains of prey" is a reference to those who attacked Jerusalem. The stouthearted (the enemies of Israel) were plundered, have sunk into their sleep, and none of their mighty men have found the use of their hands (76:5). At God's rebuke, their chariots and horses were in deep sleep (76:6). God's defeat of Israel's enemies attacking Jerusalem was such that the attackers seemed paralyzed and anesthetized as if they were asleep. This is probably a description of the victory God gave Israel over the armies of Sennacherib (2 Kings 19:35; Isa. 37:26).

The Judgment of God (76:7-10) This victory of God in the battle over Jerusalem was God's judgment on the enemies of Israel. Again addressing God, Asaph says, "You, Yourself, are to be feared; and who may stand in Your presence when once You are angry?" (76:7). The enemies of Israel should have feared God when they made Him angry because they attacked Jerusalem. So Asaph says to God, "You caused judgment to be heard from heaven; the earth feared and was still, when God arose to judgment, to deliver all the oppressed of the earth" (76:8-9). On this occasion, and for that matter on other occasions as well, when God rises to judge and His judgment is heard from heaven, the people of the earth fear and stand still.

Instead of translating verse 10, "Surely the wrath of man shall praise you; but the remainder of your wrath you shall gird yourself" (76:10), some translations and some commentators take the first part of verse 10 ("the wrath of man") as a reference to the wrath of God. Thus, the point of the verse is that *God's wrath* results in believers praising Him, and what wrath He did not use this time, He will strap on His belt like a sword to use later. The context is about God's wrath, not man's wrath (see 76:7) as is the later part of verse 10.

A Vow to God (76:11-12) Asaph invites the people of Israel to not only make vows to the Lord but also to pay them (76:11a). He adds, "Let all who are around Him bring presents to Him who ought to be feared" (76:11b). The righteous are to fear the Lord in the sense that they stand in awe of Him, as well as being afraid of Him if they disobey Him. To say the same thing another way, those who fear the Lord should make vows of praise and sacrifice to the Lord, as one might bring presents to a King (Rom. 12:1). Furthermore, God shall cut off the spirit of the princes who oppose Him; He is awesome to the Kings of the earth (76:12). Those who opposed the Lord should fear the judgment of the Lord.

Summary: When God gives the victory, give Him the praise and, perhaps, a present.

A point to ponder: Both the righteous and the wicked should fear God because He is a God who judges sin (76:7, 11).

Psalm 77: When Your Problems Keep You Awake

Psalm 77 is a lament psalm written by Asaph. In it, Asaph's problems keep him awake (77:2).

A Cry for Help (77:1-9) Asaph says in the day of his trouble (77:2a), he cried out to God (77:1), stretching out his hand "in the night without ceasing" (77:2b). He remembered God but that troubled him too (77:3a) because God did not answer his prayer (77:7-9). He felt overwhelmed (77:3). He says God held his eyelids open, meaning he could not sleep. He had insomnia! He was so troubled that he could not speak (77:4).

When he thought about the past (77:5), he remembered his meditation and song in the night (77:6). With a series of questions, he wants to know if the Lord has cast him off forever, will be favorable no more (77:7), cease being merciful forever, failed to keep his promises (77:8), forgotten to be gracious and let His anger shut up His tender mercies (77:9). In short, Asaph feels overwhelmed with trouble and abandoned by God. God was not answering his prayers as he had done in the past. He was in the depths of despair. In the middle of the night, he saw no hope.

Contemplation of God and His Work (77:10-20) Even though he was in anguish, Asaph deliberately decided to remember God's works and wonders (77:10-11). He would remember them, meditate on God's work, and *talk* of His deeds (77:12).

To be more specific, he will remember, meditate on, and talk about God's way in the sanctuary (God is holy), God's greatness (77:13), God's wonders among peoples (77:14), and God's redemption of His people, the sons of Jacob and Joseph (77:15).

Earlier in the psalm, Asaph mentions "ancient times" (77:5). At this point, he speaks about what God did in Exodus. He says the waters were afraid and the depths trembled (77:16). The clouds poured out water. Thunder was heard and lightning was seen (77:17). As a result of the thunder and lightning, the earth trembled and shook (77:18). It was God who was working in the crossing of the Red Sea (77:19). It was God who led His people "like a flock by the hand of Moses and Aaron" (77:20).

The fact that the psalm ends with Asaph's contemplation of God's greatness indicates that he was distracted from his pain by focusing on God's performance in the past.

Summary: When your problems keep you awake at night, remember, meditate on, and talk about God's person and work as revealed in the Scripture.

A point to ponder: It is not enough to remember or even meditate on God's work and wonders; it is a critical part of the process to *talk* about them (Jos. 1:8).

Psalm 78: When You Read the Old Testament #1

Psalm 78 is a didactic psalm written by Asaph. In it, Asaph reviews the history of Israel (78:12-64).

An Invitation to Learn (78:1-8) Asaph invites his people to listen (78:1) to parables of old (78:2, cited in Mt. 13:35), which their fathers told them (78:3) so they could tell their children (78:4), as God told them to do (78:5) so that coming generations (78:6) would trust and obey God (78:7) and not be like the stubborn, rebellious, unfaithful generation of the past (78:8).

The Rebellion of Ephraim (78:9-11) The children of Ephraim retreated from obedience (78:9), refusing to keep God's Law (78:10) and forgetting His wonderful works (78:11).

Unfaithfulness of Israel (78:12-64) God did marvelous things in Egypt (78:12). He divided the Red Sea (78:13), led them by a cloud and by fire (78:14), and split the rock to give them water to drink (78:15-16), but they rebelled (78:17), tested (78:18), spoke against (17:19), and questioned God (78:20). Therefore, God was angry (78:21), because they did not trust Him (78:22). Yet He provided food for them (78:23-30a) and while it was still in their mouth, the wrath of God struck down the choice men of Israel (78:30b-31). Because they still did not believe God, their years were filled with futility and fear (78:33).

Seeing the judgment of God, some of the people sought Him (78:34), remembering He was their Redeemer (78:35). Yet they lied, flattering God (78:36) without a steadfast heart that was faithful to God's covenant (78:37), but God forgave them (78:38) remembering that they were but flesh (78:39).

God's children provoked, grieved (78:40), and tempted Him (78:41). They did not remember His power in the plagues in Egypt (78:42-51), His guidance and protection in the wilderness (78:52-54), or His provision of victory in the conquests (78:55). Instead they tested, provoked, and disobeyed God (78:56). They were unfaithful like their fathers (78:57). They provoked Him and moved Him to jealousy with their idols (78:58). God was furious (78:59). He forsook the Tabernacle during the period of the Judges (78:60) and delivered Israel into the hands of their enemy, the Philistines (78:61; 1 Sam. 4:4-11). Some of God's people were killed (78:62), fire consumed their young men, maidens were not given in marriage (78:63), priests fell by the sword, and their widows made no lamentation (78:64).

The Faithfulness of God (78:65-72) Like a man who had been asleep, God woke up (78:65) and defeated His enemies (78:66). This time, He rejected the tribes of Joseph and Ephraim (78:67), chose the tribe of Judah and Mount Zion, that is, the city of Jerusalem (78:68), built His Temple (78:69), and chose David, who had been a shepherd (78:70), to shepherd His people (78:71). David shepherded Israel according to the integrity of his heart and guided them by the skillfulness of his hands (78:72; see 1 Kings 9:4).

Summary: When you read the Old Testament, learn from Israel's unfaithfulness and God's faithfulness.

This psalm traces Israel's history from Zoan (78:12), a city in Egypt, to Zion (78:68), Jerusalem. It reviews the history of Israel, from slavery in Egypt to the reign of David. Three psalms review Israel's history (78, 105, 106).

A point to ponder: Learn from the past to avoid repeating it.

Psalm 79: When You Think Vengeance is Appropriate

Psalm 79 is an imprecatory psalm written by Asaph in response to an attack on Jerusalem and the sacking of the Temple by Babylon in 586 BC (see Ps. 74). In it, Asaph asks for vengeance because God's people have been slaughtered and God's name has been slandered (79:6-7, 12).

A Lament over the Destruction (79:1-4) Asaph laments the destruction of Jerusalem and the defilement of God's holy Temple (79:1). The dead bodies of God's saints and servants are food for birds and beasts (79:2; see Jer. 7:33). Their blood was shed like water and no one is left to bury them (79:3). For bodies to be left unburied was the ultimate humiliation, treating them like a dead animal for whom no one cares. The psalmist complains, "We have become a reproach to our neighbors, a scorn, and derision to those who are around us" (79:4).

A Plea for Forgiveness and Vengeance (79:5-12) Asaph asks, "How long, Lord? Will You be angry forever? Will Your jealousy burn like fire?" (79:5). He wonders how long God will be angry with His people and allow them to suffer defeat, destruction, and humiliation. How long will God's jealousy burn like fire?

Asaph asks God to pour out His wrath on the nations that do not know Him and the kingdoms that do not call on His name (79:6) because they destroyed Jerusalem and laid waste to His Temple (79:7). He is asking for just judgment.

Asaph also asks for forgiveness of the sins of his forefathers and mercy because they have been humiliated (79:8). The previous generations had committed idolatry and had failed to keep the sabbatical year for the land, which was the cause of the captivity and the suffering of this generation (2 Chron. 36:14-21). He asks for forgiveness and deliverance for the Lord's namesake (79:9).

Asaph asks, "Why should the nations say, 'Where is their God?'" He asks God to avenge the death of His servants (79:10). Asaph asks God to hear the groaning of the prisoner, to preserve those appointed to die (79:11), and return sevenfold (abundantly) the reproach (the insults and taunting) with which they have reproached God (79:12). He is leaving vengeance up to the Lord. This plea for punishment is also a request for God to honor a provision of the Abrahamic covenant in which God promised to curse those who curse Abraham's descendants (Gen. 12:2-3).

A Promise to Praise (79:13) Asaph concludes by promising God that His people, the sheep of His pasture, will praise Him to all generations and give thanks to Him forever (79:13). The helpless sheep promise the sufficient Shepherd perpetual public praise.

Summary: When you think vengeance is appropriate because God's people have been slaughtered and God's name has been slandered, it is proper to pray for forgiveness, deliverance, and vengeance.

A point to ponder: Even when vengeance is appropriate, it should be left to the Lord (Rom. 12:19-21).

Psalm 80: When You Need Spiritual Restoration

Psalm 80 is a lament psalm written by Asaph. In it, Asaph seeks spiritual restoration (80:3, 7, 19).

An Appeal to the Shepherd (80:1-7) Asaph asks the Shepherd of Israel, who dwells between the cherubim and who has led Joseph like a flock, to hear his prayer, to shine forth (80:1), to stir up His strength before Ephraim (Northern Kingdom), Benjamin (Southern Kingdom), and Manasseh (Transjordan) to save us, meaning deliver us from physical danger (80:2), to restore us (spiritually), and to cause His face to shine on us (be favorable) so we will be delivered (80:3; Num. 6:25).

Asaph laments God's discipline on Israel. He asks, "O Lord God of hosts, how long will You be angry against the prayer of Your people?" (80:4). God's discipline has been like giving them tears to eat and drink, a reference to the manna and water that God supplied for Israel in the wilderness (80:5). It has resulted in strife with Israel's neighbors and laughter (mocking) among Israel's enemies (80:6). This may refer to the defeat of Samaria by the Assyrians in 722 BC.

Asaph pleads, "Restore us, O God of hosts; cause your face to shine, and we shall be saved!" (80:7). Except for addressing God as "O God of hosts" instead of "O God," verse 7 is identical to verse 3. Asaph repeats the request for spiritual restoration and favor so that they will be physically delivered.

Appeal to the Vinedresser (80:8-19) Changing the metaphor for God (see "Shepherd" in 80:1), Asaph appeals to God as a vinedresser. As a vinedresser, God brought a vine (Israel) out of Egypt, made room to plant it (80:8), caused it to take deep root, and filled the land (Canaan) with it (80:9). The hills were covered with its shadow and the mighty cedar with its boughs, that is, branches (80:10). Her branches spread from the sea, meaning the Mediterranean, to the river, that is, the Euphrates (80:11).

Again, Asaph laments God's discipline on Israel. This time, he asks, "Why have you broken down her hedges, so that all who pass by the way pluck her fruit?" (80:12). God broke down Israel's protective wall, allowing Israel's enemy to consume her.

Asaph asks the Vinedresser to return, look down from heaven to see what's going on, and visit His vine (80:14) and the vineyard which He planted and the branches He made strong for Himself (80:15). He tells God that His vineyard is burned with fire, cut down, and perishes at the rebuke of His countenance (80:16). So, he asks the Vinedresser to let His hand be upon the man of His right hand, upon the son of man who He made strong for Himself (80:17). The man of God's right hand (see verse 2 where the Hebrew word "Benjamin" means "son of my right hand") and the son of man (see Ex. 4:22) are references to Israel. Asaph adds, "Then we will not turn back from You; revive us and we will call upon Your name" (80:18). Revive (Hebrew: preserve, that is, our life) us and we will faithfully call on Your name.

For the third and final time, Asaph pleads, "Restore us, O Lord God of hosts; cause your face to shine, and we shall be saved!" (80:19). Except for addressing God as "O Lord God of host" instead of "O God" or "O God of Hosts," verse 19 is identical to verses 3 and 7. Asaph repeats the request for spiritual restoration and favor so that they will be physically delivered.

Summary: When you need spiritual restoration, appeal to God, as your Shepherd and Vinedresser, to restore you and be favorable toward you so that you might be delivered.

A point to ponder: We need to be restored to bear fruit, which benefits others.

Psalm 81: When You Want to Celebrate the Lord

Psalm 81 is a praise psalm written by Asaph. In it, Asaph celebrates the Lord (81:1-3).

A Call to Celebration (81:1-5a) Asaph calls the people to "Sing aloud to God our strength; make a joyful shout to the God of Jacob" (81:1), raise a song with the timbrel, harp, lute (81:2). This song accompanied by musical instruments is *to God*, our source of strength, not just *to people* (see Eph. 5:19).

Asaph adds, "Blow the trumpet at the time of the new moon, at the full moon on our solemn feast day" (81:3). The new moon marked the beginning of the month. Israel was instructed to celebrate (Lev. 23:41) the beginning of the seventh month by blowing trumpets (Lev. 23:24). The full moon marked the fifteenth day of the month. Israel was instructed to celebrate the Feast of Tabernacles on the fifteenth day of the seventh month (Sept./Oct.; Lev. 23:34). In other words, this verse refers to the Feast of Tabernacles. The reason ("for") they were to blow the trumpets is because they were instructed to do so in the Law (81:4; see the verses in Leviticus). God gave them this feast, which He established after the Exodus, as a testimony (81:5a).

A Communication from the Lord (81:5b-16) God begins to speak. He says in Egypt, He heard a language He did not know, that is, acknowledge (81:5b). He delivered Israel from their burden of slavery (81:6). He reminds them that when they were in trouble, they called and He delivered them from Egypt, gave them the Law at Sinai (here called the place of thunder), and tested them in the wilderness, that is, at the waters of Meribah (81:7).

God commands Israel to listen to Him (81:8). They are not to worship any other god (81:9) because He is the Lord their God who brought them out of the land of Egypt and who will fill their mouth if they open it wide (81:10).

God complains that His people did not obey Him (81:11). He says, "So I gave them over to their own stubborn heart, to walk in their own councils" (81:12).

God contemplates what would have happened had they listened to Him and walked in His ways (81:13). He would have subdued their enemies (81:14). Even if those who hated Him would have pretended submission to Him, their fate would have endured forever (81:15). As for Israel, He would have fed them with the finest of wheat and satisfied them with honey from the rock (81:16).

Summary: When you want to celebrate the Lord, sing to Him and listen to Him so that you will learn to obey Him.

A point to ponder: If we, like Israel, do not listen to the Lord, we will miss His blessings and not be satisfied.

Psalm 82: When You Are Facing an Unjust Judge

Psalm 82 is a wisdom psalm written by Asaph. In it, Asaph is facing an unjust judge (82:2).

The Judge of the Judges (82:1) Asaph begins with a simple statement: "God stands in the congregation of the mighty; He judges among the gods" (82:1). The "mighty" and the "gods" are references to the same group of people. The Hebrew word translated "gods" (*elohim*) means "god, god-like, rulers, judges." In other words, in this verse, "gods" is a reference to human judges. Human judges represent God to establish justice. Those who have stood before a human judge in court understand that they are "mighty;" they are "gods."

Asaph pictures all the judges gathered together in a congregation, standing before God, who judges them. Human judges have a Judge! To say the same thing another way, the Judge judges human judges.

The Indictment of the Judges (82:2-7) Asaph asks human judges, "How long will you judge unjustly and show partiality to the wicked?" (82:2). Instead of just judgments, some judges judge unjustly by showing partiality. To make matters worse, they show partiality to the wicked. They were not practicing justice; they were perverting justice.

Asaph advises human judges, "Defend the poor and the fatherless; do justice to the afflicted and the needy" (82:3) and "deliver the poor and needy; free them from the hand of the wicked" (82:4). Instead of handing down unjust judgments that favor the wicked, human judges should be defending the poor, fatherless, afflicted, and needy and delivering them from the wicked.

Asaph accuses these unjust human judges in Israel of not knowing (the Law of Moses), not understanding (justice), and walking in darkness (82:5a). Because they had the Law, the judges in Israel should have been the wisest judges, but because they did not know the Law or understand justice, they were living in darkness (not in the light of the Law), blind to justice. Consequently, "all the foundations of the earth are unstable" (82:5b). Unjust judges produce an unstable society.

Asaph asserts, "I said 'You are gods' and all of you are children of the Most High, but you shall die like men and fall like the one of the princes" (82:6-7). These unjust judges may be "gods" (individuals with power by God's authority), even God's sons (God's representatives), but they will die just like other people, including princes, and when they die, they will face the Most High Judge. They may be high and mighty but are not the Most High.

When Jesus was charged with blasphemy because He claimed to be the Son of God, He quoted Psalms 82:6 (Jn. 10:34) to remind them that God called Israel's judges "gods." His argument is that if God called mere men "god," it would not be blasphemy to say that the Son, who was sent into the world by the Father, is God.

A Prayer for Justice (32:8) Asaph concludes, "Arise O God, Judge of the earth; for You shall inherit all nations" (82:8). When the righteous Judge comes, He will establish justice (96:13; 98:9) among all the nations of the earth. Jesus will fulfill this (Jn. 5: 22).

Summary: When facing an unjust judge, remember the Most High Judge will judge that judge.

A point to ponder: There is injustice in the world now, but one day, God will judge injustice and establish justice on earth.

Psalm 83: When You Pray for Your Enemies

Psalm 83 is a lament psalm written by Asaph. In it, Asaph prays for his enemies, who are also God's enemies (83:2-3).

A Plea for God's Action (83:1-8) Asaph pleads for God to not be still (83:1) because (for) His enemies have risen (83:2) and are plotting against God's people (83:3). Their intent is clear. "They have said, 'Come and let us cut them off from *being* a nation, that the name of Israel may be remembered no more'" (83:4). Furthermore, they have formed a confederacy against God (83:5). Enemies of God's people are enemies of God.

Asaph lists the members of the confederacy: "The tents of Edom and the Ishmaelites; Moab [the descendants of Lot] and the Hagrites [the descendants of Hagar]; Gebal [either another name for Byblos, a town in Lebanon, or the mountainous region south of the Dead Sea], Ammon [also the descendants of Lot], and Amalek; Philistia with the inhabitants of Tyre; Assyria also has joined with them; They have helped the children of Lot. Selah" (83:6-8). All of these present enemies are nations that are on the borders of Israel and Judah.

A Petition for Judgment (83:9-12) Asaph asks God to deal with His present enemies as He has dealt with His enemies in the past, and he lists those past enemies. He says, "Deal with them as *with* Midian [see Gideon in Judges 7-8], as *with* Sisera [a Canaanite commander], as *with* Jabin [the Canaanite king] at the Brook Kishon, who perished at En Dor, *who* became *as* refuse on the earth (see Deborah and Barak in Judges 4-5). Make their nobles like Oreb and like Zeeb [Midianite commanders; see Judges 7:25], Yes, all their princes like Zebah and Zalmunna [Midianite kings; Judges 8:5-6, 12, 18], who said, 'Let us take for ourselves the pastures of God for a possession'" (83:9-12). All these victories were during the period of the Judges. Asaph is asking God to defeat these present enemies as He has defeated enemies in the past.

A Purpose for the Judgment (83:13-18) Asaph specifies the details of the defeat of these enemies. He prays that God would drive them away like chaff in the wind (83:13), that God would pursue them like a fire sweeping through a forest (83:14), that God would frighten them with His storm (83:15), and that God would "fill their faces with shame" so that they may seek His name (83:16). He wants God to pursue them, frighten them, and let them be ashamed so that they will turn to Him. Asaph's first concern is their salvation.

Asaph adds, "Let them be confounded and dismayed forever (because their plans failed); Yes, let them be put to shame and perish [not as individuals, but as nations conspiring against Israel], that they may know that You, whose name alone *is* the LORD, *are* the Most High over all the earth" (83:17-18). Asaph's ultimate goal is for God's reputation as the sovereign Lord to be known worldwide.

Summary: When you pray for your enemies who are also God's enemies, ask God to defeat them and save them for God's glory.

A point to ponder: The ultimate issue is not just our safety or their salvation; it is God's glory.

Psalm 84: When You Are On Your Way to Church

Psalm 84 is an ascent (ascending to the Temple) psalm written by an unknown author. In it, the author is on his way to the Temple in Jerusalem (84:5-7).

Passion for God's House (84:1-4) The author of this psalm is on his way to the Temple in Jerusalem, which houses the very presence of God, to pray. It begins by talking about the loveliness of the Temple (84:1) and the longing to see it (84:2a), but the passion is not just for God's house; it is for God Himself (84:2b). The poet envies the sparrow, who has a home, and the swallow, who has a nest for its young in the courtyard of Temple (84:3). Blessed ("happy," as in 1:1) are those who live in the rooms surrounding the Temple because they can praise God in the Temple (84:4).

Pilgrimage to God's House (84:5-7) Blessed ("happy;" see 84:4) are those whose strength is in the Lord and whose heart is set on a pilgrimage to His house (His presence) (84:5). On the way to the Temple, "As they pass through the Valley of Baca, they make a spring; the rain also covers it with pools" (84:6). The Hebrew word translated "Baca" means "weeping." The anticipation of going to the Temple turns their weeping into a blessing. It is like a refreshing spring or pool of water. Moreover, "They go from strength to strength; each one appears before God in Zion" (84:7). They grow stronger and stronger as they get closer and closer to Zion, that is, Jerusalem.

Prayer in God's House (84:8-12) Addressing Him as the God of hosts and the God of Jacob (Israel), the psalmist asks God to give ear and hear his prayer (84:8) for "our shield" and to look upon the face of "Your anointed" (84:9). The shield and the anointed are references to the king.

The psalmist adds, "For a day in your courts is better than a thousand. I would rather be a doorkeeper in the house of my God than dwell in the tents of the wicked" (84:10). One day in God's house (presence) is better than thousands of days anywhere else. Nothing can compare with being in God's house (presence). The psalmist would rather be a lowly servant in the house of God than live in luxury in the tent of the wicked.

The reason ("for") for wanting to be in the Temple of God rather than the tent of the wicked is: "For the Lord God is a sun and a shield; the Lord will give grace and glory; no good thing will He withhold from those who walk uprightly" (84:11). Like the sun, God provides light and warmth. Like a shield, God provides protection. The king is the shield in verse 9 and the Lord is the shield in verse 11. God gives grace, glory, and good things to those who walk uprightly. He gives grace (unmerited, undeserved favor) for enablement, glory, honor, and good gifts, such as refreshments (see verse 6), to those who walk in harmony with His will.

The psalmist concludes, "O Lord of hosts, blessed is the man who trusts in You!" (84:12). This psalm opens and closes by calling God "Lord of hosts." Those who trust in the Lord are the ones who receive all the blessings mentioned in verse 11. The word "blessed" ("happy") appears three times in this psalm (84:4, 5, 12), once in each part of it.

Summary: On your way to the house of God, you will be blessed (happy) if you go with a passion to be with the Lord and a prayer of trust in the Lord.

A point to ponder: Attending church should be a delight, not just a duty. It will be if your heart is where it should be.

Psalm 85: When You Need Restoration Again

Psalm 85 is a thanksgiving psalm written by the sons of Korah. In it, they need restoration again (85:1-4).

A Review of God's Past Restoration (85:1-3) Addressing the Lord, the psalmist says: "You have been favorable to Your land, You brought back the captivity of Jacob (85:1), You have forgiven the iniquity of Your people, You have covered all their sin (85:2), You have taken away all Your wrath, You have turned from the fierceness of your anger" (85:3). Bringing back the captivity of Jacob is probably a reference to God bringing back Israel after the Babylonian captivity. These verses constitute a thanksgiving to God for no longer being angry, for forgiving Israel of her sins, and for restoring her to the land of Palestine.

A Request for God's Present Restoration (85:4-7) Even after God restored Israel, they sinned again and needed restoration. Thus, the psalmist requests, "Restore us, O God of our salvation and cause Your anger toward us to cease" (85:4). He asks, "Will You be angry with us forever? Will you prolong Your anger to all generations? (85:5); will You not revive us again, that your people may rejoice in you?" (85:6). He adds, "Show us your mercy, Lord, and grant us Your salvation" (85:7). This is a request for God not to be angry, but to be merciful, to restore them, to revive (Hebrew: preserve) them so that His people will rejoice in Him.

A Reflection on God's Future Restoration (85:8:13) Having prayed for restoration, the psalmist says, "I will hear what God the Lord will speak, for He will speak peace to His people and to His saints; but let them not turned back to folly" (85:8). He is confident the Lord will speak peace and prevent His people from returning to their folly again.

The psalmist describes this future spiritual restoration in detail. He says, "Surely His salvation is near to those who fear Him, that glory may dwell in our land" (85:9). "Mercy and truth have met together; righteousness and peace have kissed" (85:10). "Truth shall spring out of the earth and righteousness shall look down from heaven" (85:11). "Yes, the Lord will give what is good; and our land will yield its increase" (85:12). "Righteousness will go before Him, and shall make His footsteps our pathway" (85:13). God's future restoration will include glory (the presence of God), mercy, truth, righteousness, peace, and that which is good. This will be fully fulfilled in the Millennium.

Summary: When you need restoration again, review God's past restoration, request restoration again, and reflect on the kind of restoration God gives, namely, truth, righteousness, mercy, and peace.

After Nehemiah led the children of Israel back to the land, rebuilt the wall, and restored the people, he returned to Persia. When he returned to the land, he discovered that the people needed to be restored again (see Neh. 13).

A point to ponder: When we stray from truth, righteousness, mercy, and peace, God will restore us because He is a God of mercy (85:7); He will preserve us so that we may rejoice in Him (85:6).

Psalm 86: When Your Life is Threatened

Psalm 86 is a lament psalm written by David. In it, David's life is threatened (86:2).

A Plea for Protection (86:1-7) David pleads with the Lord <u>to hear</u> his prayer because he is poor and needy (86:1), <u>to preserve</u> his life because he is holy (living a righteous life) and the Lord is his God (86:2a), <u>to save</u> him because he trusts the Lord (86:2b), <u>to be merciful</u> because he cries to the Lord all day long (86:3), <u>to rejoice</u> his soul because the Lord lifts up his soul (86:4), is good, ready to forgive, and abundant in mercy to all who call upon Him (86:5), and <u>to give ear</u> to his prayer and supplication (86:6), because in the day of trouble, he will call upon the Lord and the Lord will answer him (86:7). In this subsection, as poor and needy, holy, and as a servant who is in trouble, David pleads with the Lord to protect him and deliver him, because He is merciful.

A Praise of God (86:8-10) David says, "Among the gods, there is none like you, O Lord; nor are there any works like Your works" (86:8). All the nations that the Lord has created shall come and worship and glorify the Lord (86:9), because He is great and does wondrous things (86:10).

A Petition for Understanding (86:11-13) David asks the Lord to teach him His ways (86:11a) so that he can walk in God's truth, have a united heart to fear God's name (86:11b), praise God with all of his heart, and glorify God's name forever (86:12), because the Lord is merciful and has delivered David from certain death (86:13).

A Prayer for Strength (86:14-17) David explains that the proud have risen against him and a mob of violent men have has sought his life because they did not set God before them (86:14), but the Lord is a God full of compassion, grace, long-suffering, mercy, and truth (86:15). So he asks the Lord to be merciful to him, to give him strength, to deliver him (86:16), and to show him a sign for good so that those who hate him may see it and be ashamed because the Lord has helped him and comforted him (86:17).

Summary: When your life is threatened, plead with the Lord for protection, praise Him, and ask for understanding and strength because He is a God full of mercy.

God's name appears in this psalm nine times (see "the Lord" in verses 1, 3, 4, 5, 6, 11, 12, 15, and 17).

A point to ponder: This psalm highlights again that when we are in trouble (86:7), we need an understanding of God's will (86:11) and the strength to do it (86:16).

Psalm 87: When You Contemplate the City of God

Psalm 87 is a praise psalm written by the sons of Korah. In it, the authors contemplate the city of God (87:3).

The Glory of Zion (87:1-3) The psalmist says God founded the holy mountain, a reference to Jerusalem (87:1; see Isa. 14:32), and loves the gates of Zion, a reference to Jerusalem (87:2). No wonder he adds, "Glorious things are spoken of you, O city of God!" (87:3; Isa. 2:2-4; Isa. 4:2-6; Isa. 28:16).

The glory of Jerusalem is that it is the city of God. God founded it and chose it (1 Kings 11:13) to make His earthly residence there in the Temple. He particularly loves the gates of Jerusalem because it is through the gates people come to the Temple where He dwells. Glorious things were spoken of Jerusalem, mainly because of the Temple being there. The Jerusalem of old foreshadows the New Jerusalem (Rev. 21:2-22:5).

The Population of Zion (87:4-6) At this point, God speaks, saying, "I will make mention of Rahab and Babylon to those who know Me; Behold, O Philistia and Tyre, with Ethiopia: 'This *one* was born there.'" Rahab is a nickname for Egypt and the city of Tyre refers to the nation of Syria. God mentions five Gentile nations that say they know Him and were born in Jerusalem. Since they were obviously born someplace else, this is a reference to a second birth (see Jn. 3:10). During the reign of Hezekiah, Gentiles visited the Temple in Jerusalem.

The psalmist adds, "And of Zion, it will be said, 'This one and that one were born in her; and the Most High shall establish her'" (87:5). This verse refers to those who were physically born in Jerusalem, namely Jews. Thus, God will establish Jerusalem's population consisting of Jews and Gentiles (Isa. 2:2-4).

The psalmist continues, "The Lord will record when He registers the peoples: 'This *one* was born there'" (87:6). God registers the people who have been born again in a record.

The Joy in Zion (87:7) The psalmist concludes, "Both the singers and the players on instruments *say,* 'All my springs *are* in you'" (87:7). The springs in Jerusalem, including water for survival and refreshment, are the source of joy. Joy comes from Jerusalem because God dwells in Jerusalem.

Summary: When you contemplate the city of God, where God dwells, you will see that He is the source of salvation and joy for Jews and Gentiles.

John Newton's great hymn "Glorious Things of Thee Are Spoken" is based on this Psalm.

> Zion, city of our God;
> God, whose word cannot be broken,
> formed thee for his own abode.
> On the Rock of Ages founded,
> what can shake thy sure repose?
> With salvation's walls surrounded,
> thou mayst smile at all thy foes.

A point to ponder: Like Abraham, we wait "for the city which has foundations, whose builder and maker is God" (Heb. 11:10), that is, the New Jerusalem. This world is not my home!

Psalm 88: When You Feel Alone and Abandoned

Psalm 88 is a lament psalm written by Heman, the Ezrahite (1 Kings 4:31; 1 Chron. 15:16-19). In it, the author feels alone and abandoned (88:8).

The Cry of Heman (88:1-9) Addressing God as Lord and the God of his salvation, Heman reminds God that he has cried out to Him day and night (88:1) and asks Him to answer his cry (88:2), because his soul is full of trouble and his life draws near to death (88:3). The fact that he is still praying and that he calls God the God of his salvation indicates that although God has not answered his prayer, Heman is trusting the Lord to answer his prayer and deliver him from death.

Heman describes his crisis as being considered by others as about to die, as a man who has no strength (88:4), and as being like a slain man already lying in the grave (88:5a). He goes on to say that God no longer remembers him, has cut him off (88:5b), has laid him in the lowest pit (88:6), has laid His wrath on him, has afflicted him (88:7), has put his acquaintances far from him, and has made him an abomination to them (88:8a). He says he is shut up and cannot get out (88:8b) and his eyes waste away because of his affliction (88:9a).

Heman has been forsaken by his friends, feels God has abandoned him, and he is knocking on death's door. He feels alone and miserable.

The Complaint of Heman (88:9b-12) Heman complains that he has called on the Lord daily (88:9b), indicating that he has asked and God has not answered. He asks rhetorical questions that expect a negative answer: "Will You work wonders for the dead? Shall the dead arise and praise you?" (88:10) "Shall Your lovingkindness be declared in the grave?" Or your faithfulness in the place of destruction?" (88:11). "Shall Your wonders be known of the dark? And Your righteousness in the land of forgetfulness?" (88:12). If he dies, Heman will no longer be able to praise the Lord in the land of the living. He is not denying that he can praise the Lord after he dies. He simply desires to praise the Lord on this side of the grave.

The Consternation of Heman (88:13-18) For the third time, Heman mentions crying out to the Lord (88:13; see verses 1 and 2) and the Lord has not answered (88:14). He says that he has been afflicted and has been ready to die for a long time (88:15a). He has suffered from the terrors of God to the point that he is distraught (18:15b). God's fierce wrath has gone over him and God's terrors have cut him off (18:16), engulfing him like a flood of water (18:17). Furthermore, he says, "Loved ones and friends, You have put far from me" (88:18). The psalm ends with Heman feeling alone and abandoned, cut off from loved ones and the Lord.

Summary: When you feel alone and abandoned by God, keep praying and trusting the Lord.
A point to ponder: Never give up on the Lord. Keep praying. He knows what He is doing.
Because of how it ends, this psalm has been called one of the saddest psalms in the Psalter. Moreover, the psalmist felt that he was at death's door. Note the number of times there is a reference to death (see "pit" in verses 4 and 6; "dead" in verses 5 and 10; "grave" in verse 5; "darkness" in verse 6; "depths" in verse 6; "place of destruction" in verse 11; "dark" in verse 12 and "land of forgetfulness" in verse 12).

Psalm 89: When You Question God's Faithfulness

Psalm 89 is a royal psalm written by Ethan, the Ezrahite. In it, Ethan questions God's faithfulness (89:49).

The Covenant of God (89:1-4) The psalmist says he will sing of the mercies of the Lord forever and make known God's faithfulness to all generations (89:1) because He is merciful and faithful (89:2). God says He has made a covenant with David (89:3) and his seed (89:4; see 2 Sam. 7).

The Character of God (89:5-18) The Lord's faithfulness will be praised in heaven and in the assembly of the saints (89:5), because He is incomparable (89:6), great (89:7), mighty (89:8), sovereign (89:9), victorious over Rahab (Egypt; 89:10), the Creator (89:11-12), strong (89:13), righteous, just, full of mercy and truth (89:14). Blessed are those who walk in the light of His countenance (89:15). They rejoice in His name and exalt in His righteousness (89:16), because His glory is their strength and in His favor, they are exalted (89:17). Their king and shield belong to the Holy One (89:18). In the Lord, they had joy, exaltation, glory, strength, and security.

The Promise of God (89:19-37) Concerning David, God promised to exalt him (89:19-20), establish him, strengthen him (89:21), give him victory (89:22-23), be faithful and merciful to him (89:24), and expand his territory (89:25). He shall cry to the Lord, his Father, God, and rock of salvation (89:26) and God will make him His firstborn and the highest King of the earth (89:27). His throne shall be eternal (89:28-29). If his sons are disobedient, God will punish them (89:31-32), but will not take His lovingkindness from them nor allow His faithfulness to His covenant made with David to fail (89:33-35). His throne shall be eternal (89:36-37). The Davidic Covenant will ultimately be fulfilled in the Son of David, Jesus Christ.

An Appeal to God (89:38-51) It appears God is furious with David (89:38), has broken His covenant with David, has cast David's crown to the ground (89:39), has brought his strongholds to ruin (89:40), made his enemies rejoice (89:42), has not sustained him in battle (89:43), has made his glory cease (89:44), shortened his life, and covered him with shame (89:45).

So the psalmist asks a series of questions: "How long, Lord? Will you hide Yourself forever? Will Your wrath burn like fire?" (89:46). "For what futility have You created all the children of men?" (89:47). "What man can live and not see death? Can he deliver his life from the power of the grave?" (89:48). "Lord, where is Your former lovingkindnesses, which You swore to David in Your truth?" (89:49). In short, the psalmist is questioning God's faithfulness to the covenant He made with David because of some humiliating defeat suffered by a Davidic king. As a result of a defeat, the poet was distressed, despondent, and disillusioned.

The psalmist pleads, "Remember, Lord, the reproach of Your servants (89:50) with which Your enemies have reproached Your anointed" (89:51). The psalmist poured out his pain and pleaded with the Lord, indicating that he still trusted the Lord's faithfulness. Notice the references to God's mercy (89:1, 2, 14, 24, 28; "lovingkindness" in verses 33 and 49 is the same Hebrew word) and faithfulness (89:1, 2, 5, 8, 24, 33).

The doxology, "Blessed be the Lord forevermore! Amen and Amen," closes book III.

Summary: When you question God's faithfulness, review His character and promises, remind Him of His promises, request Him to remember His promises, and be reassured that God is faithful even when it appears He is not.

A point to ponder: God's promises depend on God's character, not our circumstances.

Psalm 90: When You Reflect on the Brevity of Life

Psalm 90 is a lament psalm written by Moses. In it, Moses reflects on the brevity of life (90:3-6).

The Eternality of God (90:1-2) God has been the dwelling place (refuge; a protective shelter) for His people in all generations (90:1), because He is the eternal God who existed before the creation of the world (90:2).

The Brevity of Human Life (90:3-6) In contrast to the eternality of God is the brevity of human life on this earth. People return to the dust (90:3). Even if they lived for 1000 years (Methuselah lived 969 years), that is like one day or even part of the day (a four-hour watch in the night) to God (90:4; 2 Pet. 3:8). Their life is like something carried away in a flood which only takes a moment (90:5a). Their entire life is like one night of sleep (90:5b). They are like a blade of grass that grows up in the morning, flourishes through the day, and is cut down and withered in the evening (90:5c-6). Human life is short.

The Judgment of God (90:7-12) The reason ("for") life is so short is because of the judgment of God. We are terrified and consumed by His anger (90:7). Our sins, even our secret sins, are before Him (90:8). All our days pass in God's wrath and we finish our years like a sigh (90:9). Moses saw God's anger against sin (Ex. 32:1-14; Deut. 3:26).

Sin shortens life. The normal lifespan of a human being is 70 or 80 years, full of labor and sorrow, soon cut off when we fly away like a fleeting bird (90:10). Moses, who wrote this Psalm, lived to be 120 and Joshua died at 110. God promises a longer life to those who live godly: "The fear of the Lord prolongs days, but the years of the wicked will be shortened" (Prov. 10:27).

Yet, who understands the power of God's anger? Who understands God's wrath against sin and, therefore, gives Him the reverence ("fear") due Him (90:11)?

In light of the brevity of human life because of God's wrath on sin, Moses asks, "Teach us to number our days that we may gain a heart of wisdom" (90:12). If we understood the brevity of life, we would wisely use the few days we have to serve the Lord and not live in sin.

A Prayer for Mercy (90:13-17) Moses asks the Lord to have compassion (90:13) and satisfy us early with His mercy "that we may rejoice and be glad all our days" (90:14).

Moses asks the Lord to make us glad "according to the days in which You have afflicted us, the years in which we have seen evil" (90:15), that is, let us be glad for as long as we were sad.

Moses asks the Lord to let His work appear to us and His glory to our children (90:16). May God's eternal work and glory be revealed to us and to our descendants. Let us see that which lasts beyond our lives and generation.

Moses asks the Lord to let the beauty of the Lord be upon us and establish the work of our hands (90:17). May our work have eternal, not transitory, value.

Summary: When you reflect on the brevity of life, you will realize life is short because of God's judgment on sin and you will ask God for mercy to satisfy you early with His mercy, to make you glad, and to establish your work.

A point to ponder: Reflecting on the brevity of life should motivate us to improve the quality of each day of our life.

Psalm 91: When You Are Exposed to Danger

Psalm 91 is a trust psalm written by an anonymous author. In it, the author is exposed to danger (91:3, 5-6, 10).

God's Protection (91:1-2) The psalmist says, "He who dwells in the secret place of the Most High shall abide under the shadow of the Almighty" (91:1). The "secret place" is the most private place of the Most High (the sovereign Ruler), that is, the Holy of Holies in the Tabernacle (see 27:5). Those who live aware of the presence of God abide under the shadow (like being under the wing of a bird, see 91:4) of the Almighty (the all-powerful One). The psalmist adds, "I will say of the Lord, 'He is my refuge and my fortress; my God, in Him will I trust'" (91:2). In these two verses, the psalmist uses four names to refer to God: Most High God, Almighty, Lord, God. The psalmist trusts the Lord to be his refuge (his place of safety in the time of danger) and his fortress (his defense against an attack). In short, the psalmist trusts the sovereign, all-powerful God for his protection.

God's Deliverance (91:3-13) The Lord will deliver us from the snare of the fowler (the trap set for a bird) and the perilous pestilence, that is, deadly diseases (91:3). Like a mother bird, He covers us with His feathers so that we take refuge under His wings (91:4a). His truth is our shield and buckler (91:4b; Eph. 6:14). A buckler was a shield that surrounded a person.

Therefore, you shall not be afraid of the terror in the night (91:5), the arrows that fly during the day, pestilence that walks in darkness, nor the destruction that lays waste at noon (91:6). Even when you see a thousand, yea ten thousand, fall near you, know it will not harm you (91:7) and that you are looking at the reward of the wicked, those who do not trust the Lord (91:8). God protects those who trust Him at all times (91:5-6) and in all kinds of danger (91:6). Nothing can harm us without God's permission, nor will rebels escape His retribution.

Because you have made the Lord your dwelling place and refuge (91:9), no evil shall befall you, nor shall any plague come near your dwelling (91:10). The reason ("for") is God puts His angels in charge over you to keep you in all of your ways (91:11). They will bear you up, lest you dash your foot against a stone, that is, stub your toe (91:12). During the temptation of Christ, Satan misquotes Psalm 91:11-12 (Mt. 4:6). Jesus refused to tempt God by deliberately putting Himself in a dangerous situation. The point here is those who dwell with the Lord and make Him their refuge will trample underfoot the lion, the cobra, the young lions, and the serpent (91:13; Lk. 10:19). To sum up, God will deliver you from danger.

God's Assurance (91:14-16) The Lord says because you know Me and love Me, I will deliver you (91:14), answer your prayers (91:15a), honor you (91:15b), satisfy you with long life, and show you My deliverance (91:16). The Hebrew word translated "love" in verse 14 means "to love, be attached to, to long for" (BDB). It comes from a root word that means "cling" (Strong).

Summary: When you are exposed to danger, remember that God assures those who know Him, love Him and trust that He will protect them and deliver them from all kinds of danger.

Are there exceptions to this provision? The point is that nothing can happen to those who love and trust the Lord without His permission. The exceptions (such as Job's experience) are for our good (Rom. 8:28) and God's glory (Jn. 9:3).

A point to ponder: Those who cling to the Lord (91:14) are not afraid (91:5) of any kind of danger because they know that a sovereign, all-powerful God tenderly protects them like a mother bird tucks her little ones under her wing.

Psalm 92: When You See the Defeat of Your Enemies

Psalm 92 is a praise psalm written by an anonymous author. In it, the author sees the defeat of his enemies (92:11).

Praise God (92:1-3) It is good to give thanks to the Lord, to sing praises to the name of the Most High (92:1), to declare His lovingkindness in the morning, and to declare His faithfulness every night (92:2). The psalmist adds, "On an instrument of ten strings, on the lute, and on the harp, with harmonious sound," which indicates that this psalm was part of a public meeting.

For His Works (92:4-6) The psalmist explains ("for") that the Lord has made him glad through His works and that he will triumph in God's works (92:4), which are great and His thoughts are very deep (92:5). The Hebrew word translated "triumph" means "overcome, cry out, shout for joy" (see "sing for joy" in the NASB and the NIV). The psalmist is saying it is good to give thanks, sing praise, declare God's lovingkindness and faithfulness and sing for joy because of God's works and very deep thoughts, which he undoubtedly learned from God's Word. The Word of God enabled the psalmist to understand the works of God, that is, what God was doing. The psalmist goes on to say, "A senseless man does not know, nor does a fool understand this" (92:6). Fools do not understand God's Word or works (1 Cor. 2:14).

For His Judgment on the Wicked (92:7-9) For example, what the psalmist understands and the fool does not is that when the wicked spring up like grass and flourish, in the end they will be destroyed forever (92:7), but the Lord will be on high forevermore (92:8). As the psalmist explains ("for") the workers of iniquity shall be scattered and God's enemies shall perish (92:9).

For His Blessing on the Righteous (92:10-15) The psalmist says that his horn (strength) has been exalted like a wild ox, he has been anointed with fresh oil (for service) (92:10), his eyes have seen and his ears have heard his desire on his enemies (92:11). God has blessed him by allowing him to see the defeat and destruction of his enemies rather than him seeing death.

Using the figure of several types of trees, the psalmist describes the blessings of the righteous. They will flourish (Hebrew: blossom) like a palm tree and grow like a cedar (be strong) in Lebanon (92:12). Those who are planted in the house of the Lord (draw near to Him) shall flourish (Hebrew: blossom) in God's court (92:13), which is the court that counts. They shall bear fruit in their old age, stay fresh (Hebrew: be fertile), and flourish (Hebrew: prosper; 92:14). God will bless them with strength and fruitfulness.

The psalm begins by declaring God's lovingkindness and faithfulness (92:2). It concludes by declaring His uprightness, saying, "He is my rock and there is no unrighteousness in Him" (92:15).

Summary: When you see the defeat of your enemies, who are also God's enemies, publicly praise God for His righteousness, lovingkindness, faithfulness, just judgment, and blessings.

A point to ponder: Thank God for what He has done, and praise Him for who He is.

Psalm 93: When You See the World out of Control

Psalm 93 is an enthronement psalm (47:1-9, 93, 95-99) written by an anonymous author. In it, the author sees the world out of control (93:1, 3).

The Sovereignty of the Lord (93:1-2) The psalmist abruptly proclaims, "The Lord reigns" (93:1a), meaning He is sovereign over the world. Barnes suggests that apparently, the psalmist had been meditating on the dark things that occur in the world, things that are seen irreconcilable with the idea that there is a just government over the world, and suddenly, like a flash of lightning in a storm it occurred to him that the Lord reigns over all. The Lord is in control!

As the sovereign King, the Lord is "clothed with majesty" (93:1b). The Hebrew word translated "majesty" means "lifted up." It was used of a column of rising smoke (Isa. 9:18). The idea here is that God is exalted.

As the sovereign King, the Lord is "girded" with strength (93:1c). As an ancient monarch might have a sword strapped to his side, the sovereign King of the universe is girded with the power needed to be victorious.

Because the sovereign, all-powerful King reigns, "Surely the world is established so that it cannot be moved" (93:1d). The world is established; it is immovable because God is in control. There is no power that can wrench control from the Lord. As if to underscore this point, the psalmist adds, "Your throne is established from old; you are from everlasting" (93:2). In other words, God's rule and reign were established in eternity past and He Himself is eternal, all of which means His control has always been and always will be. It is not going to change.

The Power of the Lord (93:3-4) The psalmist looks around and sees the world out of control. He says, "The floods have lifted up, O Lord, the floods have lifted up their voice; the floods lift up their waves" (93:3). The picture is of wind that has stirred up the waves, which, when they pound against the shore, make a roaring noise. The floods in this verse are said to represent the god Baal (the Canaanites believed that Baal overcame the sea), nations coming against Israel, or a rebellious uprising against God. At any rate, the storms of life make it seem as if things are out of control. Who can control the stormy sea?

The psalmist looks up and sees, "The Lord on high is mightier than the noise of many waters, than the mighty waves of the sea" (93:4). The Lord is more powerful than the raging, roaring, mighty waves of the sea. The Lord is in control.

The Holiness of the Lord (93:5) The psalmist concludes, "Your testimonies are very sure; holiness adorns Your house, O Lord, forever" (93:5). God's Word is sure, that is, God will be faithful to do what He said He would do. His character (holiness) guarantees that God will be faithful to His Word forever.

Summary: When you see the world out of control because of the storms of life, remember that a sovereign, all-powerful, holy, eternal God is in control.

A point to ponder: The Ultimate Power in the universe is a holy Power, not an unholy, corrupt power like the lesser powers on the earth.

Psalm 94: When You See the Wicked Triumph

Psalm 94 is a lament psalm written by an anonymous author. In it, the author sees the wicked triumph (94:3).

A Prayer for Judgment (94:1-7) The psalmist asks the Lord, as Judge and avenger, to shine forth (94:1) and to rise up to punish the proud (94:2). He asks, "How long will the wicked triumph?" (94:3).

The reason the psalmist asks for judgment is that the wicked arrogantly boast (94:4), afflict God's people (94:5), slay widows, murder the fatherless (94:6), and say the Lord does not see what they are doing (94:7).

A Warning to the Wicked (94:8-11) The psalmist instructs senseless fools to wise up (94:8). The Creator of the ear hears; the Creator of the eye sees (94:9), and He corrects the nations (94:10). Make no mistake, "The Lord knows the thoughts of man, that they are futile" (94:11).

The Blessing of the Righteous (94:12-23) The Lord blesses those who learn from His Law (94:12). He will give rest to the righteous and judge the wicked (94:13), because He is faithful to His people (94:14) and will do what is just (94:15a). Those who are upright in heart will follow righteousness (94:15).

The psalmist asks who will stand up for him against the wicked (94:16). The answer is the Lord. Unless the Lord had helped him, his soul would have settled in silence (he would have died; 94:17) and his foot would have slipped in His walk with the Lord, but God's mercy held him up (94:18) and in the multitude of the anxieties within him, the Lord's comfort delighted his soul (94:19).

The psalmist asks if the wicked, who devises evil by law, shall have fellowship with God (94:20). He points out that they gather together (make alliances with each other) to condemn the innocent who are righteous (94:21). His comfort is that the Lord has been his defense, the rock of his refuge (94:22), and will judge the wicked (94:23). The psalmist chooses to trust the Lord until He executes vengeance on the wicked.

Summary: When you see the wicked triumph, ask God for justice, warn the wicked of coming judgment, and remember that the Lord blesses the righteous and judges the wicked.

A point to ponder: Like the psalmist, we should not take vengeance; we should let the Lord do it because He has said, "Vengeance is mine, and recompense; their foot shall slip in due time" (Deut. 32:35).

Psalm 95: When You Praise the Lord as King

Psalm 95 is an enthronement psalm (47:1-9, 93, 95-99) written by an anonymous author. In it, the author praises the Lord as King (95:2-3).

It consists of 1) a call to praise (95:1-5) and 2) a call to obedience (95:6-11). There are two exhortations (95:1, 6), each one containing a reason for the exhortation ("for" in verses 3 and 6).

A Call to Praise (95:1-5) Four times in the first two verses, the psalmist says, "Let us." He says, "Oh come, let us sing to the Lord! Let us shout joyfully to the Rock of our salvation. Let us come before His presence with thanksgiving; let us shout joyfully to Him with psalms" (95:1-2). The call is for the congregation ("us") to sing and shout with joy and thanksgiving to the Lord, who is the Rock of salvation. The expression "Rock of salvation" combines the ideas of stability and deliverance. Evidently, the congregation had experienced deliverance for which they are exhorted to thank the Lord.

The psalmist gives the reason for the praise ("for"). He says, "For the Lord is the great God and the great King above all gods" (95:3). The reason for the praise is not just the deliverance; it is for who God is. He is the sovereign King above all other so-called gods. As the psalmist goes on to say, "In His hands are the deep places of the earth; the heights of the hills are His also. The sea is His, for He made it; and His hands formed the dry land" (95:4-5). The pagans venerated various gods, who supposedly ruled over different parts of the earth, such as the mountains and the sea, but it is the Lord who created the land and the seas, and all of creation is in His hands, meaning He is in control of them all. He is the real ruler. Therefore, He is the one to be praised.

A Call to Obedience (95:6-11) The second exhortation is for the congregation to worship, bow down, and kneel before the Lord our Maker (95:6). The Hebrew word translated "worship" means to "bow down, prostrate oneself." Thus, the three verbs, worship, bow down, and kneel, describe physically prostrating oneself before God in honor, submission, and obedience.

The reason for submission is that the Lord is not only our Maker (95:6), but He is our Shepherd, and we are the sheep of His pasture (95:7a). As the Shepherd, He provides and protects. The psalmist adds, "Today if you will hear His voice" (95:7b), meaning hear and heed.

The voice of the Lord says, "Do not harden your hearts as in the rebellion, as in the day of trial in the wilderness, when your fathers tested Me; they tried Me, though they saw My works. For forty years, I grieved with that generation and said, 'It is a people who go astray in their hearts, and they do not know My ways.' So I swore in My wrath, 'They shall not enter My rest'" (95:7b-11; quoted in Heb. 3:7-9). "Rebellion" and "trial" are references to Rephidim. Moses called Rephidim Meribah (Hebrew: rebellion) and Massah (Hebrew: trial) because at Rephidim the Israelites murmured that there was no water (see Ex. 17:1-7). In short, obey the Lord; do not harden your hearts like the wilderness generation who hardened their hearts, provoked God, and consequently didn't enter the Promised Land, here called "My rest." They had not learned God's ways, that as their Shepherd, He would provide for them.

Summary: When you praise the Lord as King, make sure you are obeying Him.

A point to ponder: Don't make the serious mistake of murmuring instead of praising.

Psalm 96: When You Reflect on the Future of the World

Psalm 96 is an enthronement psalm (47:1-9, 93, 95-99) written by an anonymous author. In it, the author reflects on the world's future (96:13).

A Call to Praise the Lord (96:1-6) The psalmist calls all the earth to sing a new song to the Lord (96:1). A "new song" (33:3, 40:3, 96:1, 98:1, 144:9, 149:1) is a song about His new blessings (98:1; see Lam. 3:23). They are to "Sing to the Lord, bless His name; proclaim the good news of His salvation from day to day" (96:2) and "declare His glory among the nations, His wonders among all people" (96:3). The whole earth is to praise the Lord and proclaim the good news of His salvation every day. There will come a day when the knowledge of the Lord will fill the earth (Isa. 11:9), a fulfillment of God's promise to Abraham that through him all the nations of the earth would be blessed (Gen. 12:3).

The reason ("for") for praising the Lord is that He is great, greatly to be praised, and feared above all gods (96:4). As the psalmist goes on to explain, the so-called gods are lifeless idols, but the Lord is the Creator of the heavens (96:5). Therefore, "honor and majesty are before Him; strength and beauty are in His sanctuary" (96:6). He is to be honored because He is almighty and the beauty of creation comes from Him.

A Call to Honor the Lord (96:7-10) The psalmist calls all the earth to give the Lord the glory due to His name (96:8a), strength (96:7), and an offering (96:8b). They are invited to worship (honor) the Lord in the beauty of holiness and tremble before His name (96:9; see these phrases also in 29:1-2). They are invited to honor the Lord not only with praise but also with offerings.

The psalmist calls the nations to proclaim, "The Lord reigns; the world also is firmly established, but it will not be moved; He shall judge the people righteously" (96:10). The Lord is not only in control now, He will judge righteously in the future. Justice is coming

A Call to Rejoice before the Lord (96:11-13) The psalmist says, "Let the heavens rejoice and let the earth be glad; let the sea roar and all its fullness (96:11), let the field be joyful, and all that is in it. Then all the trees of the woods will rejoice before the Lord" (96:12). Let the heavens, the earth, the sea, the fields, and all the trees of the woods rejoice before the Lord. All of creation, including the plants and animals, should rejoice because they will benefit from the righteous rule of the Lord (Rom. 8:19-22).

The reason ("for") for such rejoicing is that "He is coming, for He is coming to judge the earth. He shall judge the world with righteousness and people with His truth" (96:13). The Lord is coming to the earth to judge all the people of the earth with righteousness and truth. Justice is coming. This will literally be fulfilled at the Second Coming of Jesus Christ. In the meantime, all are to rejoice in the coming Judge and just judgment.

Summary: When you reflect on the world's future, call the world to praise the Lord, honor the Lord, and rejoice before the Lord because of who He is and because He is coming to righteously judge the world.

A point to ponder: The world, probably your world, contains injustice, but remember: justice is coming.

Psalm 97: When You Reflect on the Coming of the Lord

Psalm 97 is an Enthronement psalm (47:1-9, 93, 95-99) written by an anonymous author. In it, the author reflects on the coming of the Lord (97:1).

The Reign of the Lord (97:1) The psalmist announces, "The Lord reigns" (97:1a). The Lord reigns now, but since the whole creation is now groaning (Rom. 8:22) and here the earth is rejoicing, this psalm is describing the Lord's reign on earth which will take place when Jesus Christ returns (compare verse 7 with Heb. 1:6). Thus, the psalmist says, "Let the earth rejoice; let the multitude of the isles be glad!" (97:1b). When the Lord reigns on the earth, the whole earth, even the smallest parts of it ("isles"), will rejoice.

The Judgment of the Lord (97:2-9) God's throne sits on the foundation of righteousness and justice. His judgments are just. He is surrounded by "clouds and darkness" (97:2). He is surrounded by "impenetrable clouds." From Him comes the fire that devours His enemies (97:3). When He judges, the earth trembles (97:4), the mountains melt like wax (97:5), the heavens declare His righteousness, and all the people see His glory (97:6). This describes the judgment just before God establishes His kingdom.

As if to applaud God's judgment, the psalmist says, let those who serve and boast in the carved images of idols be put to shame (97:7a). He adds, "Worship Him, all you gods" (97:7b). In Hebrews 1:6, the latter part of Psalm 97:7 is translated, "Let all the angels of God worship Him" and is applied to the Son at His Second Coming. When Israel hears this, they will rejoice because of the Lord's judgments (97:8), the Lord is the Most High, and the Lord is exalted for above all gods (97:9).

The Response to the Lord (97:10-12) The psalmist invites those who love the Lord to hate evil, reminding them that the Lord preserves His saints and delivers them out of the hand of the wicked (97:10). Using the imagery of a farmer sowing seed, the psalmist says light is sown for the righteous and gladness for the upright in heart (97:11).

Since the Lord preserves, delivers, and sows righteousness and gladness for the righteous, they should "rejoice in the Lord" and "give thanks at the remembrance of His Holy name" (97:12). Thus, the response of the righteous to the reign and righteous judgment of God should be to hate evil, rejoice in the Lord, and give thanks. The psalm begins and ends with rejoicing.

Summary: When you reflect on the coming of the Lord to execute righteous judgment and establish a righteous rule, hate evil, rejoice in the Lord, and give thanks.

A point to ponder: Unrighteousness exists now, but praise the Lord, He is coming to judge the unrighteousness and rule with righteousness.

Psalm 98: When You are Called to Sing to the Lord

Psalm 98 is an Enthronement psalm (47:1-9, 93, 95-99) written by an anonymous author. In it, the author calls people to sing to the Lord (98:1, 5).

A Call to Sing the Lord as the Deliverer (98:1-3) The psalmist invites people, "Oh, sing to the Lord a new song!" (98:1a). A "new song" (33:3, 40:3, 96:1, 98:1, 144:9, 149:1) is a song about His new blessings (98:1; see Lam. 3:23). In this case, the blessing is the deliverance of Israel (see "victory" in verse 1 and "salvation" in verse 2).

The reason for singing a new song: the Lord has done marvelous things, He has gained the victory (98:1b), He has made known His salvation (deliverance), He has revealed His righteousness to the nations (98:2), He has remembered His mercy and faithfulness to the house of Israel (98:3), and all the ends of the earth have seen His salvation (deliverance, 98:3). In these three verses the word "salvation," which means "deliverance," appears twice. The call is for people to sing to the Lord as a Deliverer who has won a marvelous victory. The victory is the Lord's final victory over His enemies before He establishes His kingdom on earth.

A Call to Sing to the Lord as the King (98:4-6) The next subsection begins and ends with the phrase "shout joyfully" (98:4, 6). It begins by saying, "Shout joyfully to the Lord all the earth; break forth in song, rejoice, and sing praises" (98:4). The psalmist adds, Sing to the Lord with the harp (98:5), with trumpets, and with the sound of a horn (98:6a). "Shout joyfully before the Lord, the King" (98:6b). The Lord is King now, but this psalm anticipates God establishing His kingdom on the earth (98:9). That is when the earth will shout joyfully before the Lord.

A Call to Sing to the Lord as the Judge (98:7-9) The psalmist proclaims, "Let the sea roar, in all its fullness, the world and those who dwell in it" (98:7); let the rivers clap their hands; let the hills be joyful together before the Lord" (98:8). Nature as well as people will rejoice when Jesus Christ returns to rule as King in His kingdom on the earth. Everyone and everything should enthusiastically praise the Lord.

The reason ("for") the entire world and all of nature should rejoice together before the Lord is that "He is coming to judge the earth. With righteousness He shall judge the world and the people with equity" (98:9).

Summary: When you are called to sing to the Lord, sing to Him as the Deliverer, King, and Judge.

A point to ponder: Expand the list of things to sing praise to the Lord for, including His salvation (deliverance), His coming rule, and righteous judgment.

Psalm 99: When You See an Answer to Prayer

Psalm 99 is an Enthronement psalm (47:1-9, 93, 95-99) written by an anonymous author. In it, the author sees an answer to prayer (99: 6-8)

Praise the Lord for His Greatness (99:1-3) In the first stanza, the psalmist says, "The Lord reigns; let" ... (99:1) and "The Lord is great; let" ... (99:2).

Since the Lord reigns, "let the peoples tremble! He dwells *between* the cherubim; Let the earth be moved!" (99:1). In the Old Testament, the Lord dwelt in the Holy of Holies. The only piece of furniture in the Holy of Holies was the Ark of the Covenant (something like a cedar chest). On the top of the Ark was a lid called the Mercy Seat, which had two golden cherubim facing each other. The psalmist is saying in the presence of the Lord, let the people tremble in reverential fear and let the earth be moved. The Lord is so great He could shake the earth. Therefore, people should tremble before Him.

Since the Lord is great in Zion (Jerusalem) and "high above all the peoples" (99:2), "let them praise Your great and awesome name—He *is* holy" (99:3). The Lord is not only great in Israel, He is above all the people of the earth. Therefore, they should praise His great and awesome name. The Hebrew word translated "holy" means "set apart." When applied to God, it is a reference to His transcendence.

Praise the Lord for His Justice (99:4-5) The Lord, at this point called the King, is not only great, He loves justice (99:4). Addressing the Lord, the psalmist says, "You have established equity; You have executed justice and righteousness in Jacob" (Israel) (99:4). Then addressing the people, the psalmist exhorts, "Exalt the Lord our God, and worship at His footstool—He is holy" (99:5). The people of God should exalt and worship the Lord at His footstool (Jerusalem) because He loves justice, equity, and righteousness. These are manifestations of His holiness.

Praise the Lord for Answering Prayer (99:6-9) Moses, Aaron, and Samuel called on the Lord and He answered them (99:6). Notice the description the psalmist gives of the people who got answers to prayer. In the first place, the Lord spoke to them out of the pillar of the cloud, and they kept the commandments He gave them (99:7), but that does not mean that they did not sin. As the psalmist goes on to explain, "You answered them, O Lord our God; You were to them God-who-Forgives, though You took vengeance on their deeds" (99:8). The Lord forgave them when they sinned, but that did not exempt them from the consequences of their sin. The Lord is not only just and holy, He is also merciful.

The psalmist concludes, "Exalt the Lord our God, and worship at His holy hill (Jerusalem); for the Lord our God is holy" (99:9). Verse 9 is a slight modification of verse 5. The point of this stanza is if God answered the prayers of Moses, Aaron, and Samuel, He will answer the prayers of those who call upon Him (Jas. 5:17).

Summary: When you see an answer to prayer, praise the Lord for His greatness, justice, holiness, and mercy.

A point to ponder: When God answers prayer, do not just thank Him for the answer; praise Him for who He is, the great, just, merciful God.

Psalm 100: When You Come to God's House

Psalm 100 is a thanksgiving psalm written by an anonymous author. It begins with a theme (100:1), amplified in two short stanzas of two verses each (100:2-3 and 100:4-5). Each stanza speaks of praising God in His house (see "Come before His presence with singing" in verse 2 and "Enter into His gates with thanksgiving, *and* into His courts with praise" in verse 4). In the Old Testament, "come before His presence" meant coming to the Tabernacle or the Temple. The gates and courts are references to the Temple. In the New Testament, the Lord dwells in believers. So, this psalm is applied to us when we come together in church.

Praise the Lord The psalmist invites all the people in all the lands of the earth to "make a joyful noise to the Lord" (100:1). In the context of the psalm, the shout is a shout of praise.

Because He is God (100:2-3) The psalmist says, "serve the Lord with gladness" (100:2a), and "come before His presence with singing" (100:2b). All are encouraged to sing to the Lord (see "shout to the Lord" in verse 1). Paul speaks of "singing and making melody in your heart to the Lord" (Eph. 5:19) and "singing with grace in your heart to the Lord" (Col. 3:16). When we sing in church, we are not only singing to one another, we are singing to the Lord. The psalmist says we are to not only to sing but to serve the Lord with great joy.

This singing to the Lord is to be done with knowledge. The psalmist says, "Know that the Lord, He is God; it is He who is made us and not we ourselves; we are His people and the sheep of His pasture" (100:3). We are to sing to the Lord knowing that He is God, the Creator and Shepherd to His people who are His sheep. We did not make ourselves; He created us and, as a Shepherd, provides and protects us. The people of God should praise God because He is God.

Because He is Good (100:4-5) The psalmist says, "Enter His gates with thanksgiving and into His courts with praise. Be thankful to Him and bless His name" (100:4). The Israelites are called to enter the gates of Jerusalem and the courts of the Temple with thanksgiving and praise.

The reason ("for") is that He is good (100:5a). More specifically, "His mercy is everlasting and His truth endures to all generations" (100:5b). The goodness of God includes giving us His mercy and truth (verse 5), as well as giving us His provisions and protection (verse 3). No wonder we should thank the Lord, praise Him, and bless His name.

Verse 3 captures the essence of this Psalm. It speaks of the Lord being our Creator and Shepherd. We are to praise Him for being the former and thank Him for being the latter.

Summary: When you praise the Lord in His house, praise Him because He is God and good, giving us mercy, truth, provisions, and protection. Praise Him for who He is and what He has done.

A point to ponder: We thank God for His blessings but are less likely to praise Him for creating us.

Psalm 101: When You are Put in Charge

Psalm 101 is a royal psalm written by David. In it, David is put in charge as king (101:5-6, 8).

David's Personal Promise (101:1-4) David promises that he will personally sing praises to the Lord concerning His mercy and justice (101:1). Furthermore, he promises, "I will behave wisely in a perfect way. Oh, when will you come to me? I will walk within my house with a perfect heart" (101:2). David's desire, yea, David's determination was that when God came to visit, He would find that with a perfect heart toward the Lord, David behaved wisely in his house.

The other side of the same coin is, "I will set nothing wicked before my eyes; I hate the work of those who fall away; it shall not cling to me. A perverse heart shall depart from me; I will not know wickedness" (101:3-4). He desires a perfect heart (101:2), not a perverse heart (101:4). He is determined to set nothing wicked before his eyes nor let it cling to him that he might not know (experience) wickedness.

David's Public Policy (101:5-8) Concerning his public policy as king, David says, "Whoever secretly slanders his neighbor, him I will destroy; the one who has a haughty look and a proud heart, him I will not endure" (101:5). As king, David says he will not tolerate, yea he will deal severely, with those who have a proud heart, a haughty look, and a slanderous tongue. David wants righteousness in his realm.

David goes on to say, "My eyes shall be on the faithful of the land, that they may dwell with me; he who walks in a perfect way, he shall serve me" (101:6). David says he will choose those who are faithful to the Lord and live blameless lives to serve him in his cabinet. The negative side of that same coin is, "He who works deceit shall not dwell within my house; he who tells lies shall not continue in my presence" (101:7). He would not choose a deceiver or a liar to serve in his presence or dwell in his house. David desires to surround himself with counselors who are faithful, righteous, honest, and truthful.

David concludes, "Early I will destroy all the wicked of the land, that I may cut off all the evildoers from the city of the Lord" (101:8). He will not only not have wickedness in his house, early in his administration, but he will also cut off evildoers from the city of the Lord (Jerusalem) and for that matter from the entire land of Palestine.

Summary: When you are in charge, be a godly person, surround yourself with godly people, and make godly decisions.

A point to ponder: Part of living a godly life is surrounding yourself with godly people.

Psalm 102: When You Suffer Affliction

Psalm 102 is a lament psalm written by David. In it, David suffers affliction (102:3-7).

A Prayer for Intervention (102:1-2) David asks the Lord to hear his cry (102:1) and not hide His face in the day of his trouble but answer him speedily (102:2).

A Description of Affliction (102:3-11) David says his days are consumed like smoke, his bones are burned like a hearth (he has a fever; 102:3), his heart is withered like grass so that he forgets to eat (102:4), his bones cling to his skin (he is losing weight; 102:5), he is like a pelican in the wilderness and an owl in the desert (102:6), and he is alone at night like a sparrow alone on the housetop (102:7). His suffering includes a fever, weakness, sleeplessness, and aloneness.

Moreover, his enemies reproach him all day long, swearing against him (102:8). Consequently, he has eaten ashes like bread (the ashes on his head as a sign of mourning had fallen in his food) and mingled his drink with weeping (102:9). On top of all of that, he feels that God in His wrath has cast him away (102:10), and his days are like a shadow that lengthens (shadows lengthen as the day ends) and he withers away like grass (102:11). He feels like his life is coming to an end.

Praise for Answered Prayer (102:12-17) The Lord, however, endures forever (102:12) and will have mercy on Zion, that is Jerusalem (102:13) so the godly take pleasure in her stones (102:14), and all the nations and kings of the earth will fear the Lord (in the kingdom; 102:15) because the Lord will appear in His glory and answer the prayer of the destitute (102:17).

Praise for God's Arrival (102:18-22) People in the future will praise the Lord (102:18), for the Lord will look down from heaven (102:19) to hear the groaning of the prisoner, to release those appointed to death (102:20), to declare His name in Zion (102:21) when the people and the kingdoms of the world are gathered together to serve the Lord (102:22).

Prayer for Strength (102:23-28) In the meantime, David prays for strength (102:23) and a longer life (102:24) from Him who laid the foundation of the earth and created the heavens with His hands (102:25), Who endures when the heavens and earth perish, Who changes them like people change an old garment for a new one (102:26), and who Himself never changes and lives forever (102:27). Psalm 102:25-27 is addressed to God, but these verses are quoted in Hebrews and applied to Christ (Heb. 1:11-12). After the Millennium, God will create a new heaven and a new earth (2 Pet. 3:10-13; Rev. 21:1). The universe is changeable and temporary, but God (the Son) is unchangeable and eternal. The Creator will outlast the creation. The eternal God gives strength and a longer life to temporary man. Furthermore, the children of God's servants will continue and their descendants will be established before Him (102:28).

Summary: When you suffer physical and emotional affliction, even to the point of death, do not hesitate to ask God to intervene quickly and remember He is the eternal God who gives strength and longevity.

Point to ponder: Contemplating God's ceaseless and changeless character is a great comfort to God's children when they suffer affliction. It puts affliction in the context of eternity.

Psalm 103: When You Bless the Lord

Psalm 103 is a praise psalm written by David. In it, David blesses the Lord (103:1-2).

A Personal Call to Bless the Lord (103:1-18) David tells himself to bless the Lord. He declares, "Bless the Lord, O my soul; and all that is within me, bless His holy name!" (103:1). He adds, "Forget not all of His benefits" (103:2), including forgiveness, healing (103:3), deliverance from death, kindness and mercy (103:4), satisfaction with good things, and renewed strength (103:5).

At this point, David no longer speaks about his personal blessings; he begins to talk about how the Lord has blessed the nation of Israel. He is blessing the Lord for national blessings.

The Lord executes justice for the oppressed (103:6), made known His ways to Moses (the Law) and His acts (during the Exodus and the wilderness wanderings) to the children of Israel (103:7). He has been merciful, gracious, slow to anger, and abounding in mercy (103:8; see Ex. 34:6). He does not keep His anger forever (103:9), and has not dealt with them according to their sins (103:10). As the heavens are high above the earth, so great is God's mercy toward those who fear Him (103:11). As far as the east is from the west, so far does He remove our sins from us (103:12). As a father pities His children, so the Lord pities all who trust Him (103:13), because He remembers that they are dust (103:14).

God separates our sins from us as far as the East is from the West, not as far as the North is from the South. If people travel either north or south, they arrive at a pole and can proceed no further north or south, but if they travel east or west, they never reach such a point. This indicates that our sins are infinitely separated from us.

We are frail and short-lived, like grass and flowers (103:15), when a hot summer wind passes over them (103:16), but the mercy and righteousness of the Lord are strong from everlasting to everlasting to those who fear Him (103:17) and obey Him (103:18). God's anger is temporary (103:9); His mercy is forever (103:17).

A Universal Call (103:19-22) Observing that the Lord has established His throne in heaven and His kingdom rules over all (103:19), David calls on the angels who excel in strength and do God's Word to bless the Lord (103:20). He urges all the angels who do God's pleasure to bless the Lord (103:21). In fact, he calls all of God's works in all the places of His dominion to bless the Lord (103:22a). The call is for heaven and earth to bless the Lord.

David concludes by calling himself to bless the Lord. He ends with, "Bless the Lord, O my soul!" (103:2b).

Summary: When blessing the Lord, call yourself and all in the universe to bless the Lord for all of His benefits, including forgiveness, healing, deliverance from death, lovingkindness, mercy, satisfying us with good things, renewed strength, justice for the oppressed, for making known His ways and acts, and for being slow to anger.

A point to ponder: We don't praise the Lord for all the reasons that we should.

Psalm 104: When You Contemplate the Creation

Psalm 104 is a praise psalm written by an unknown author. In it, the author contemplates creation (104:5-32).

Praise for the Creation (104:1-23) The psalmist invites himself to bless the Lord, who is great, who is clothed with honor and majesty (104:1), and who covers Himself with light as a garment and stretches out the heavens like a curtain (104:2).

The Lord created the heavens. He <u>builds</u> His chamber above the clouds, <u>makes</u> the clouds His chariot, <u>walks</u> on the wings of the wind (104:3), and <u>makes</u> His angels spirits (104:4).

The Lord created the earth. He <u>laid</u> the foundation of the earth (104:5), <u>covered</u> it with deep water (104:6a) as a mother covers her infant, <u>separated</u> the waters on the earth from those above the earth (105:6b-7; Gen. 1:6-8), <u>separated</u> the dry ground from the waters on the earth so that they would never overrun the earth (104:8-9; Gen. 1:9-13), <u>created</u> springs (104:10) so that animals could quench their thirst (104:11), <u>provided</u> trees for the birds who sing among the branches (104:12), supplied rain so vegetation could grow (104:13), <u>caused</u> the grass to grow for cattle and vegetation, including wine, oil, and bread, for people (104:14-15; Gen. 1:11–13), <u>planted</u> trees (104:16) where the birds make their nests (104:17), <u>established</u> the hills for animals (104:18), <u>appointed</u> the moon for seasons (104:19; Gen. 1:14–19), <u>made</u> darkness for the night (104:20-21), and sun for the day (104:22) so that men could work (104:23).

Praise the Creator (104:24-32) Turning his attention from the creation to the Creator, the psalmist says the Lord's works, which are His possessions, are many and wise (104:24), including the sea with its hidden treasures (104:25) ships, and Leviathan (sea monsters; 104:26). All sea creatures are dependent upon the Lord for their food and life (104:27-29). By His Spirit, they are created (104:30). Creation depends on the Creator for birth, life, and food.

The psalmist prays that the Lord's glory would endure forever, that He would rejoice in His works (104:31), because, after all, when He looks on the earth, it trembles, and when He touches the hills, they smoke (104:32).

The Proper Response of the Psalmist (104:33-35) In light of the great, marvelous, and wise creation by the sovereign Creator of the universe, the psalmist promises to sing praises to the Lord as long as he lives (104:33) and prays that his meditation may be sweet to the Lord (104:34) and that sinners be judged (104:35a). The psalmist promises to praise God with his mouth and his mind.

The psalmist concludes, "Bless the Lord, O my soul! Praise the Lord!" (104:35b; see 104:1). This is the first time of 23 times "Praise the Lord" (Hebrew: hallelujah) occurs in the Psalms (105:45; 106:1, 48; 112:1; 113:1, 9; 115:18; 116:19; 117:2; 135:1, 3, 21; 146:1, 10; 147:1, 20; 148:1, 14; 149:1, 9; 150:1, 6). It only occurs four times in the New Testament (Rev. 19:1, 3, 4, 6), all in the context of the Second Coming of Christ. The proper response to the wonders of God's creation is to please the Creator and not sin against Him.

Summary: When you contemplate the creation, praise the Lord for His creation, praise the Creator, please Him with your mouth and mind, and pray for the judgment of sinners.

A point to ponder: We are often too busy to contemplate the creation.

Psalm 105: When You Read the Old Testament #2

Psalm 105 is a praise psalm written by an unknown author. In it, the author reviews the history of Israel (105:7-41).

Israel's Praise (105:1-6) The psalmist calls Israel (105:6) to give thanks to the Lord, call upon His name, make His deeds known (105:1), sing psalms to Him (105:2), glory in His holy name, rejoice (105:3), seek the Lord and His strength (105:4), and remember His works (105:5-6).

God's Faithfulness (105:7-41) The psalmist reviews the history of God's faithfulness to Israel.

1) To Abraham. The Lord, our sovereign God (105:7), remembers His covenant with Abraham, Isaac, and Jacob forever (105:8-10), saying, "To you, I will give the land of Canaan (105:11), when you were few in numbers and strangers to it (105:12). As they journeyed from one nation to another (105:13), He protected them (105:14) saying, "Do not touch My anointed one and do my prophets no harm" (105:15; Gen. 20:7).

2) To Joseph. When He called for a famine (105:16), He sent Joseph, whom they sold as a slave (105:17-18). He was tested (105:19), released from prison (105:20), and made a ruler (105:21) to teach the elders wisdom (105:22).

3) In Egypt. In Egypt (105:23), the Lord increased His people greatly (105:24), turned the hearts of the Egyptians to hate His people (105:25), sent Moses and Aaron (105:26), who performed wonders (105:27), sent darkness (105:28), turned water to blood (105:29), sent frogs 105:30), sent a swarm of flies and lice (105:31), gave hail for rain (105:32), struck their vines and fig trees (105:33), sent locusts (105:34), who ate all the vegetation and devoured the fruit of the land (105:35), destroyed all the firstborn (105:36), and brought His people out of Egypt with silver and gold (105:37). The Egyptians were glad when they departed (105:38). This account of the plagues in Egypt is not in chronological order and only eight of the ten plagues are listed.

4) In the wilderness. In the wilderness, "He spread a cloud for covering and fire to give them light in the night" (105:39). When the people asked, "He brought quail and satisfied them with the bread of heaven" (105:40). "He opened the rock, and water gushed out; it ran in the dry places like a river" (105:41).

Praise God for His Faithfulness (105:42-45) "Praise the Lord!" (105:45b). He remembered His promise to Abraham (105:42), brought His people out of Egypt (105:43), and gave them the lands of the Gentiles (105:44), so they might "observe His statutes and keep His laws" (105:45a).

Three times, the psalmist says God remembers (105:5, 8, 42). In other words, God has been faithful.

Summary: When you read the Old Testament, remember that God remembers His covenant with Abraham and praises Him for His faithfulness.

Three psalms review Israel's history (78, 105, 106).

A point to ponder: We should remember and reflect on how God has been faithful to us and praise Him for His faithfulness.

Psalm 106: When You Read the Old Testament #3

Psalm 106 is a wisdom psalm written by an unknown author. In it, the author reviews the history of Israel (106:6-46).

Israel's Praise (106:1-5) The psalmist says, "Oh, give thanks to the Lord, for He is good! For His mercies endure forever" (106:1). When he asks who can praise Him (106:2), he says those who are righteous (106:3). Then he asks that the Lord remember him with the favor God has toward His people and visit him with salvation (106:4), that he may see the benefits of God's chosen ones, that he may rejoice, and that he may glory in God's inheritance (106:5).

Israel's Unfaithfulness (106:6-46) The psalmist says we have sinned with our fathers (106:6).

1) At the Red Sea. They rebelled at the Red Sea (106:7). God saved them (106:8), by rebuking the Red Sea (106:9-10) and drowning the Egyptians (106:11). Then they believed God's Word and sang His praise (106:12).

2) In the Wilderness. These events are not in chronological order. They are listed from the lesser to the more serious. The people soon forgot God's works (106:13), lusted exceedingly and tested God (106:14), who gave them their request, but sent leanness into their soul (106:15; Num. 11:4-34). When they envied Moses and Aaron, God judged them (106:16-18; Num. 16:12-14). They worshiped a molten image (106:19-20; Ex. 32:4), forgetting what God had done for them in Egypt (106:21-22). God would have destroyed them had it not been for Moses's prayer (106:23). They despised the land and did not believe (106:24) nor obey God's Word (106:25). Therefore, God raised His hand in an oath against them to overthrow them (106:26), and their descendants (106:27; Num. 14:26-35). They joined themselves to Baal, ate sacrifices made to the dead (106:28; Num. 25:3), and provoked God to anger (106:29). When the plague broke out among the people and Phinehas intervened, the plague stopped (106:30) and that was accounted to him for righteousness and to all generations forever (106:31; Num. 25; justification by works is justification before people, see "you see" in Jas. 2:24). They angered God at Mariah (Hebrew: "water of strife" (106:32), because they rebelled against His Spirit (106:33; Num. 20:2-13).

3) In the Land. They did not destroy the people as the Lord had commanded them (106:34), but learned the works of the Gentiles (106:35). They served idols (106:36), sacrificed their sons and daughters to demons (106:37), shed innocent blood, sacrificed to idols (106:38), and thus were defiled (106:39; Deut. 32:17).

4) During the Judges. Therefore, God kindled His wrath against them (106:40) and gave them into the hand of the Gentiles (106:41), who oppressed them (106:42). He delivered them many times, but they rebelled and were brought low because of their sin (106:43). Nevertheless God heard their cry (106:44), remembered His covenant, and relented according to His mercy (106:45-46).

Israel's Plea (106:47-48) The psalmist pleads for Israel to be saved and gathered (106:47) and concludes by blessing and praising God. This is the conclusion of Book IV.

Three psalms review Israel's history (78, 105, 106).

Summary: When you read the Old Testament, see the unfaithfulness of God's people and the faithfulness of God, plead for restoration, and praise God for His faithfulness.

A point to ponder: God remains faithful, even when we are unfaithful (2 Tim. 2:13).

Psalm 107: When You See God's Wonderful Works

Psalm 107 is a wisdom psalm written by an unknown author. In it, he sees God's wonderful works (107:4-32).

The Praise of God (107:1-3) The psalmist says, "Oh, give thanks to the Lord, for He is good! For His mercies endure forever" (107:1; see 106:1). He adds, "Let the redeemed of the Lord say so" (107:2a). The Lord has redeemed Israel from her enemies and gathered her (107:2b-3).

The Deliverance of God (107:4-32) The psalmist presents four pictures of God's deliverance. Each picture contains a problem, a prayer (the same one: 107:6, 13, 19, 28), deliverance, and thanksgiving (the same statement each time: 107:8, 15, 21, 31).

1) A Wanderer. When Israel was wandering (107:4), hungry, thirsty, and discouraged (107:5), they cried to the Lord and He delivered them out of their distress (107:6) and led them to a city (107:7). Give thanks to the Lord for His goodness and wonderful works (107:8), because He satisfies the hungry soul with goodness (109).

2) A Prisoner. When Israel was in prison (107:10) because they rebelled (107:11) and there was none to help (107:12), they cried to the Lord and He saved them out of their distress (107:13) and brought them out of the shadow of death (107:14). Give thanks to the Lord for His goodness and wonderful works (107:15), because He has cut the bars of iron in two (107:16).

3) Sickness. When Israel was foolish because of their sin (107:17) and they were sick, even to death (107:18), they cried to the Lord and He saved them (107:19), healing them (107:20). Give thanks to the Lord for His goodness and wonderful works (107:21); give sacrifices of thanksgiving and declare His works (107:22).

4) A Sailor. When Israel was like a sailor (107:23) in the midst of the storm (107:24-26) and they were at their wits' end (107:27), they cried to the Lord and He delivered them (107:28) calming the storm (107:29) and guiding them to their desired haven (107:30). Give thanks to the Lord for His goodness and wonderful works (107:31) and publicly praise Him (107:32).

Based on these verses, the rabbis said there were four occasions when it was appropriate to give a thank offering: for a safe return from a voyage, for a safe return from a desert journey, for recovery from illness, and for being released from prison.

The Providence of God (107:33-43) The Lord is in control. He turns rivers into wilderness (107:33), turns fruitful land into barrenness because of the wickedness of those who live there (107:34), turns wilderness into pools of water (107:35), makes the hungry establish a city for a dwelling place (107:36), sow those fields so that they may yield a fruitful harvest (107:37), and greatly blesses His people with increased herds (107:38). God controls nature so that it can be either be a blessing or a curse.

God is also in control over people. He humbles the mighty (107:39-40), and exalts the poor (107:41). When the righteous see it, they rejoice; the unrighteous keep silent (107:42). When the wise see all of these things, they will understand the lovingkindness of the Lord (107:43).

Summary: When you see God's wonderful works to people, publicly give thanks for the goodness of the Lord (107:8, 15, 21, 31).

A point to ponder: The Lord delivers lost travelers, prisoners, the sick, and sailors in a storm when they call upon Him. He delivers people in trouble, even when it's their fault. The wise understand the grace and mercy of God.

Psalm 108: When You Wake Up in the Morning

Psalm 108 is a psalm of trust written by David. In it, David speaks about waking up in the morning (108:2).

David's Praise (108:1-5) Addressing God, David says, "O God, my heart is steadfast; I will sing and give praise, even with my glory" (108:1). He adds, "Awake, flute and harp! I will awaken the dawn" (108:2). David desires to sing praises to the Lord with the flute and the harp before sunrise. The expression "even with my glory" means "with my honor." In other words, David considered it his honor to wake up singing praises to the Lord.

Furthermore, he says, "I will praise you, O Lord among the peoples and I will sing praises to you among the nations" (108:3). Having praised God first thing in the morning, David desires to praise God among the people throughout the day.

The reason ("for") for David's praise is that God's mercy is great above the heavens and His truth reaches to the clouds (108:4). God's mercy and truth are sky-high; nevertheless, David says, "Be exalted, O God, above the heavens and your glory above all the earth" (108:5).

David's Prayer (108:6-13) David asks, "That your beloved may be delivered, save with your right hand and hear me" (108:6). The reference to God's right hand is a figurative way of speaking about His power. David is asking God to hear his prayer so that God's power can deliver him.

God answers David. David says, "God has spoken in His holiness: 'I will rejoice; I will divide Shechem and measure out the Valley of Succoth. Gilead *is* Mine; Manasseh *is* Mine; Ephraim also *is* the helmet for My head; Judah *is* My lawgiver'" (108:7-8). God says He takes pleasure ("I will rejoice") in delivering His people and He divided the land of Palestine among the Israelites. God adds, "Moab *is* My washpot; over Edom, I will cast My shoe; over Philistia, I will triumph" (108:9). God has control over the three Gentile nations of Moab, Edom, and Philistia. "Washpot" is a figure of speech expressing contempt and control. Casting His shoe over Edom is a way of saying He will conquer them.

David asks, "Who will bring me *into* the strong city? Who will lead me to Edom? *Is it* not *You*, O God, *who* cast us off? And *You*, O God, *who* did not go out with our armies?" (108:10-11). The strong city refers to Sela (also known as Petra), the capital of Edom. It was renowned for being inaccessible and impregnable. Evidently, the Israeli army went out to conquer Edom, but God did not go with them, and therefore they were defeated. David acknowledges that only the Lord can give them victory.

So David prays, "Give us help from trouble, for the help of man is useless. Through God we will do valiantly, for *it is* He *who* shall tread down our enemies" (108:12-13). Having been defeated, David realizes that help from the army is useless; God gives the victory.

Summary: When you wake up in the morning, praise God for His mercy and truth and ask Him to hear your prayer for help in your trouble.

A point to ponder: If God is not working, "the help is useless."

Psalm 109: When You Are Wounded by Wicked Words

Psalm 109 is an imprecatory (imprecatory means "to invite a curse on someone") psalm written by David. In it, David speaks about being wounded by wicked words (109:2-3, 22).

The Silence of God (109:1-5) Apparently, David had asked for God's intervention and He had kept silent. So David asks, "Do not keep silent, O God of my praise" (109:1).

The reason for David's request is that wicked, deceitful men have lied about him (109:2), spoken hateful words about him, and fought him without a cause (109:3). David has loved them and been a man of prayer (109:4), but they have returned evil for good and hatred for his love (109:5). David is declaring his innocence and praying for God's intervention and his vindication.

The Judgment of God (109:6-20) David asks God to judge his enemies. Changing from the plural ("them") to the singular ("him"), David asks God to set a wicked man over his enemy, let him have an accuser (109:6), let him be found guilty, let his prayer become sin (109:7), let his days be few, let another take his office (109:8; applied to Judas in Acts 1:20), and let his children be fatherless and his wife a widow (109:9). David is praying for justice. His enemy has killed others (109:16). A just judgment is that the killer be killed. This is the judgment on his person.

David prays for his enemy's children to become beggars (109:10). This is the natural consequence of sin. The sins of the fathers affect the children (Ex. 20:5).

David prays for his enemy's property to be seized (109:11), that no one extends mercy to him or his children (109:12), that his prosperity be cut off (109:13), and his parents be punished for their sins (109:14-15). Why does David ask that no one extend mercy to the *children* of his enemies? They could be adult children who participated in sin, just like his enemy's parents.

David asks for such judgment because his enemy did not show mercy but persecuted the poor and slew the broken in heart (109:16). So as he loved cursing, let him be cursed (109:17-19). David adds, "Let this be the Lord's reward to my accusers, and to those who speak evil against any person" (109:20). David's enemy was not just his own enemy; he persecuted and killed others. David did not seek personal vengeance. He vented his feelings before the Lord, knowing that vengeance belonged to the Lord. He asks for a just judgment on evil.

The Mercy of God (109:21-31) David asks to be delivered by the Lord's mercy for the Lord's sake (109:21), because he is poor, needy, and has a wounded heart (109:22). David describes his life as ebbing like a lengthening shadow and his life as being shaken off as easily as a man shakes off a locust (109:23). He is weak from fasting (109:24) and has become a reproach to his enemies (109:25). So he prays for the Lord to help him and deliver him according to His mercy (109:26) that his enemies may know that the Lord did it (129:27). He prays for his enemies to be cursed and ashamed and God's servants to be blessed and rejoice (109:28-29). David promises to publicly praise the Lord (109:30) because He delivered him from those who condemn him (109:31).

Summary: When you are wounded by wicked words (lies), do not seek personal revenge; ask God to judge your enemy and deliver you so that they may know the Lord blesses His servants.

A point to ponder: God promises to bless those who follow Him when they are cursed, so they should ask God for deliverance; His reputation is at stake.

Psalm 110: When You Want a Picture of the Messiah

Psalm 110 is a messianic psalm written by David. This is one of the most-quoted psalms in the New Testament. See Jesus' use of this psalm (Mt. 22:41-45; Mk. 12:35-37; Lk. 20:41-44) and Peter's exposition of it (Acts 2:34–36, 5:30–31). In this Psalm, David paints a picture of the Messiah (110:1, 4).

The Messiah as King (110:1-3) David declares, "The Lord said to my Lord, 'Sit at my right hand, till I make your enemies your footstool'" (110:1). In the Hebrew text, the first appearance of the word "Lord" ("the Lord") in this verse is the personal name of God (Yahweh, God the Father) and the second occurrence of the word "Lord" ("my Lord") is the Hebrew word that means "Lord" (Adonai). In other words, this is a conversation between God and David's Lord, someone greater than David. According to Jesus, this is a reference to the Messiah (Mt. 22:41–45; Mk. 12:35–37; Lk. 20:41–44). Peter plainly says this is a reference to Jesus (Acts 2:34–36, 5:30–31), and the author of Hebrews says this is not a reference to an angel (Heb. 1:13) but to Jesus (Heb. 10:10–13).

God (God the Father) says to the Messiah (Jesus), "Sit at my right hand [the place of honor], till I make your enemies your footstool." At the Second Coming, the enemies of Jesus will be subject to Him. Jesus will not only subject His enemies to Him, He shall rule over them from Zion, that is, Jerusalem (110:2). In the day of His power, His people should be holy volunteers "from the womb of the morning" (110:3). They will willingly join His reign, be holy in contrast to the unholy people the Messiah will subdue, and they will be young ("from the womb of the morning") and fresh ("dew").

The Messiah as Priest (110:4) The Messiah will not only be a King, He will be a priest forever according to the order of Melchizedek (110:4), who was both king and priest (Gen. 14:18). The author of Hebrews says this is a reference to Jesus (Heb. 5:5-11; 6:20; 7:1-28). This verse answers the question, "How can the Messiah, who is a descendant of David (9:7), also be a priest who had to be a descendant of Aaron?" The Messiah is a priest by divine decree ("the Lord has sworn" and will not change His mind), not by human descent.

The Messiah as Warrior (110:5-7) In the day of His wrath, the Messiah shall execute kings (110:5), judge among the nations, fill the places with dead bodies, and execute the heads of many countries (110:6). This will be fulfilled at the Second Coming of Christ (Rev. 19:19-21). The Messiah "shall drink of the brook by the wayside" (be refreshed) and "shall lift up the head," that is, be victorious (110:7).

Summary: When you want to see a picture of the Messiah, look at the King-priest Warrior of Psalm 110.

A point to ponder: The messianic psalms are those that predict the coming of the Messiah, including His crucifixion (Ps. 22), His resurrection (Ps. 16), His priestly ministry according to the order of Melchizedek at the right hand of the Father (Ps. 110), and His coming reign (Ps. 2).

Psalm 111: When You Praise the Lord for His Works

Psalm 111 is a praise psalm written by an unknown author. It is an acrostic; each line begins with the succeeding letter of the Hebrew alphabet. In it, the author praises the Lord for His works (111:1-9, esp. 2, 3, 7).

The Praise of the Lord (111:1) "Praise the Lord! I will praise the Lord with my whole heart, in the assembly of the upright and in the congregation" (111:1). The psalmist promises to praise the Lord publicly and proclaims that others should also do so.

The Works of the Lord (111:2-9) The psalmist proclaims that the works of the Lord are great, studied by all who have pleasure in them (111:2), honorable, and glorious (111:3a). He adds, "And His righteousness endures forever" (111:3b). The Lord is to be praised for what He has done and who He is. He has done great, glorious works and He is righteous.

The Lord "has made His wonderful works to be remembered; the Lord is gracious and full of compassion" (111:4). Again, the psalmist focuses on what the Lord has done and who He is.

The Lord "has given food to those who fear Him; and He will ever be mindful of His covenant" (111:5). The Hebrew word "fear" means 1) to be afraid, terrified, 2) to stand in awe, 3) to reverence, 4) to honor. The expression "the fear of the Lord" refers to those who know the Lord, reverence the Lord, and are afraid of the Lord when they are disobedient. Again, the psalmist speaks of what the Lord has done and who He is. He gives food and is faithful.

The Lord "has declared to His people the power of His works, in giving them the heritage of the nations" (111:6). The Lord demonstrated His power in delivering Israel from Egypt and giving them the land of Palestine, here called "the heritage of the nations."

The Lord's works are "verity [truth] and justice; all His precepts are sure [reliable]" (111:7). What He does is just and what He says is dependable; God is faithful.

The Lord's works "stand fast forever and ever, and are done in truth and uprightness" (111:8). God's works are firmly established.

The Lord "has sent redemption to His people; He has commanded His covenant forever; holy and awesome is His name" (111:9). The redemption spoken of here is the deliverance from Egypt. He has redeemed and has given His covenant; He is holy.

The Fear of the Lord (111:10) The psalmist concludes, "The fear of the Lord is the beginning of wisdom; a good understanding have all those who do His commandments. His praise endures forever" (111:10; see Job 28: 28; Prov. 1:7, 9:10). Those who know, trust, and obey the Lord have spiritual understanding and the beginning of wisdom. Praise God forever.

Summary: When you praise the Lord for His works, also praise Him for who He is, the righteous, gracious, compassionate, faithful God.

A point to ponder: We should not just praise the Lord for what He has done and who He is in our private prayer life we should publically praise the Lord by telling others what He has done and who He is.

Psalm 112: When You Count Your Blessings

Psalm 112 is a praise psalm written by an unknown author. It is an acrostic; each line begins with the succeeding letter of the Hebrew alphabet. In it, the author counts his blessings (112:2-9).

The Praise of God (112:1) "Praise the Lord! Blessed is the man who fears the Lord, who delights greatly in his commandments" (112:1). The expression "the fear of the Lord" refers to those who know the Lord, reverence the Lord, and are afraid of the Lord when they are disobedient. This fear includes delight! They who <u>fear</u> the Lord <u>delight</u> greatly in His commandments. Such people are blessed ("happy;" the same word is in 1:1) because they trust the Lord and obey His word.

The Blessing of the Righteous (112:2-9) The psalmist lists the blessings of those who delight in God's commandments. Their descendants will be mighty on the earth and those who are upright will be blessed (112:2). They will have prosperity and their righteousness will endure forever (112:3). They will have light and not darkness; they (some translations and commentaries take this as a reference to the blessed and others take it as a reference to the Lord; the flow of the passage indicates this refers to the blessed) are gracious, full of compassion, and righteous (112:4). They will deal graciously (they lend money, etc.) with their neighbors. Discretion guides their affairs (112:5). They will never be shaken and their righteousness will be in everlasting remembrance (112:6). They will not be afraid of evil tidings because their heart is steadfast, trusting in the Lord (112:7). Their heart is established; they will not be afraid (112:8). Because they give to the poor, they are honored now and their righteousness endures forever (112:9).

To sum up: Those who are obedient to God's commandments are righteous (112:3, 4), gracious, full of compassion (112:4-5), and are generous to the poor (112:9). Their blessings include blessed descendants (112:2), material prosperity (112:3a), enduring righteousness (112:3b), spiritual light (112:4), discretion (112:5), emotional stability (112:6-8), honor (112:9); they will see their enemies perish (112:10), and receive eternal rewards (112:3, 6, 9).

The Judgment of the Wicked (112:10) On the other hand, the wicked will see the blessings of the righteous and be grieved, gnashing their teeth and melting away. "The desire of the wicked shall perish" (112:10). The desire of the righteous will prevail (112:8); the desire of the wicked will perish (112:10).

Summary: When you count your blessings, praise the Lord for each one.

A point to ponder: The obedient are not only personally blessed; they bless others (they are gracious).

Psalm 113: When You See the Lord Do the Unusual

Psalm 113 is a praise psalm written by an unknown author. In it, the author records seeing the Lord do the unusual (113:7-9). Psalms 113-118 are called the Hallel Psalms (Hebrew: praise; "hallelujah" means "praise the Lord"), a collection of songs sung during the holy days of Israel, including Passover, Pentecost, and Tabernacles. For example, at Passover, Psalms 113-114 were sung before the meal and Psalms 115-118 were sung after the meal.

A Call to Praise (113:1-3) "Praise the Lord! Praise, O servants of the Lord, praise the name of the Lord" (113:1). In the Scripture, the term "name" often signifies the character of the person (9:10). Praising the name of the Lord is praising the nature, character, and attributes of the Lord.

The Lord is to be praised forever: "Blessed be the name of the Lord from this time forth and for evermore!" (113:2).

The Lord is to be praised universally: "From the rising of the sun to its going down the Lord's name is to be praised" (113:3). The rising and setting of the sun is not a description of the day, that is, from dawn to dusk; it is a description of East and West, indicating the universal praise of the Lord.

The Causes for Praise (113:4-9) The first reason the Lord is to be praised is that He is the exalted Sovereign: "The Lord is high above all nations (sovereign); His glory above the heavens" (exalted; 113:4). He is Great.

The second reason the Lord is to be praised is because He humbles Himself. The psalmist asks, "Who is like the Lord our God, who dwells on high, who humbles Himself to behold the things that are in the heavens and in the earth?" (113:5-6). Even though the Lord is the exalted sovereign of the universe, He "humbles himself" (Phil. 2:5-8). He condescends to care for His creatures.

For example, "He raises the poor out of the dust and lifts the needy out of the ash heap, that He may seat him with the princes, with the princes of His people" (113:7-8). The Lord occasionally exalts the very poor, those who eke out an existence by searching the rubbish heaps ("out of the dust"), to positions of wealth and influence. He puts the underprivileged in a place of privilege.

Another example of God's concern for people is that "He grants the barren woman a home, like a joyful mother of children" (113:9a). In ancient times, a barren woman was a sad woman. The Lord grants children to barren women, making them joyful mothers (Sarah, Rebekah, Rachel, and Hannah are illustrations.)

The Lord is concerned for the poor and for the childless. The psalmist closes with the same exhortation with which he opened this Psalm: "Praise the Lord!" (113:9b). The Lord is to be praised because He blesses those who have no hope from any other source. He is gracious.

Summary: When you see the Lord do something unusual, such as taking someone from being extremely poor to being highly influential or giving a barren couple children, bless the name of the Lord.

A point to ponder: The Lord sometimes does the unusual for His children.

Psalm 114: When You See the Lord is Present

Psalm 114 is a praise psalm written by an unknown author. It was sung before the Passover meal. In it, the author sees the Lord's presence (114:2).

The Exodus from Egypt (114:1-3). "When Israel went out of Egypt, the house of Jacob from a people of strange language, Judah became His sanctuary and Israel His dominion" (114:1-2). The house of Jacob and Judah are names for Israel. When Israel was in Egypt, they were among a people who spoke a strange language compared to theirs, but they were the Lord's sanctuary and dominion. He dwelt among them and ruled over them. The point is, when Israel came out of Egypt, God's presence was with them. This was an appropriate song to be sung at Passover, which commemorated Israel's departure from Egypt.

The Experience of Israel (114:3-6) Describing what happened to Israel, the psalmist says, "The sea saw it and fled; Jordan turned back. The mountains skipped like rams, the little hills like lambs" (114:3-4). This is a poetic description of the Exodus from Egypt, the crossing of the Jordan River, and the giving of the Law on Mount Sinai. The psalmist personifies the Red Sea, saying it *saw* the presence of the Lord and *fled* from Israel by parting its waters. The Jordan River accommodated Israel by backing up to allow them to cross into the Promised Land. Mount Sinai quivered like a scared animal when God's presence appeared to Moses.

The psalmist asks, "What ails you, O sea, that you fled? O Jordan, that you turned back? O mountains that you skipped like rams? O little Hills, like lambs? (114:5-6). Again, using the poetic language of personification, the psalmist directly asks the sea and the mountains a series of questions. The answer to his questions is the presence of the Lord (114:1-2).

An Exhortation to the Earth (114:7-8) The psalmist exhorts, "Tremble, O Earth, at the presence of the Lord, at the presence of the God of Jacob, who turned the rock into a pool of water, the flint into a mountain of waters" (114:7-8). If the earth is to tremble at the presence of the Lord, surely the people on the earth should fear the Lord, the One who provides for His people. On two occasions, God miraculously provided water for Israel in the wilderness by bringing it out of a rock (Ex. 17:6; Num. 20:11)! The implication is we are to praise the Lord.

Summary: When the Lord is present, you see Him use His power to provide for His people.

A point to ponder: If the Lord can part the waters of the Red Sea and the Jordan River, if He can make mountains quiver and quake in His presence if He can provide water out of a rock, He has the power to meet our needs as we seek His presence and trust Him.

Psalm 115: When You Hear God Has Been Inactive

Psalm 115 is a praise psalm written by an unknown author. It was sung after the Passover. In it, the author hears that God has been inactive (115:2).

A Comparison Between God and Idols (115:1-8) "Not unto us, O Lord, not unto us, but to Your name give glory, because of Your mercy, because of Your truth" (115:1). People glory in what they do when they should be glorying in the mercy and truth of the Lord. William Wilberforce marked the passing of the bill to abolish the slave trade in England by meditating on this verse.

The psalmist asks, "Why should the Gentiles say, 'So where is their God?'" (115:2). Apparently, the Gentiles, those who do not know God, ridiculed the God of Israel because of His inactivity. The psalmist answers, "But God is in heaven; He does whatever He pleases" (115:3). Just because God has not done something you think He should does not mean He is not in control. He is sovereign ("in heaven") and acts according to His mercy and truth.

The silver and gold idols that men make with their hands (115:4) have mouths that do not speak, eyes that do not see (115:5), ears that do not hear, noses that do not smell (115:6), hands that do not handle, feet that do not walk, "nor do they mutter through their throat" (115:7). God is in heaven; idols are on earth. God is alive; idols are dead. God speaks, hears, and acts; idols are incapable of speaking, hearing, or acting, even if they are made out of valuable gold (see 135:15-18).

Moreover, those who make idols are like idols, and so is everyone who trusts in idols (115:8). People become like the things they worship, and idol worshipers are as powerless as their idols.

A Call to Trust God (115:9-11) Repeating the same exhortation three times, the psalmist calls on all of Israel, the house of Aaron (the priests), and all those who fear the Lord to "Trust in the Lord; He is their help and shield," that is, protection (115:9-11). The repetition is for emphasis. We are to trust the Lord rather than idols because He helps and protects us.

A Confidence in God's Blessing (115:12-18) When we trust the Lord, we discover He *has* been mindful of us and *will* bless us, as well as Israel, the priests (115:12), and those who fear Him, both small and great (115:13). God blesses all who trust Him.

The prayer wish of the psalmist is that the Lord may give you and your children increase (Psalm 115:14) and that the Lord, who made heaven and earth, may bless you (115:15).

The psalmist concludes with the declaration that the heavens belong to the Lord, the earth is given to the children of men (115:16), and those who have died do not get to praise the Lord on the earth (115:17), "But we will bless the Lord from this time forth and for evermore. Praise the Lord!" (115:18).

Summary: When you hear God has been inactive, remember that He is alive, sovereign, and there is neither help nor protection in any other source, so trust the Lord and praise Him.

A point to ponder: There is no other place to go! (Jn. 6:68).

Psalm 116: When You Face Trouble, Sorrow, and Death

Psalm 116 is a praise psalm written by an unknown author. It was sung after the Passover meal. In it, the author faces trouble, sorrow, and death (116:3).

A Promise to Pray (116:1-2) "I love the Lord because He has heard my voice and my supplication (116:1) because He has inclined His ear to me" (116:2a). The psalmist loves the Lord because the Lord answered his prayer. "Therefore I will call upon him as long as I live" (116:2b). Because the Lord has answered his prayer, he will pray for the rest of his life.

A Proclamation of the Deliverance (116:3-11) The psalmist explains that when he was facing trouble, sorrow, and imminent death (116:3), he called on the Lord for deliverance (116:4). The Lord answered (16:1-2). The psalmist proclaims that the Lord is gracious, righteous, and merciful (116:5). He preserves the simple (the naïve) and saved (delivered) the psalmist (116:6). The use of the word "simple" suggests the psalmist was near death because he had been gullible. Addressing himself, he says, "Return to your rest," adding, "For the Lord has dealt bountifully with you" (116:7). Then, addressing the Lord, he says, "For you have delivered my soul from death, my eyes from tears, and my feet from falling" (16:8). Because the Lord has delivered him, the psalmist says he will walk before the Lord in the land of the living (116:9), adding, "I believe, therefore I spoke, 'I am greatly afflicted'" (116:10). The belief in verse 10 is the belief that the Lord would deliver him from death to the land of the living (verse 9). Paul quotes, "I believed, therefore, I spoke" (116:10a) in 2 Corinthians 4:13 as proof the Lord will resurrect believers. The psalmist also says, "I said in my haste, 'All men are liars'" (116:11). Apparently, he is referring to the fact that when other people told him he was going to die, he called them liars.

A Promise to Praise (116:12-19) The psalmist asked, "What shall I render to the Lord for all of His benefits toward me?" (116:12). His answer is that he will take up the cup of salvation (a cup of wine was used as an expression of thanks; the third cup in the Passover was called the "cup of salvation"), call upon the name of the Lord (116:13), and publicly pay his vows (praise) to the Lord (116:14). A thank offering was a public offering that reminded others of God's goodness.

The psalmist inserts, "Precious in the sight of the Lord is the death of His saints" (116:15). To the Lord, the death of a saint is not trivial. In this case, He delivered the psalmist from death.

The psalmist goes on to say that, since he is God's servant, the Lord has loosed his bonds (116:16), he will offer the Lord the sacrifice of thanksgiving, call on the name of the Lord (116:17), and publicly pay his vows to the Lord (116:18-19a). He concludes with an exhortation for others to "Praise the Lord! (116:19b).

Summary: When you face trouble, sorrow, and death, call on the Lord for deliverance and when He delivers you, learn the lesson of prayer (pray for the rest of your life), publicly praise the Lord, and invite others also to praise the Lord.

A point to ponder: We have all faced trouble, sorrow, and life-threatening situations, prayed, experienced deliverance, and when the same thing happened again, our first response was to worry. Answered prayer should teach us always to pray and not lose heart (Lk. 18:1).

Psalm 117: When All Are Called to Praise the Lord

Psalm 117 is a praise psalm written by an unknown author. Psalm 117 is the shortest psalm in the Psalter and the middle chapter in the Bible. In it, the author calls everyone to praise the Lord (117:1).

A Call to Praise (117:1) "Praise the Lord, all you Gentiles! Laud Him, all you peoples!" (117:1). Obviously, the psalmist is calling *everyone* to praise the Lord. Several factors underscore the point. The Hebrew word translated "Lord" is the personal name of the God of Israel. He is the Creator and, therefore, the God of all. The word "Gentiles" are all of those who are not Jews, but "all you peoples" would include the Jews. The psalmist invites everyone, including Gentiles and all the people on the planet, to praise the Lord. As one commentator put it, all nations without exception and all peoples without distinction are to praise the Lord.

The Hebrew word translated "praise" means "to boast, be boastful, praise," and the one rendered "laud" means "to laud, praise, commend, congratulate." In Romans 15, Paul quotes this verse to prove that the Gentiles should glorify God for His mercy (Rom. 15:9-11).

The Cause for Praise (117:2) "For His merciful kindness is great toward us, and the truth of the Lord endures forever" (117:2a). The reason ("for") for praising the Lord is that He is kind. Everyone is to praise God for His kindness toward Israel ("toward us").

Traditionally, the Hebrew word translated "merciful kindness" has been defined as "goodness, kindness" (BDB), "kindness, merciful" (Strong), "kindness" (Young's Literal Translation), "merciful kindness" (KJ; NKJV). More recently, the tendency has been to include the concept of love in the definition of the word (see "lovingkindness" in the NASB; "love" in the NIV; "steadfast love" in the ESV). It is now common among commentators to render it "loyal love," indicating God's covenant loyalty to His people. Kindness is the most basic meaning of the word; "merciful kindness" is the idea.

The Lord is to be praised because He is kind and because His truth endures forever. The Hebrew word translated "truth" means "faithfulness, truth." Thus, some translations render this verse as the truth of God endures forever (KJV; ASV; NASB; NKJV), while other translations render it as the faithfulness of God endures forever (NIV; ESV).

The psalm closes as it begins with an exhortation to praise the Lord (117:2b).

Summary: When all are called to praise the Lord, they should praise Him for His merciful kindness and eternal truth.

A point to ponder: We should not only praise the Lord but also call all people to praise the Lord.

> From all that dwell below the skies,
> Let the Creator's praise arise;
> Let the Redeemer's name be sung
> Through every land, by every tongue.
> Eternal are Thy mercies, Lord;
> Eternal truth attends Thy word;
> Thy praise shall sound from shore to shore,
> Till suns rise and set no more.
> —*Isaac Watts*

Psalm 118: When You Are in Distress

Psalm 118 is a praise psalm written by an unknown author. In it, the author is in distress (118:5).

Praise for God's Mercy (118:1-4) "Oh, give thanks to the Lord for He is good! For His mercy endures forever" (118:1). A general exhortation to give thanks to the Lord for He is good and His mercy endures forever is followed by an exhortation for Israel (118:2), the house of Aaron (the priest; 118:3), and those who fear the Lord (118:4) to say, "His mercy endures forever" ("Let ... say" in verses 2, 3, 4, is antiphonal, a verse sung responsively). The statement, "His mercy endures forever," appears four times in the first four verses.

Praise for God's Deliverance (118:5-21) The psalmist says he was in distress (Hebrew: strait, tight), he called on the Lord, and the Lord answered him and set him in a broad (Hebrew: broad, roomy, wide) place (118:5). Since the Lord was <u>with</u> him, he did not need to fear what people would do to him (118:6; quoted in Heb. 13:6). Since the Lord is <u>for</u> him, he is confident he will see his desire on those who hate him (118:7). It is better to trust the Lord than put confidence in man (118:8) or princes (powerful people; 118:9).

The psalmist says the nations surrounded him, but in the name of the Lord, he will destroy them (118:10-12; repeated three times for emphasis). Addressing his enemies, he says, "You pushed me violently that I might fall, but the Lord helped me" (118:13). He adds, "The Lord is my strength and song, and He has become my salvation," that is, deliverance (118:14; quoted from Ex. 15:2; quoted in Isa. 12:2; see 2 Tim. 4:17-18).

The psalmist declares, "The voice of rejoicing and salvation is in the tent of the righteous because the hand of the Lord does valiantly" (118:15-16; Ex. 15:6). He is confident that he will not die; he will live, because even though the Lord has disciplined him severely, He has not given him over to death (117:18). He adds that he will go to the gates of righteousness and praise the Lord (118:19-20), because the Lord has answered him and become his deliverance (118:21).

Praise for God's Victory (118:22-29) "The stone which the builders rejected has become the chief cornerstone" (118:22). The psalmist compares himself to a rejected stone that became one of the most important stones in the building. Jesus applied this verse to Himself (Mt. 21:42; Mk. 12:10-11; Lk. 20:17); Peter and Paul also applied it to Jesus (Acts 4:11; 1 Pet. 2:7; see also Eph. 2:20). The Lord's doing is marvelous and in that day of victory, we should rejoice and be glad in it (118:23-24).

The psalmist prays for deliverance and prosperity (118:25) and declares, "Blessed is he who comes in the name of the Lord!" (118:26), a statement shouted by the people as Christ entered Jerusalem on a donkey (Mt. 21:9; Mk. 11:9; Lk. 19:38; Jn. 12:13; see also Mt. 23:39; Lk. 13:35).

The psalmist declares that since God is the Lord who gives light, sacrifices should be given to Him (118:27) and addressing God, he says, "You are my God and I will praise You; You are my God, I will exalt You" (118:28). The psalm ends with the same statement made at the beginning. "Oh, give thanks to the Lord for He is good! For His mercy endures forever" (118:29).

Summary: When you are in distress, pray for deliverance and praise God for His goodness and mercy and victory when it comes.

A point to ponder: We can pray for deliverance (118:5) even when our distress is caused by divine discipline (118:18), knowing that God is good and His mercy endures forever.

Psalm 119:1-8: When You See the Benefits of Obeying

Psalm 119 is a wisdom psalm written by an unknown author. It is the longest chapter in the Bible. It is an acrostic; in each stanza of eight verses, each verse begins with the same letter of the Hebrew alphabet. A number of different terms are used for the Word (law, testimonies, commandments, precepts, statutes, judgments, path, ways, word), and every verse, except verses 84, 90, 121, 122, and 132, mentions at least one of them. Except for the first three verses, every verse is addressed to or mentions the Lord.

Psalm 119:1-8 is the first stanza in this long acrostic (all of Ps. 119). Each verse begins with the Hebrew letter *aleph* (English a). In this stanza, the psalmist talks about the benefits of obeying the Word (see verses 1, 2, 3, 4, 5, 6, 7, 8).

The Benefit of Obedience (119:1-3) "Blessed are the undefiled in the way who walk in the law of the Lord!" (119:1). Those who obey the Law of the Lord are blessed (Hebrew: happy; 1:1). The Hebrew word translated "law" (*torah*) means "law, direction, instruction." It refers to the Pentateuch or Deuteronomy. Jesus used it of the whole Old Testament (Jn. 10:34).

"Blessed are those who keep His testimonies, who seek Him with their whole heart!" (119:2). Those who wholeheartedly obey God's testimonies are blessed (Hebrew: happy; 1:1). The Hebrew word translated "testimonies" means "testimony, witness."

"They also do no iniquity; they walk in His way" (119:3). Obedient people walk in God's way and, thus, avoid iniquity, which leads to a happy life.

The benefit of obeying God's Word is happiness.

The Desire for Obedience (119:4-6) Addressing the Lord, the psalmist says, "You have commanded us to diligently keep Your precepts" (119:4). The Hebrew word translated "diligently" means "exceedingly, much." The Lord commands constant, complete obedience.

Since the Lord commands consistent obedience, the psalmist says, "Oh that my ways were directed to keep Your statutes!" (119:5). The Hebrew word translated "statutes" means "statute, ordinance, limit, something prescribed." The Lord commands obedience; the psalmist desires it.

Moreover, the psalmist says, "Then I will not be ashamed, when I look into Your commandments" (119:6). The psalmist desires to be obedient so that he might not be ashamed.

The Determination to be Obedient (119:7-8) The psalmist concludes this stanza with determination to be obedient (see "I will" in verses 7 and 8).

"I will praise you with uprightness of heart when I learn your righteous judgments" (119:7). The Hebrew word translated "judgments" means "decision, sentence."

"I will keep Your statutes; Oh do not forsake me utterly!" (119:8). The word "statutes" appears in verses 5 and 8. The psalmist is determined to be obedient, but he recognizes he needs God's help to do so. Hence, he asks God not to forsake him.

Note the various terms used for the Word of God: law, testimonies, ways, precepts, statutes, commandments, and judgments.

Summary: When you see the benefits of obeying God's Word, it makes you desire and determined to be consistently obedient.

A point to ponder: The benefits of obedience include happiness, avoidance of sin, direction in life, not being ashamed, and praise.

Psalm 119:9-16: When You Desire a Pure Life

Psalm 119:9-16 is another stanza in a long acrostic (all of Ps. 119). Each verse begins with the Hebrew letter *beth* (English b). In this stanza, the psalmist expresses his desire for a pure life (119:9, 10, 11).

The Question (119:9a) The psalmist begins this stanza with the question, "How can a young man cleanse his way?" (119:9a). The question does not mean that the young man has previously sinned. Instead, the psalmist asks how a young man can make his future path pure.

The Answer (119:9b-16) The psalmist answers his question by saying, "By taking heed according to Your word" (119:9b). The way to live a pure life is to obey the Word of life. The remainder of the stanza explains what needs to be done to be obedient.

1) Seek the Lord. "With my whole heart I have sought You; Oh, let me not wander from Your commandments!" (119:10). The first and foremost thing a young man must do to be obedient to the Word of God is to seek the God of the Word. Obedience is not a matter of just obeying the Bible; it is first wholeheartedly seeking the Lord for His power not to wander from His commandments.
2) Learn the Word. "Your word I have hidden in my heart, that I might not sin against You" (119:11). The Hebrew word translated "hidden" means "to hide, treasure, store up." The Word is to be stored up in the head and heart like putting valuables treasure in a safe. Again, the emphasis is on a personal relationship with the Lord. The point of having God's Word in our hearts is that we not sin against Him, rather than just not breaking a rule in His revelation.
3) Lean on the Lord. "Blessed *are* You, O LORD! Teach me Your statutes" (119:12). To learn the Word so as not to sin, it is necessary to lean on the Lord to teach you.
4) Speak the Word. "With my lips, I have declared all the judgments of Your mouth" (119:13). A critical key to learning the Word so as not to sin is to speak the Word. God told Joshua that the Law should not depart from His mouth, not just His mind (Jos. 1:8).
5) Rejoice in the Word. "I have rejoiced in the way of Your testimonies, as *much as* in all riches" (119:14). To be successful in obeying the Word of God, there must be as much joy in going God's way as there would be in winning the lottery.
6) Meditate on the Word. "I will meditate on Your precepts, and contemplate Your ways" (119:15). Another critical element in being obedient to the Word is learning to meditate on the Word day and night (see 1:1).
7) Delight in the Word. "I will delight myself in Your statutes; I will not forget Your word" (119:16). What we delight in, we do not forget.

Summary: When you desire a pure life, be obedient to the Word of God by learning the Word, speaking the Word, meditating on the Word and delighting in the Word and by seeking the God of the Word and leaning on Him to give you the power to be obedient.

A point to ponder: A pure life begins with the question of how to do it, which indicates a desire to do it. Those who hunger and thirst for righteousness shall be filled (Mt. 5:6).

Psalm 119:17-24: When You Want to Know the Word

Psalm 119:17-24 is another stanza in a long acrostic (all of Ps. 119). Each verse begins with the Hebrew letter *gimal* (English g). In this stanza, the psalmist desires to know the Word (119:18, 19).

A Prayer for Understanding (119:17-18) "Deal bountifully with Your servant, *that* I may live and keep Your word" (119:17). In this stanza, the psalmist first asks the Lord to deal with him in such a way that he may live so that he may obey God's Word. Then he prays, "Open my eyes, that I may see wondrous things from Your law" (119:18). The Hebrew word translated "open" means to "uncover, reveal, disclose" and the one rendered "marvelous" means "to be beyond one's power, difficult to understand, wonderful, marvelous." The psalmist is praying for the Lord to reveal to him the difficult-to-understand, yet wonderful, things in His Word.

A Desire for Understanding (119:19-20) "I *am* a stranger in the earth; do not hide Your commandments from me" (119:19). The psalmist says the earth is not his home; he is a stranger here. So he asks God not to hide His Word from him; he needs it as a map to know how to travel through life. He adds, "My soul breaks with longing for Your judgments at all times" (119:20). The psalmist says he has a constant, deep desire for the Word of God.

A Delight in Understanding (119:21-24) In the latter part of this stanza, the psalmist draws a contrast between the proud and himself: "You rebuke the proud—the cursed, who stray from Your commandments" (119:21). The proud stray from the Word and consequently are judged. The psalmist adds, "Remove from me reproach and contempt, for I have kept Your testimonies. Princes also sit *and* speak against me" (119:22-23a). He asks that the reproach, contempt, and slander of princes be removed from him because he has obeyed the Word of God. These proud princes stray from the Word of God and slander the servant of God.

In contrast to the proud, the psalmist says of himself, "*But* Your servant meditates on Your statutes. Your testimonies also *are* my delight *and* my counselors" (119:23b-24). He delights in, meditates on, and uses the Word as his counselor. He doesn't walk around thinking about what his enemies were saying about him; he delights in and meditates on what God says.

Summary: When you want to know the Word of God, ask God for an understanding of it, desire it, meditate on it, and obey it.

A point to ponder: Since God is the One who enlightens our eyes so that we can understand His Word (Eph. 1:17-18), every time we read the Word, we should begin with a prayer, "Open my eyes that I may behold wondrous things from Your law."

Psalm 119:25-32: When You Feel Discouraged

Psalm 119:25-32 is another stanza in a long acrostic (all of Ps. 119). Each verse begins with the Hebrew letter *daleth* (English d). In this stanza, the psalmist is discouraged (119: 25, 28).

Prayer for Preservation (119:25-27) "My soul clings to the dust; revive me according to Your word" (119:25). The psalmist felt so low, he describes it as clinging to the dust. He was so discouraged he felt as if he were dead and buried. So he asks God to revive him. The Hebrew word translated "revive" means "to restore to life, preserve." He is asking that his life be persevered. The phrase "according to Your word" means restore me to the level of life Your Word requires.

"I have declared my ways, and You answered me; teach me Your statutes" (119:26). It worked! The psalmist prayed (verse 25) and the Lord answered (verse 26). Now the psalmist asks the Lord to teach Him the Word, adding, "Make me understand the way of Your precepts; so shall I meditate on Your wonderful works" (119:27). Once he understands the Word, he will meditate in God's works as recorded in God's Word.

Prayer for Strength (119:28-29) "My soul melts from heaviness; strengthen me according to Your word" (119:28). For the second time in this stanza, the psalmist describes his state (see verse 25). The Hebrew word translated "melts" means "drop, drip, tears" and the one rendered "heaviness" means "grief, heaviness, sorrow" (see "weeps because of grief" in the NASB; "weary with sorrow" in the NIV; "melts with sorrow" in the ESV). The psalmist has a heavy heart; he is discouraged. It is possible that he is describing constant weeping (see "drip, tears"). This time, instead of asking to be preserved, he asks to be strengthened according to God's Word, which means to the level God's Word promised (see verse 25). In addition, the psalmist asks, "Remove from me the way of lying, and grant me Your law graciously" (119:29). He is asking that any deception be removed and graciously replaced by God's Word.

The Performance of the Psalmist (119:30-32) In the last three verses of this stanza, the psalmist speaks of his past ("I have chosen" in verse 30), his present ("I cling" in verse 31), and his future ("I will run" in verse 32).

"I have chosen the way of truth; Your judgments I have laid *before me*" (119:30). The psalmist asks the Lord to teach him (verse 26) and to give him an understanding of His word (verse 27). Having meditated on God's works (verse 27) and having been strengthened by the Lord (verse 28), the psalmist has chosen to obey the Word.

"I cling to Your testimonies; O LORD, do not put me to shame!" (119:31). This stanza begins with the psalmist clinging to the dust (verse 25). Now he is clinging (same Hebrew word as in verse 25) to the Word and is asking God not to put him to shame, that is, be disappointed.

"I will run the course of Your commandments, for You shall enlarge my heart" (119:32). Having been preserved (verses 25 and 26) and strength (verse 28), the psalmist promises to be obedient to the Word of God.

Summary: When you feel discouraged, ask the Lord to restore you to life, meditate on His works, ask for strength, and cling tenaciously to the Word.

A point to ponder: Discouraged people have a tendency to cling to the dust and sorrow of their discouragement rather than tenaciously cling to God's Word.

Psalm 119:33-40: When You Want to be Obedient

Psalm 119:33-40 is another stanza in a long acrostic (all of Ps. 119). Each verse begins with the Hebrew letter *he* (English h). In this stanza, the psalmist wants to be obedient (119:33, 34).

Prayer for Enlightenment (119:33-34) "Teach me, O LORD, the way of Your statutes, and I shall keep it *to* the end" (119:33-34). The psalmist desires to be taught and is determined to obey all of his life. As if to emphasize that, He adds, "Give me understanding, and I shall keep Your law; indeed, I shall observe it with *my* whole heart" (119:34). He desires and is determined to obey the Lord with his whole heart all of his life.

Prayer for Enablement (119:35-37) The psalmist not only prays for enlightenment, he also prays for enablement. "Make me walk in the path of Your commandments, for I delight in it" (119:35). Even though he desires to obey and delights in obeying, he recognizes that he needs God's enablement to actually do it. In the next several verses, he in essences repeats this request.

"Incline my heart to Your testimonies, and not to covetousness" (119:35). Keep in mind he has already expressed a desire and determination to be obedient (verses 33-35), yet he realizes he is capable of coveting something else. So, even though he desires to be obedient, he asks that his heart be inclined to obedience.

"Turn away my eyes from looking at worthless things, *and* revive me in Your way" (119:36). The Hebrew word translated "looking" means "to look at, inspect, give attention to, consider." Job made a covenant with his eyes to not look upon a young woman (Job 31:1; see Isa. 31:15). The issue is not merely seeing something worthless; it is looking at something *with an intent* (see "to lust" in Mt. 5:28). Here the psalmist is asking the Lord to turn his eyes away from considering worthless things and revive (Hebrew: preserve) him (see 119:25) in God's way.

Prayer for Establishment (119:38-40) "Establish Your word to Your servant, who *is devoted* to fearing You" (119:38). Even though the psalmist fears (reverences) the Lord and considers himself the Lord's servant, he still needs God's enablement to establish him in the Word. (It is possible that the Hebrew construction means "so I will fear;" see the NASB; NIV; ESV).

"Turn away my reproach which I dread, for Your judgments *are* good" (119:39). He needs to be established in God's good judgments because, as one commentator said, he dreads the "reproach on inconsistency" (JFB).

"Behold, I long for Your precepts; revive me in Your righteousness" (119:40). He longs for God to revive (Hebrew: preserve) him in His righteousness.

Summary: When you want to be obedient to God's Word, pray that God will enlighten you, enable you, and establish you in it.

A point to ponder: Desire and determination are not enough to be obedient; God's work is needed, which we obtain by praying for it.

Psalm 119:41-48: When You Have Been Reproached

Psalm 119:41-48 is another stanza in a long acrostic (all of Ps. 119). Each verse begins with the Hebrew letter *waw* (English v). In this stanza, the psalmist has been reproached (119:42).

Prayer for Mercy (119:41-43) "Let your mercies come also to me, O Lord—Your salvation according to your word" (119:41). In this passage, the word "salvation" means deliverance. The psalmist is praying for deliverance based on God's mercy and according to His Word. The phrase "according to your word" is a reference to the fact that God promised to bless those who obey His Word (Deut. 28:1-13).

The psalmist says, "So shall I have an answer for him who reproaches me, for I trust in Your word" (119:42). Because he trusted in the Lord, unbelievers reproached him. So when the Lord, by His mercy, delivers him from whatever situation he is in, he will have an answer for those who reproach him.

The psalmist adds, "And take not the word of truth utterly out of my mouth, for I have hoped in your ordinances" (119:43). He is asking for God's mercy to speak as he ought to speak.

The Promise of the Psalmist (119:44-48) As a result of the answer to the prayer for mercy, the psalmist promises to do a number of things (see "I will" in verses 44-48).

1. Be obedient. "So shall I keep your law continually, forever and ever" (119:44). The psalmist promises to constantly obey God's Word and do it for the rest of his life.

2. Walk in liberty. "And I will walk at liberty, for I seek Your precepts" (119:45). Because he seeks God's Word, the psalmist is confident that he will live a life of liberty from the sin that would restrain him from obedience.

3. Talk about God's Word. "I will speak of your testimonies also before kings, and will not be ashamed" (119:46). The psalmist promises not to be ashamed of God's Word, even before powerful people. He will not be intimidated from speaking God's Word.

4. Delight in God's Word. "I will delight myself in Your commandments, which I love" (119:47). His obedience to the Word of God will not be just because it is his duty, but because it is his delight. The psalmist adds, "My hands also I will lift up to Your commandments, which I love" (119:48a). Lifting up the hands is an external expression of his internal joy. This is another way of saying he delights in the Word of God. These last two statements deal with his delight in the Word, and both end with "Your commandments, which I love." Out of his love for the Word comes his delight. Out of his delight comes obedience.

5. Meditate on the Word. "And I will meditate on your statutes" (119:48b). Because he delights in the Word, he meditates on it, walks in it, and talks about it.

Summary: When you are reproached because you are obeying the Word of God, pray for mercy to be delivered from the reproach and be more determined than ever to meditate on it, obey it, and talk about it.

A point to ponder: Those who love the Word delight in it. Those who delight in it meditate on it. Those who meditate on it obey it. Those who obey it live a life of liberty. Those who live a life of liberty talk about the Word of God openly. If you are not openly discussing the Word of God, guess what the root problem is?

Psalm 119:49-56: When You are Mocked

Psalm 119:49-56 is another stanza in a long acrostic (all of Ps. 119). Each verse begins with the Hebrew letter *zayin* (English z). In this stanza, the psalmist has been mocked (119:51).

The Prayer of the Psalmist (119:49) "Remember the word to Your servant, upon which You have caused me to hope" (119:49). The promises in the Word had given the psalmist hope (expectation). So he asked God to remember His promises that the expectations that he had received from the Word might be realized. This is like a child asking his father to remember a promise he made.

The Problem of the Psalmist (119:50-51) The psalmist says, "This is my comfort in my affliction, for your Word has given me life" (119:50). The promises in the Word of God give the servant of God expectation, comfort, and life in his affliction. He adds, "The proud have me in great derision, yet I do not turn aside from Your law" (119:51). The Hebrew word translated "derision" means to "scorn, mock, deride." The psalmist is being mocked because of his obedience to the Word, but the derision did not deter him.

Practice of the Psalmist (119:52-56) He explains, "I remembered your judgments of old, O Lord, and have comforted myself" (119:52). When the psalmist was mocked, laughed at, and ridiculed, he took comfort in God's promise to judge the proud. The psalmist did not feel sorry for himself because he was mocked. He was sad for the mockers! He says, "Indignation has taken hold of me because of the wicked, who forsake Your law" (119:53). The Hebrew word translated "indignation" means "burning heat, raging heat" (BDB). Luther translated it "I am burnt up." It comes from a word that means "horror, terrible" (Strong). The psalmist was horrified; he trembled because of the judgment (verse 52) that would come upon those who had forsaken God's Law (verse 53). As for him, there was a song in his heart. He says, "Your statutes have been my song in the house of my pilgrimage" (119:54). In his life, considered as a journey to another world ("my pilgrimage"), his consolation and source of joy has been in the promises of God's Word. Therefore, "I remember your name in the night, O Lord, and keep Your law" (119:55). When he laid his head on his pillow at night, he remembered the Lord and during the day, he was obedient to His Word.

He closes this stanza by explaining, "This has become mine because I kept Your precepts" (119:56). His expectation (see "hope" in verse 49), his comfort (verse 50), his sheer joy (verse 54), his steadfastness (verse 51) is his because he was obedient to God's precepts.

Summary: When you are mocked for being obedient to God's Word, trust the Lord to judge the proud, wicked mockers and take comfort in, be steadfastly obedient to, and delight in God's Word.

A point to ponder: When we are mocked, we think, "Woe is me," when we ought to be thinking, "Woe is them."

Psalm 119:57-64: When You are Encircled by Enemies

Psalm 119:57-64 is another stanza in a long acrostic (all of Ps. 119). Each verse begins with the Hebrew letter *heth* (English ch). In this stanza, the psalmist is encircled by his enemies (119:61).

The Prayer of the Psalmist (119:57-58) "You are my portion, O Lord; I have said that I would keep Your words" (119:57). Prior to the occasion described in this stanza, the psalmist said that since the Lord was his portion (a Hebrew word used of a parcel of land) in life, he would to be obedient to God's Word. Now he says, "I entreated your favor with my whole heart; be merciful to me according to Your word" (119:58). He was not only obedient to the Word of God, but he sought the grace of God with all that was within him. So now he asks for God to be merciful to him in the situation he now finds himself.

The Predicament of the Psalmist (119:59-62) Before describing the predicament he is in, the psalmist says, "I thought about your ways and turned my feet to your testimonies" (119:59). Having given careful consideration to how he would live his life, the psalmist decided to walk in the ways of the Lord. He adds, "I made haste and did not delay to keep Your commandments" (119:60). Once he decided to obey God's Word, he did it quickly without delay.

As for his current situation, the psalmist says, "The cords of the wicked have bound me, but I have not forgotten Your law" (159:61). The Hebrew word translated "bound" means "surround." The specifics of the situation are unknown, except that when enemies hindered him, he did not forget to be obedient to the Word. Whatever the enemies did, they did not intimidate him or deter him from obedience. Moreover, he adds, "At midnight I will rise to give thanks to you because of Your righteous judgments" (119:62). He was not only obedient, he was thankful, even in the middle of the night (see also Acts 16:25), for God's righteous decisions.

The Partners of the Psalmist (119:63-64) As if to add support to his claim of obedience, the psalmist says, "I am the companion of all who fear You and those who keep Your precepts" (119:63). As the adage goes, "A man is known by the company he keeps." People seek friends in accordance with their values and preferences: "Birds of a feather flock together."

The psalmist concludes this stanza with, "The Lord Earth, O Lord, is full of Your mercy; teach me Your statutes" (119:64). Enemies surround the psalmist, but he sees not only his enemies but the mercy of the Lord everywhere. He mentions the mercy of God at the beginning of this stanza (119:58) and at the end of it (119:64). Perhaps this is a reference to seeing God's mercy in the lives of his companions (119:63). At any rate, his great desire in this situation is that the Lord would teach him His word. Even though he has repeatedly said in this stanza that he has been obedient (verses 57, 59, 60, 61), he asks God to teach him the Word! In every new situation in life, there are new truths to be learned from God's Word (Jas. 1:5).

Summary: When enemies encircle you, ask God for His mercy, make sure you are obedient to His Word, be grateful in the middle of the night, stay close to your friends who stay close to the Lord, and ask God to teach you His truth in that situation.

A point to ponder: When we are surrounded by opposition, we tend to focus on it, rather than seeing God's mercy and seeking God's wisdom.

Psalm 119:65-72: When Someone Lies About You

Psalm 119:65-72 is another stanza in a long acrostic (all of Ps. 119). Each verse begins with the Hebrew letter *teth* (English t). In this stanza, someone has told a lie against the psalmist (119:69).

The Prayer of the Psalmist (119:65-68) "You have dealt well with Your servants, O Lord, according to Your word" (119:65). Based on the principles and promises of His Word, God had been good to His servant, the psalmist. So the psalmist prays, "Teach me good judgment and knowledge, for I believe your commandments" (119:66). Because he has believed in God's Word, he asks God for good judgment in making decisions and for knowledge.

This prayer includes a confession. God had been good to the psalmist (119:65), but the psalmist had not always followed the Lord. He confesses, "Before I was afflicted I went astray, but now I keep Your word" (119:67). Notice the order: going astray, being afflicted, and now obeying the Word. The psalmist also confesses, "You are good and do good; teach me Your statutes" (119:68). He who is eternally good has done good to His servant (119:65). Thus, the psalmist requests that God teach him His Word.

The psalmist makes two prayer requests (see "teach" in verses 66 and 68). He requests knowledge of the Word (119:68) and good judgment (119:66). The two go together.

The Enemies of the Psalmist (119:69-70) At this point, the psalmist says, "The proud have forged a lie against me, but I will keep Your precepts with my whole heart" (119:69). Apparently, the affliction mentioned earlier (119:67) was those proud people who lied about the psalmist. The lies against him did not prevent him from wholeheartedly obeying God's truth. He understands that he is not the problem; they are. For he says, "Their heart is as fat as grease, but I delight in Your law" (169:70). The expression "their heart is as fat as grease" is a figurative way of saying that they are insensitive to spiritual truth. In contrast to the insensitivity of the proud to God's Word, the psalmist delights in it.

The Benefit to the Psalmist (119:71-72) "It is good for me that I have been afflicted, that I may learn Your statutes" (119:71). Rather than his affliction (probably the lies spoken against him) harming him, it was good for him because that experience taught him more of God's Word. In fact, he was willing to go so far as to say, "The law of Your mouth is better to me than thousands of coins of gold and silver" (119:72). What came out of the mouth of the proud (lies) is not to be compared to the priceless Law that comes out of God's mouth. His experience with the lies of the proud had taught him to appreciate God's Word.

Summary: When someone lies about you, if you ask God to teach you His Word and good judgment, and you are obedient to His Word, you will discover priceless truths from the mouth of God.

A point to ponder: God is good and does good (119:68) and, therefore, all things work together for good to those who love the Lord (119:71; Rom. 8:28).

Psalm 119:73-80: When You are Mistreated by Others

Psalm 119:73-80 is another stanza in a long acrostic (all of Ps. 119). Each verse begins with the Hebrew letter *yod* (English i). In this stanza, proud people have mistreated the psalmist (119:78).

The Prayer for Understanding (119:73-74) "Your hand had made me and fashioned me; give me understanding that I may learn your commandments" (119:73). Acknowledging that the Lord is his Creator, the psalmist asks the Lord to give him an understanding of His Word. If the Lord does that, "Those who fear You will be glad when they see me, because I have hope in Your word" (119:74). When he receives understanding of the Word, he will trust (see "hope") in the Word and believers will rejoice when they see what the Lord has done in his life.

Prayer for Merciful Kindness (119:75-77) "I know, O Lord, that your judgments are right and that in faithfulness you have afflicted me" (119:75). The Hebrew word translated "afflicted" means "to oppress, humble, be afflicted, be bowed down." The affliction mentioned in this stanza is being treated wrongly with lies (119:78). As far as the psalmist is concerned, knowing the Lord is righteous and faithful, He allowed this to happen to teach him and train him. So he asks, "Let, I pray, Your merciful kindness be my comfort, according to Your Word to Your servant" (119:76). The psalmist asks for God's kindness. He adds, "Let your tender mercies come to me that I may live; for your law is my delight" (119:77). The Hebrew word translated "tender mercies" means "compassion." The psalmist asks for God's compassion to survive this affliction because he delights in the Lord.

Prayer for the Situation in General (119:78-80) In the last three verses of this stanza, the psalmist prays for the proud (verse 78), for those who fear the Lord (verse 179), and for himself (verse 80).

"Let the proud be ashamed, for they treated me wrongly with falsehood; but I have meditated on your precepts" (119:78). The psalmists had been afflicted (verse 75) by proud people who had unjustly dealt with him with "falsehood" (Hebrew: deceit, fraud, lies), but he had not concentrated on that; he meditated on God's Word, which is truth. He asks that the proud be "ashamed" (Hebrew: be put to shame, disconcerted, disappointed).

"Let those who fear You turn to me, those who know Your testimonies" (119:79). The psalmist asks for the support of those who know God's Word and who fear Him. As one commentator said, "Let Your friends be my friends" (Barnes).

"Let my heart be blameless regarding your statutes, that I may not be ashamed" (119:80). Whereas the proud should be ashamed (verse 78) because of the way they treated him, the psalmist desires that the Lord grant him the grace to be blameless concerning His Word, that he not be ashamed.

Summary: When others mistreat you, ask God for an understanding of His Word, comfort from His mercy, support from others, the grace to obey His Word, and that those who have mistreated you be put to shame.

A point to ponder: When we are mistreated, we tend to focus and meditate on the mistreatment; the psalmist chose to meditate on (verse 78) and obey (verse 80) God's truth instead of their lies.

Psalm 119:81-88: When Your Deliverance is Delayed

Psalm 119:81-88 is another stanza in a long acrostic (all of Ps. 119). Each verse begins with the Hebrew letter *kaph* (English k or c). In this stanza, the psalmist has sought deliverance, which did not come (119:81-83).

The Lament of the Psalmist (119:81-84) "My soul faints for your salvation, but I hope in Your word" (119:81). The Hebrew word translated "faints" means "spent, exhausted." Evidently, the psalmist had sought deliverance from some situation and it had not come, but he still hoped (Hebrew: to wait, to expect) in God's Word. He adds, "My eyes fail (the same Hebrew word that is translated "faints" in verse 81) from searching Your word, saying, 'When would you comfort me?'" (119:82). Being at the point of exhaustion, the psalmist wants to know how much longer he has to wait. He explains, "For I become like a wineskin in smoke, yet I did not forget Your statutes" (119:83). The psalmist felt like a shriveled-up wineskin, yet he did not forget God's Word. Wine bottles were made of leather. As they hung in the tent, the smoke from the fire dried them out. So once again, he asks, "How many are the days of your servant? When will you execute judgment on those who persecute me?" (119:84). He wants to know how much longer the delay will be, but he is confident that it will come (119:81, 83).

The Enemies of the Psalmist (119:85-87) In the next three verses, the psalmist describes three things the proud have done to him. They have plotted against him (verse 85), persecuted him (verse 86), and brought him to the point of death (verse 87).

"The proud have dug pits for me, which is not according to Your law" (119:85). Contrary to God's Law, proud people planned to trap the psalmist.

"All your commandments are faithful; they persecute me wrongly; help me!" (119:86). These proud people persecuted the psalmist, but confident that God's Word can be trusted, the psalmist pleads for God to help him.

"They almost made an end of me on the earth, and I did not forsake Your precepts" (119:87). Their persecution had been so severe and lasted so long (verse 84) that it brought the psalmist to death's door, but he was determined to trust and obey God's Word regardless of the circumstances.

The Prayer of the Psalmist (119:88) The psalmist concludes this stanza with a prayer: "Revive me according to Your lovingkindness, so that I may keep the testimony of Your mouth" (119:88). The Hebrew word translated "revive" means "to preserve." Being at death's door (119:87), he requests that he might live. His argument is not that he has been obedient to the Word, although that is true, but that God is kind. The reason he asked for the preservation of his life is so that he may continue to obey the Word.

Summary: When your deliverance is delayed, pour out your complaint to the Lord, persist in being obedient to God's Word, and pray for God's protection.

A point to ponder: The longer the deliverance is delayed, the more difficult it is to do what God says, so the test is to trust Him to the very end. Job said, "Though he slay me, yet I will trust him" (Job 13:15).

Psalm 119:89-96: When Your World is Unstable

Psalm 119:89-96 is another stanza in a long acrostic (all of Ps. 119). Each verse begins with the Hebrew letter *lamed* (English l). In this stanza, the psalmist compares his unstable world to God's stable Word (119:92).

Establishment of God's Word (119:89-91) "Forever, O Lord, Your word is settled in heaven" (119:89). The Word is firmly fixed forever in heaven. Therefore, it can be trusted. Furthermore, "Your faithfulness endures to all generations; You established the earth and it abides" (119:90). The Word is fixed and God is faithful. An illustration of God's faithfulness is the creation: "They continue this day according to your ordinances, for all are your servants" (119:91). "They" is a reference to heaven (verse 89) and earth (verse 90). Heaven and earth continue (verse 91) as God established them (verse 90) according to His Word; they are His obedient servants.

These verses declare that the Word is settled, the Lord is steadfast, and the universe is stable, but the main point is that God's Word is established, as illustrated by the fact that the earth is established according to it.

The Experience of the Psalmist (119:92-94) In contrast to the stability of the Word and the earth, the world of the psalmist has been unstable. He says, "Unless Your law had been my delight, I would have perished in my affliction" (119:92). His world was so unstable he was close to perishing in his affliction, but delighting in God's stable Word gave him stability in his unstable world. Thus, he says, "I will never forget your precepts, for by then You have given me life" (119:93). The life-giving Word gave the psalmist life in the face of death. Nevertheless, he cries, "I am yours, save me; for I have sought your precepts" (119:94). He has been delivered from death's door but needs to be delivered in his current situation.

The Enemies of the Psalmist (119:95-96) The psalmist explains, "The wicked wait for me to destroy me, but I will consider Your testimonies" (119:95). The psalmist faces the reality that there are people out to destroy him, but he chooses to concentrate on God's Word instead of theirs. After all, he says, "I have seen the consummation of all perfection, but your commandment is exceedingly broad" (119:96). The Hebrew word translated "consummation" means "end." The psalmist has seen the end of things that claimed to be perfect, but he realizes that God's Word is boundless in its value and virtues.

Summary: When your world is unstable, do not forget the stability of God's Word (verse 93), delight in it (verse 92), seek it (verse 94), and ask God to deliver you (verse 94), because God's faithfulness endures to all generations (verse 90).

A point to ponder: The only stable, for sure, thing in this world is God's Word.

Psalm 119:97-104: When You Want to Be Wise

Psalm 119:97-104 is another stanza in a long acrostic (all of Ps. 119). Each verse begins with the Hebrew letter *mem* (English m). In this stanza, the psalmist discusses the wisdom he gained from the Word (119:98-100).

The Extent of the Wisdom (119:97-100) "Oh, how I love Your law! It is my meditation all the day" (119:97). Because the psalmist loves the Law of the Lord, he meditates on it all day long and it makes him wise. In the following verses, he explains how wise it made him.

"You, through Your commandments, made me wiser than my enemies" (119:98). The psalmist says he is wiser than his enemies, not because he is smarter than they are, but because of his knowledge of the Word. The Word gave him wisdom his enemies did not have.

"I have more understanding than all my teachers, for your testimonies are my meditation" (119:99). Because he meditates on the Word all day (verse 97), he has more understanding, which he gained from God, than his human teachers.

"I understand more than the ancients because I keep your precepts" (119:100). The Hebrew word translated "ancients" means "old, elder." As a result of meditating on the Word all day, he had more understanding than old people, who had the advantage of observation and experience.

The Effects of Wisdom (119:101-104) "I have restrained my feet from every evil way, that I may keep your word" (119:101). Meditating on the Word (verses 97, 99) and obeying it (verse 100) made the psalmist wise in that it motivated him to avoid sin so that he might be even more obedient. As he explains, "I have not departed from your judgments, for Your Yourself have taught me." It was having been taught the Word that he did not depart from it.

No wonder he says, "How sweet are Your words to my taste, sweeter than honey to my mouth!" (119:103). Obedience to the Word was not a bitter pill to swallow; it was as sweet as a dessert made of honey. It was a pleasurable experience.

The psalmist concludes, "Through your precepts, I get understanding; therefore, I hate every false way" (119:104). Again, he is making the point that meditating on the Word and obeying it, made him hate living a life of falsehood. Instead, he lived a life of truth.

Summary: When you want to be wise, meditate on the Word and obey it and you will find that you are wiser than your enemies, teachers, and older people because one of the results is a desire to be more obedient to avoid sin.

A point to ponder: The key to wise living is meditation on and obedience to the Word of God.

Psalm 119:105-112: When You are in a Severe Trial

Psalm 119:105-112 is another stanza in a long acrostic (all of Ps. 119). Each verse begins with the Hebrew letter *nun* (English n). In this stanza, the psalmist is in the midst of a severe trial (119:107).

The Path of the Psalmist (119:105-106) "Your word is a lamp to my feet and a light to my path" (119:105). As a lamp with light is necessary to walk at night, so is the Word that provides "light" for walking during the day. Thus, the psalmist says, "I have sworn and confirmed that I will keep your righteous judgments" (119:106). Having experienced God's guidance, the poet is committed to obeying God's commandments.

The Plight of the Psalmist (119:107-110) The psalmist says three things about his plight: he is greatly afflicted, his life is constantly in danger, and the wicked lay a snare trap for him.

1. "I am afflicted very much; revive me, O Lord, according to Your word" (119:107). The Hebrew word rendered "revive" means "preserve." His life was threatened (see verse 109). The nature of the affliction is not given, but all believers experience trials and sometimes the trials are heavy ("afflicted very much"). The psalmist asks that his life be preserved according to the promises in God's Word. He also asks, "Accept, I pray, the free will offering of my mouth, O Lord, and teach me your judgments" (119:108). As he praises the Lord amid his trial ("the free will offering of my mouth"), he prays for God's wisdom (see Jas. 1:2-5).

2. "My life is continually in my hand, yet I do not forget Your law" (119:109). Anything in a person's hand is liable to be dropped or snatched away. In his situation, his life was in constant danger. Yet, I did not forget to think about or to obey the Word.

3. "The wicked have laid a snare for me, yet I have not strayed from your precepts" (119:110). As hunters lay traps for animals, the wicked laid a trap for the psalmist, but that did not cause him to stray from obedience to the Word.

The Performance of the Psalmist (119:111-112) The psalmist closes this stanza by describing what he has done in the midst of his affliction. He says two things.

1. "Your testimonies I have taken as a heritage forever, for they are the rejoicing of my heart" (119:11). The Hebrew word translated "heritage" means "to acquire, possess, inherit" (see "inherited" in the NASB). It is used of the possession of the Promised Land as an inheritance. To the psalmist, the Word was his wealth, his inheritance, because it brought joy to his heart.

2. "I have inclined my heart to perform your statutes forever, to the very end" (119:12). The psalmist purposed in his heart to perform what God told him to do in His word, not only through this trial but to the very end of his life. This resolve is the key to the way the psalmist handled his severe trial (see also verse 106).

Summary: When you are in a severe trial, purpose in your heart to obey the Word (verse 112), pray for God's enabling grace (verse 107), and praise Him (verse 108).

A point to ponder: In Psalm 119, the psalmist repeatedly talked about meditating on and being obedient to the Word; the key to all of that is to *purpose in your heart* to be obedient to the Lord and to pray for His grace to be able to do it.

Psalm 119:113-120: When You are Faced with Evildoers

Psalm 119:113-120 is another stanza in a long acrostic (all of Ps. 119). Each verse begins with the Hebrew letter *samek* (English s). In this stanza, the psalmist is faced with evildoers (119:113, 115, 118, 119).

The Rejection of Evildoers (119:113-115) "I hate the double-minded, but I love Your law" (119:13). The Hebrew word rendered "double-minded" means "divided, halfhearted, ambivalent" (see Jas. 1:8). Such a person doubts, waivers, and is skeptical. Those who love the law hate such a mindset because it produces evildoers (see 119:15). The psalmist adds, "You are my hiding place and my shield; I hope in your word" (119:14). The Word is his hope and the Lord is his hiding place and shield, that is, his protection, which in this context is a reference to protection from evildoers. He says, "Depart from me, you evildoers, for I will keep the commandments of my God!" (119:15). He is determined to be obedient and to depart from the disobedient.

The Request of the Psalmist (119:116-117) In this stanza, the psalmist makes two requests.

"Uphold me according to Your word, that I may live; and do not let me be ashamed of my hope" (115:16). Recognizing that God is his protection (verse 114), the psalmist now requests that the Lord uphold him as the Lord had promised in His Word so that he might live and not have a disappointed hope.

"Hold me up, and I shall be safe and I shall observe Your statutes continually" (119:117). Knowing that the Lord is his protection (verse 114), He requests that the Lord sustain him and when He does, the psalmist will be safe and constantly obedient.

The Response of the Psalmist (119:118-120) In the last part of this stanza, the psalmist says two things about the Lord and gives his response.

"You reject all those who stray from Your statutes, for their deceit is falsehood" (119:118). In Hebrew, the repetition of words such as "deceit" and "falsehood" expresses emphasis ("the Holy of Holies"). In this case, the point is that those who stray from God's statutes are utterly false. Hence, God rejects them.

"You put away all the wicked of the earth like dross" (119:119a). The dross from a furnace was cast out; it was of no value. The wicked are like that dross.

The psalmist responds, "Therefore I love your testimonies" (119:119b). His response was to love God's Word because it contains just judgment on the wicked.

The psalmist concludes this stanza, "My flesh trembles for fear of You, and I am afraid of Your judgments" (119:120). In light of God's judgments, the psalmist shuddered and stood in reverence and awe.

Summary: When faced with evildoers, depart from them, cling to the Lord for safety, and stand in awe of His judgment.

A point of view: If we love God's Law, we will hate all that is opposite and opposed to it.

Psalm 119:121-128: When You are Oppressed

Psalm 119:121-128 is another stanza in a long acrostic (all of Ps. 119). Each verse begins with the Hebrew letter *ayn* (there is no English equivalent). In this stanza, the psalmist is dealing with oppressors (119:121-122).

Prayer for Deliverance (119:121-123) "I have done justice and righteousness; do not leave me to my oppressors" (119:121). The Hebrew word translated "oppressors" (see verses 121 and 122) means "to press upon, oppress violate, defraud, do violence, extort." The psalmist proclaims his innocence (verse 121) and asks for deliverance (verse 122). "Be surety for Your servant for good; do not let the proud oppress me" (119:122). His oppressors are proud, but as God's servant, he asked for deliverance. In fact, he says, "My eyes fail from seeking Your salvation and Your righteous Word" (119:123). His eyes fail him, looking for God's deliverance ("salvation") and His righteous judgment ("righteous word") on those who oppress him.

Prayer for Understanding (119:124-125) "Deal with your servant according to Your mercy, and teach me Your statutes" (119:124). Up to this point in this stanza, the psalmist seems to be pleading for God's deliverance based on his righteousness (verse 121), his service (122), and his prayers (verse 123). Now, he asks God to deal with him according to His mercy. Moreover, he asks God to teach him the Word. He adds, "I am Your servant; give me understanding that I may know Your testimonies" (119:125). He needs God's mercy to be delivered from the oppressors and he needs God's enlightenment to understand His Word.

A Prayer for Action (119:126-128) The psalmist asked the Lord to intervene for two reasons.

First is <u>their</u> attitude toward God's Word. He says, "It is time for You to act, O Lord, for they have regarded Your law as void" (119:126). The Hebrew word rendered "void" means "to break, violate, make ineffectual." Since they have broken God's law, the psalmist asks God for God's immediate ("it is time") intervention to deliver him and judge them.

Second is <u>his</u> attitude toward God's Word. "Therefore I love Your commandments more than gold, yes, than fine gold!" (119:127). The more he sees the proud (verse 122) break God's law (verse 126) and sees the consequences of their disobedience (verse 126), the more he loves God's commandments. They are more valuable to him than the finest gold. He concludes, "Therefore all Your precepts concerning all things I consider to be right: I hate every false way" (119:128). God is not only righteous and just in this situation; His Word is right about all things. Thus, the psalmist has learned to <u>love</u> God's Word (verse 127) and <u>hate</u> "every false way" (128).

Summary: When you are oppressed by proud (verse 122), or evil (verse 126) people, pray for deliverance, an understanding of God's Word, and for God's immediate intervention.

A point to ponder: Being oppressed is not pleasant; it can be painful, but it can also be profitable if we seek wisdom from God's Word because of it.

Psalm 119:129-136: When You See Wonder in the Word

Psalm 119:129-136 is another stanza in a long acrostic (all of Ps. 119). Each verse begins with the Hebrew letter *pe* English "p"). In this stanza, the psalmist is struck by the wonder of the Word (119:129).

Desire for The Word (119:129-131) "Your testimonies are wonderful; therefore my soul keeps them" (119:129). The Hebrew word translated "wonderful" means "incomprehensible, extraordinary, wonderful." Being struck by the wonder of the Word, the psalmist says he obeys it. It is extraordinary because "The entrance of your word gives life; it gives understanding to the simple" (119:130). The Hebrew word translated "simple" means "open-minded, naïve." The Word is able to give understanding to the naïve and life to all. No wonder the psalmist says, "I open my mouth and panted, for I longed for Your commandments (119:131). The breathtaking wonder of the Word to give understanding and life causes the psalmist to deeply desire it (verse 131) and be obedient to it (verse 129).

Prayer for Mercy (119:132-135) At this point, the psalmist asks for mercy (grace, strength).

"Look upon me and be merciful to me, as Your custom is toward those who love Your name" (119:132). As one who deeply desires the Word and who loves the Lord, the psalmist asks for mercy.

"Direct my steps by Your word, and let no iniquity have dominion over me" (119:133). He needs mercy to be obedient to the Word and to be free from sin.

"Redeem me from the oppression of man, that I may keep your precepts" (119:134). He needs mercy to be delivered from the oppression of people that he might be obedient to the Word.

"Make your face to shine upon your servant, and teach me your statutes." He asks for mercy ("make your face to shine upon your servant") and for instruction from the Word.

The Sorrow of the Psalmist (119:136) "Rivers of water run down my eyes because men do not keep Your law" (119:136). The disobedience (verse 136) of his oppressors (verse 134) causes him to weep.

Summary: When you see the wonder in the Word, it ought to make you deeply desire it, be obedient to it, ask for mercy to be obedient, and to weep over the disobedient

A point to ponder: Realizing what the Word can do (giving life and understanding, even to the naïve) should make us deeply desire it and weep for the disobedient.

Psalm 119:137-144: When You are Despised

Psalm 119:137-144 is another stanza in a long acrostic (all of Ps. 119). Each verse begins with the Hebrew letter *tsadde* (English "ts"). In this stanza, the psalmist speaks of being despised (119:141).

The Praise of the Word (119:137-138) "Righteous are You, O Lord, and upright are Your judgments" (119:137). The righteous God has given a righteous Word. As if to underscore that, the psalmist adds, "Your testimonies, which You have commanded, are righteous and very faithful" (119:138). Because God's Word is right, it can be trusted.

The Plight of the Psalmist (119:139-143) In the next several verses of this stanza, the psalmist moves back and forth between his plight and his praise for God's Word.

"My zeal has consumed me because my enemies have forgotten Your words" (119:139). Because his enemies forgot God's Word (implying they did something to the psalmist that was contrary to God's Word; see verse 141), his zeal (his strength) has been consumed (exhausted). Nevertheless, the psalmist proclaims, "Your word is very pure; therefore, Your servant loves it" (119:140). Even though his enemies forgot God's Word, that did not deter him from believing that God's Word was right ("pure"); therefore, he loved it.

"I am small and despised, yet I did not forget Your precepts" (119:141). By "small" he means small in the eyes of other people (see "and despised"). His enemies look down on him, perhaps because he loves the Word of God. They also despised him. The Hebrew word translated "despised" means "to despise, hold in contempt, disdain, to be despicable, to be worthless." They did not just look down upon him, they viewed him with contempt as despicable. Yet, he did not become like them and forget God's Word (compare verse 139 with verse 141). Thus, he adds, "Your righteousness is an everlasting righteousness, and Your law is true" (119:142). He did not forget God's Word and was convinced that God's righteousness was eternal and His Word is true.

"Trouble and anguish have overtaken me, yet Your commandments are my delight" (119:143). The Hebrew word translated "trouble" means "distress, foe, enemy, oppressor." Because of the treatment of his enemies, the psalmist was overtaken with anguish. Yet even in the midst of his anguish, he delighted in the Word of God. When there was no delight in how he was being treated, he could delight in the Word of a righteous God.

The Prayer of the Psalmist (119:144) The psalmist concludes by saying, "The righteousness of Your testimony is everlasting; give me understanding and I shall live" (119:144). There is an emphasis in this stanza on the righteousness of God and the righteousness of His Word (see verses 137, 138, 142, 144). Thus, the psalmist asks God to give him an understanding of His everlasting, righteous Word so that he may live while being despised.

Summary: When you are despised, remember God and His Word are righteous, delight in it, and ask for understanding of it (see Jas. 1:2-5).

A point to ponder: "There are few things which we are less able to bear than contempt, and one of the best evidences of attachment to principle is when we adhere to what we regard as right and true, though we are despised for it by the frivolous, the worldly, the rich - by those who claim to be 'wise'" (Barnes, a 19th-century commentator).

Psalm 119:145-152: When Your Enemies Draw Near

Psalm 119:145-152 is another stanza in a long acrostic (all of Ps. 119). Each verse begins with the Hebrew letter *qoph* (English k). In this stanza, an enemy draws near the psalmist (119:150).

The Cry of the Psalmist (119:145-147a) Each of the first three verses in this stanza mentions the psalmist crying out to the Lord in prayer.

"I cry out with my whole heart; hear me, O Lord! I will keep your statutes" (119-145). The nature of his cry was a whole-hearted prayer; that is, he prays earnestly and fervently and declares his intention to obey the Word.

"I cry out to you; save me and I will keep your testimonies" (119:146). The content of his cry was that the Lord would deliver (save) him. He again declares his intention to obey the Word.

"I rise before the dawning of the morning; and cry for help" (119:147a). The time of his cry for help was before dawn.

The Confidence of the Psalmist (119:147b-149) "I hope in Your word" (147 b). The psalmist is trusting the promises of the Word. He adds, "My eyes are awake through the night watches, that I may meditate on Your word" (119:148). The ancients divided the night into military watches instead of hours. Whatever he was going through kept him awake at night, but instead of fretting through the night, he meditated on the Word.

The psalmist trusts God's promises in the Word of God, but his confidence is in the Lord. "Hear my voice according to Your lovingkindness; O Lord, revive me according to your justice" (119 149). The Hebrew word rendered "revive" means "preserve." His confidence is in the kindness and justice of the Lord to preserve him.

The Condition of the Psalmist (119:150-152) "They draw near who follow after wickedness; they are far from Your law" (119:150). The enemies drawing near to the psalmist are wicked people who disobey the law of the Lord (see 17:9, 28:3-5, 43:2). Obviously, they are intent on harming the psalmist and because they are far from God's law, they will stop at nothing.

The enemies of the psalmist are near, but so is the Lord. "You are near, O Lord, and all Your commandments are true" (119:151). The enemies who are near are wicked; the Lord who is near is righteous. His commandments are true; furthermore, they are eternal. "Concerning Your testimonies, I have known of old that You have founded them forever" (119:152). His enemies are temporary, but the Lord and His promises are eternal.

Summary: When enemies draw near, cry to the Lord for deliverance, meditate on His Word, not them, and remember the Lord is also near.

A point to ponder: When enemies draw near to us, we need to draw near to the Lord and His Word.

Psalm 119:153-160: When You Are Persecuted

Psalm 119:153-160 is another stanza in a long acrostic (all of Ps. 119). Each verse begins with the Hebrew letter *resh* (English r). In this stanza, the psalmist faces persecution (119:57).

The Prayer of the Psalmist (119:153-156) In a number of different ways, in the first part of this stanza, the psalmist asks for deliverance. It is not until verse 157 that he indicates that he needs deliverance from persecutors.

"Consider my affliction and deliver me, for I do not forget Your law" (119:153). The affliction that the psalmist mentions here is from wicked persecutors (see verse 157). He is asking for deliverance from persecutors because he does not forget God's law, which is another way of saying he obeyed.

"Plead my cause and redeem me; revive me according to Your word" (119:154). The psalmist is asking God to be his advocate. For him to ask to be redeemed and revived (Hebrew: preserved) is another way of requesting deliverance. In contrast to his obedience, he says, "Salvation is far from the wicked, for they do not seek your statutes" (119:55). Salvation is far from those who do not seek it.

"Great are your tender mercies, O Lord; revive me according to your judgments" (119:156). Again, the psalmist asks for preservation ("revive me") based on God's Word and mercy.

The Persecutors of the Psalmist (119:157-158) "Many are my persecutors and my enemies, yet I do not turn from Your testimonies" (119:157). Even though his enemies, who are his persecutors, are many, they did not deter him from obeying God's Word (119:157).

In fact, he sees who they really are. "I see the treacherous and am disgusted because they do not keep your law" (119 158). The Hebrew word translated "treacherous" means "to act or deal treacherously, deceitfully." His enemies are deceitful and disobedient persecutors. He sees them for what they really are and is disgusted, a Hebrew word which means "to be grieved, to loathe, to detest."

The Pleasure of the Psalmist (119:159-160) "Consider how I love your precepts; revive me, O Lord, according to your lovingkindness" (119:159). At the beginning of this stanza, he asked God to <u>consider</u> his affliction (verse 153). Now, he asks God to <u>consider</u> how much he loves the Word (verse 159). For the third time in this stanza, he asks God to "revive me" (Hebrew: preserve; see verses 154, 156, 159). On the one hand, he asks God to preserve him because he loves his Word; on the other hand, he pleads for God's kindness (119:159).

One of the reasons he loves God's Word (verse 159) is because, as he tells the Lord, "The entirety of Your word is truth, and every one of Your righteous judgments endures forever" (159:160). The Word teaches him that in the end, God will judge righteously according to truth.

Summary: When persecuted, pray for deliverance and remember that there will be a righteous judgment according to the truth in the end.

A point to ponder: Even though you may face a great deal of opposition to obedience (see "many" persecutors in verse 157), God is bigger than the opposition.

Psalm 119:161-168: When You Are Persecuted Without Cause

Psalm 119:161-168 is another stanza in a long acrostic (all of Ps. 119). Each verse begins with the Hebrew letter *shin* (English s or sh). In this stanza, the psalmist is persecuted without a cause (119:161).

The Persecutors of the Psalmist (119:161-163) "Princes persecute me without a cause, but my heart stands in awe of Your word" (119:161). Those in a position of authority ("Princes") were persecuting the psalmist without a cause. Regardless of what they said (see verse 163), he stood in awe of God's Word, not fearing what powerful people could do to him. He goes on to say, "I rejoice at Your word as one who finds great treasure" (119:162). He has stood in awe and rejoiced in the "great treasure" he found in the Word of God. He adds, "I hate and abhor lying, but I love Your law" (119:163). The context seems to imply that those in authority, persecuting him without a cause, were lying about him. His response was to say he hates the lies of the persecutors but loves the truth of God's Word.

The Peace of the Psalmist (119:164-165) In the midst of these trying circumstances, the psalmist praises God. In fact, he says, "Seven times a day I praise You, because of Your righteous judgments" (119:164). He didn't just praise God once a day in the morning or in the evening; he praised God all day long because, from the Word, he knew there would be a just judgment. Consequently, he could say, "Great peace have those who love Your law and nothing causes them to stumble" (119:165). Those who love the "great treasure" (verse 162) of the Word of God have the "great peace" (verse 165) of God, and nothing, such as persecution, causes them to stumble spiritually.

The Prayer of the Psalmist (119:166-168) At this point in this stanza, the psalmist addresses the Lord, not with a request, but simply with a response to His Word. "Lord, I hope for Your salvation, and I do Your commandments" (119:166). The psalmist trusts the Lord for deliverance ("salvation") from his persecutors and, in the meantime, makes sure he obeys God's commandments. In the last two verses of this stanza, the psalmist gives two reasons why he is obedient.

"My soul keeps Your testimonies and I love them exceedingly" (119:167). One of the reasons for his obedience is his love for God's Word (see "love" in verses 163 and 167).

"I keep Your precepts and Your testimonies, for all my ways were before You" (119:168). Another reason for his obedience is that he is aware that God sees all that he does.

To sum up: the psalmist is being persecuted without a cause (verse 161), but because he knew from God's Word that there would be a just judgment (verse 164), he stands in awe of the Word (verse 161), rejoices in the Word (verse 162), loves the Word (verse 163, 167), is obedient to the Word (verses 166, 167, 168), praises God all day long, and, consequently, has the peace of God in the midst of persecution.

Summary: When persecuted without a cause for being obedient to the Word of God, praise God all day, remember there will be just judgment in the end, and make sure you're being obedient to the Word of God.

A point to ponder: Jesus said, "Blessed are you when they revile and persecute you and say all kinds of evil against you falsely for my sake. Rejoice and be exceedingly glad for great is your reward in heaven, for so they persecuted the prophets who were before you" (Mt. 5:11-12).

Psalm 119:169-176: When You Spiritually Go Astray

Psalm 119:169-176 is another stanza in a long acrostic (all of Ps. 119). Each verse begins with the Hebrew letter *tau* (English t). In this stanza, the psalmist confesses that he has spiritually gone astray (119:176).

The Prayer of the Psalmist (119:169-170) "Let my cry come before you, O Lord; give me understanding according to Your word" (119:169). The psalmist requests that the Lord hear his prayer and give him an understanding of the Word. To be more specific, he says, "Let my supplication come before You; deliver me according to Your word" (119:170). In other words, the request that God hear his prayer (verse 169) is a request for deliverance according to the promise of God (verse 170).

The Promise of the Psalmist (169:171-172) As a result of understanding the Word of God and being delivered by the hand of God, the psalmist promises, "My lips shall utter praise, for You teach me Your statutes" (169:171). One of the things God taught him from the Word was that the commandments in the Word are righteous. Therefore, the psalmist says, "My tongue shall speak of Your word, for all Your commandments are righteous" (169:172).

The Plea of the Psalmist (119:173-175) The psalmist pleads for God's help (verses 173, 175), deliverance (verse 174), and restoration (verse 176).

"Let Your hand become my help, for I have chosen Your precepts" (119:173). Having chosen to be obedient to God's Word, the psalmist needs God's help to do it.

"I long for Your salvation, O Lord, and Your law is my delight" (119:174). The psalmist longs for and patiently waits for God's deliverance ("salvation") and, in the meantime, he delights in God's Word.

"Let my soul live, and it shall praise You; and let Your judgments help me" (119:175). The psalmist pleads with God to preserve his life so that he can praise Him and again asks for God's help, which comes from God's Word (verse 175) and from God's power (verse 173).

"I have gone astray like a lost sheep; seek Your servant, for I have not forgotten Your commandments" (119:176). Even though the psalmist had wandered away like a lost sheep, he had not forgotten God's commandments. So he asked God to seek him like a Shepherd looking for a lost lamb.

It has been pointed out that in this stanza, the Word affects the mind (verse 169), the mouth (verses 171, 172), the will (verse 173), the emotions (verse 174), and the conscience (verse 176; The Ryrie Study Bible).

Summary: When you spiritually go astray, ask the Lord to give you an understanding of His Word and help you do what it says, and praise when He answers that prayer.

A point to ponder: It is possible not to forget the Word (verse 176) and yet need an understanding of it (verse 169) and help to do it (verse 173).

As has been repeatedly pointed out, Psalm 119 is an acrostic. The psalmist has selected words in the order of the Hebrew alphabet to express various aspects of life, including adversaries and affliction. He shows how the Word is relevant to every area of life and how essential it is to delight in, meditate on, and obey the Word.

Psalm 120: When You Are Living Among Liars

Psalm 120 is an ascent psalm written by an unknown author. The ascent psalms (120-134, see also 84) were songs sung by pilgrims ascending to Jerusalem for the annual feasts of Passover, Pentecost, and Tabernacles. In Psalm 120, the psalmist lives among liars (120:2-3, 5), who stir up strife (120:6-7) before he journeys to Jerusalem.

A Prayer for Deliverance (120:1-2) "In my distress, I cried to the Lord and He heard me" (120:1). The psalmist begins by saying the Lord answered his prayer. The content of the prayer is given in the next verse, where the psalmist says, "Deliver my soul, O Lord, from lying lips and from a deceitful tongue" (120:2). The Lord answered the psalmist's prayer for deliverance from the lying lips of slander.

Prayer for Destruction (120:3-4) The psalmist asks, "What should be given to you, or what should be done to you, you false tongue?" (120:3). What should be given or what should be done to a lying tongue meaning, of course, a lying person?

The psalmist answers his own question: "Sharp arrows of the warrior, with coals of the broom tree" (120:4). The possessor of a lying tongue should be destroyed. The destruction is described as being hit by the warrior's sharp arrows, which would be deadly, or being burned by the charcoal made from the broom tree, which would burn hot and long.

Prayer for Peace (120:5-7) The psalmist laments, "Woe is me, that I dwell in Meshech, that I dwell among the tents of Kedar!" (120:5). Meshech was a son of Japheth (Gen. 10:2). His descendants, known as a savage, uncivilized people, settled north of Israel (Ezek. 39:1–2). Kedar was the second son of Ishmael (Gen. 25:13). His posterity, also known as a cruel and merciless people, settled in northern Arabia. Both were renowned for their warlike ways. As the psalmist explains, "My soul has dwelt too long with one who hates peace" (120:6). These liars (120:2-3) hated peace; they loved strife (120:6).

The psalmist is not saying he lived in these places. He says he lived with people, perhaps in a Gentile land, like people from these places. He lived among liars, who were barbarians and savages. In contrast to them, the psalmist says, "I am for peace; but when I speak, they are for war" (120:7).

The peace-loving psalmist, who lived among people who hated peace, is singing this song on his way to Jerusalem, the city of peace, where he could pray for peace (122:6).

Summary: When you live among liars who love strife, pray for your deliverance and their destruction and pray for and seek peace.

A point to ponder: God puts a premium on peace. So much so that a believer who is married to an unbeliever who wants a divorce is to let the unbeliever go because "God has called us to peace" (1 Cor. 7:15). Paul said, "If it is possible, as much as depends on you, live peaceably with all men" (Rom. 12:18).

Psalm 121: When You Travel

Psalm 121 is an ascent psalm written by an unknown author. The ascent psalms (120-134, see also 84) were songs sung by pilgrims ascending to Jerusalem for the annual feasts of Passover, Pentecost, and Tabernacles. In Psalm 121, the psalmist describes the protection he receives from the Lord (21:3, 5, 7) as he travels to Jerusalem.

The Source of Help (121:1-2) "I will lift up my eyes to the hills—from whence comes my help?" As the psalmist draws near to Jerusalem, he lifts his eyes to the hills on which Jerusalem and the Temple are built, and asks, "From whence comes my help?" He answers his own question, saying, "My help comes from the Lord, who made heaven and earth" (121:2). He declares that his help comes from the Creator of the universe. As Creator, the Lord is in control.

The Nature of the Help (121:3-8) Having experienced the Lord's help (121:2), the psalmist now turns his attention to Israel (note the change from "my" in verse 2 to "your" and "you" in the remainder of the Psalm, and see "Israel" in verse 4). He informs Israel, "He will not allow your foot to be moved; He who keeps you will not slumber" (121:3). Traveling over treacherous terrain, the danger was the foot would slip and the traveler would fall, but God will not allow your foot to be moved; He will protect you from falling. Furthermore, He does not slumber. To emphasize this point, the psalmist adds, "Behold He who keeps Israel shall never slumber nor sleep" (121:4). He is always on the job and alert; He does not slumber (momentarily doze off), nor does He sleep soundly. The nature of God's help is protecting His people and He is on the job day and night.

At this point, the psalmist continues the same subject of protection (see "keeper" in verse 5), but changes the figure of speech to communicate it. He says, "The Lord is your keeper; the Lord is your shade at your right hand" (21:5). As a tree protects from the burning sun, so the Lord protects His people. Hence, the psalmist can say, "The sun shall not strike you by day, nor the moon by night" (121:6). Again, the point is God's help is protecting His people day and night.

The psalmist concludes by stating his point without an additional figure of speech. He simply says, "The Lord shall preserve you from all evil; he shall preserve your soul" (121:7). The Hebrew word translated "evil" means "bad, evil, distress, injury, misery." It is evil in the sense of "giving pain, unhappiness, misery" (BDB; the Hebrew lexicon). This Psalm probably refers to dangers on the road (see verses 3 and 6). The Hebrew word translated "soul" means "life" (NIV; ESV). This is the same point he has made several times in this short psalm: the Lord will protect and preserve His people. He adds, "The Lord shall preserve your going out and your coming in from this time forth and for evermore" (121:8). In every circumstance of life ("going out" and "coming in;" outdoors and indoors), the Lord will protect His people—forever.

Summary: When you travel, trust the Lord for His protection, which He gives to His people perpetually.

A point to ponder: When you get on an airplane, in a car, or out of bed, ask the Lord for "journeying mercies."

As someone has pointed out, believers can trust the Lord for protection from the perils of the pilgrimage, for He is not too great to care, nor are we too insignificant to be noticed.

Psalm 122: When Praying for the City

Psalm 122 is an ascent psalm written by David. The ascent psalms (120-134, see also 84) were songs sung by pilgrims ascending to Jerusalem for the annual feasts of Passover, Pentecost, and Tabernacles. In Psalm 122, the psalmist is in Jerusalem (122:2), praying for the city (122:6).

The Pleasure of the Psalmist (122:1-2) The songs of ascent to Jerusalem began with Psalm 120. In that Psalm, the psalmist laments where he is before the journey. In it, he expresses a desire for peace (120:7). In the next Psalm, the psalmist is on the journey to Jerusalem (121:1). In this psalm, he has arrived in Jerusalem after the journey. He says, "Our feet have been standing within your gates, O Jerusalem" (122:2). Now he says, "I was glad when they said to me, 'Let us go into the house of the Lord'" (122:1). Once at Jerusalem, he expresses the pleasure of entering the Temple ("house of the Lord"). Going to Jerusalem was not just a duty; it was a delight. There is a stark contrast between the lament of Psalm 120 and the joy of Psalm 122. It is the before and after of being in the house of the Lord.

The Praise of Jerusalem (122:3-5) "Jerusalem is built as a city that is compact together" (122:3). This is the city that unifies ("compact together") the people of Israel. There was a sense of community there. Jerusalem is "where the tribes go up, the tribes of the LORD, to the testimony of Israel, to give thanks to the name of the Lord" (122:4). The people of Israel went to the Temple of God in Jerusalem to give thanks to Him. The psalmist explains ("for") "For thrones are set there for judgment, the thrones of the house of David" (122:5). One of the reasons for the praise of Jerusalem and the thanksgiving of the people is that the throne of David is in Jerusalem.

The Prayer for Jerusalem (122:6-9) The psalmist exhorts, "Pray for the peace of Jerusalem; may they prosper who love you" (122:6). He exhorts the people of Israel to pray for the security of Jerusalem so that they who love her can continue to enjoy her. Then he desires peace for those who love Jerusalem and those who live in Jerusalem. He says, "Peace be within your walls, prosperity within your palaces" (122:7). He desires peace and prosperity for the residents of Jerusalem. "For the sake of my brethren and companions, I will now say, 'Peace *be* within you'" (122:8). The reason he seeks peace for the residents of Jerusalem is, "Because of the house of the Lord our God I will seek your good" (122:9). He sought the good (peace and prosperity) of the people of Jerusalem because the Temple was there.

Summary: When praying for the city, especially the city of Jerusalem (but not only the city of Jerusalem; 1 Tim. 2:1-2), pray for the peace and prosperity of the people.

A point to ponder: Today, to pray for the peace of Jerusalem is to pray for the return of Christ because there will be no peace in Jerusalem until the Prince of Peace comes (Rev. 22:20). We should also pray for churches to have peace so they will prosper.

Psalm 123: When You Are Treated with Contempt

Psalm 123 is an ascent psalm written by an unknown author. The ascent psalms (120-134, see also 84) were songs sung by pilgrims ascending to Jerusalem for the annual feasts of Passover, Pentecost, and Tabernacles. In Psalm 123, the psalmist and others were treated with contempt (123:3-4).

Prayer for Mercy (123:1-2) "Unto You I lift my eyes, O You who dwell in the heavens" (123:1). This is an ascent psalm; the psalmist is on his way to Jerusalem. Jerusalem contained the Temple, considered to be the dwelling place of God. Yet the Israelites knew that God did not live in a man-made building; He dwelt in the heavens as the sovereign over the earth. The psalmist lifts his eyes up because God is in heaven and also as an expression of looking to God to meet his need, which he expresses in verse 2.

"Behold, as the eyes of servants look to the hand of their masters, as the eyes of a maid to the hand of her mistress, so our eyes look to the Lord our God, until He has mercy on us" (123:2). As slaves and maids looked to the hand of their masters and mistresses to supply all of their needs, so the people of God look to Him for mercy (verse 3) until He gives it (verse 2).

Reason for Mercy (123:13-4) "Have mercy on us, O Lord, have mercy on us! For we are exceedingly filled with contempt" (123:3). The psalmist asks for mercy and gives the reason ("for") for the request, namely, that he and others are filled with contempt. The Hebrew word translated "contempt" means "contempt" (BDB), "despised" (Strong). The Israelites were being exceedingly despised, probably because of their trust in the Lord.

The psalmist adds, "Our soul is exceedingly filled with the scorn of those who are at ease, with the contempt of the proud" (123:4). He further describes their experience is being filled with scorn. The Hebrew word translated "scorn" means "mocking, derision" (BDB), "scoffing, scorn" (Strong). The contempt (verse 3) was the attitude; the mocking and scorning was the action (verse 4). In both cases, there was an abundant amount of it (see "exceedingly" in verses 3 and 4).

Who were the people treating the Israelites with such contempt and scorn? The psalmist says two things about them. They were proud and they were at ease. The psalmist and others were making the long, hard trip over tough terrain to Jerusalem while proud pagans were comfortable at home mocking them. The Israelites were being ridiculed for their religious practice of going to Jerusalem.

Summary: When treated with contempt and being mocked for your faith, ask God for mercy.

A point to ponder: It should come as no surprise that believers are despised, criticized, ridiculed, and mocked for following the Lord because He said, "In the world, you will have tribulation" (Jn. 16:33). In that same verse He also said, "Be of good cheer, I have overcome the world" and "in Me, you may have peace" (Jn. 16:33).

Psalm 124: When You Are Delivered from Annihilation

Psalm 124 is an ascent psalm written by David. The ascent psalms (120-134, see also 84) were songs sung by pilgrims ascending to Jerusalem for the annual feasts of Passover, Pentecost, and Tabernacles. In Psalm 124, Israel has been delivered from annihilation (124:3, 4-5).

The Nature of the Deliverance (124:1-5) David declares, "If it had not been the Lord who was on our side" (124:1a). As the rest of the psalm indicates, Israel had been delivered from extinction. The deliverance was of such a nature that only the Lord could have done it.

"Let Israel now say, 'If it had not been the Lord who was on our side'" (124:1b-2a). This is an antiphonal psalm (a verse sung responsively). The deliverance was not from some natural disaster; it was from men attacking Israel. The point is that the Lord delivered Israel from a dire situation that only He could have done.

Using several figures of speech, David describes just how dangerous the situation was. For example, he says, "Then they would have swallowed us alive when their wrath was kindled against us" (124:3). The Hebrew word translated "swallowed" is the one that was used of the earth opening up and swallowing people alive (Num. 16:30). When Israel's enemy was filled with wrath and came at them with overwhelming force, they would have been annihilated had it not been for the Lord's intervention.

Using another figure of speech, David says, "Then the waters would have overwhelmed us, the stream would have gone over our soul" (124:4). Israel's angry enemy came at them like a torrent of water that would have drowned them had the Lord not intervened. To emphasize the point, David repeats it. "Then the swollen waters would have gone over our soul" (124:5).

Praise for the Deliverance (124:6-8) "Blessed be the Lord, who has not given us as prey to their teeth" (124:6). David is praising the Lord for not allowing Israel's angry enemy to tear her to pieces like a vicious animal tears its prey with its teeth.

Changing the figure of speech, David says, "Our soul has escaped as a bird from the snare of the fowlers; the snare is broken and we have escaped" (124:7). David is praising the Lord for allowing Israel to escape the trap laid by their enemy. It was as if they had been in a trap, like a trap set for a bird, but because of the Lord's intervention, they were able to escape the trap.

David concludes by saying plainly, "Our help is in the name of the Lord, who made heaven and earth" (124:8). Their help came not from a human deliverer but from the Divine Deliverer, who is the Creator of heaven and earth and, thus, controls all things.

Summary: When delivered from annihilation, praise God for His deliverance, who delivers as only He can.

A point to ponder: When we face the annihilation of our life, our marriage, our job, etc., the Lord is able to deliver us when no one else can.

Psalm 125: When You Contemplate Your Security

Psalm 125 is an ascent psalm written by an unknown author. The ascent psalms (120-134, see also 84) were songs sung by pilgrims ascending to Jerusalem for the feasts of Passover, Pentecost, and Tabernacles. In Psalm 125, the psalmist contemplates his security (125:1).

The Protection of the Believers (125:1-3) "Those who trust the Lord are like Mount Zion, which cannot be moved, but abides forever" (125:1). Assuming that Jerusalem ("Mount Zion") is invincible and eternal, the psalmist compares believers to Jerusalem. Like Jerusalem, they cannot be moved and abide forever. Believers are eternally secure. Then he adds another comparison to Jerusalem, saying, "As the mountains surround Jerusalem, so the Lord surrounds His people from this time forth and evermore" (125:2). As the *mountains* surrounding Jerusalem provided protection from their enemies, so the *Lord* forever surrounds His people to protect them.

In short, the Lord secures and protects believers.

To say the same thing another way, "For the scepter of wickedness shall not rest on the land allotted to the righteous, lest the righteous reach out their hands to iniquity" (125:3). The expression "the scepter of wickedness" refers to the power of wickedness. As God promised to protect Israel from their enemies, as long as they obeyed Him, those who trusted the Lord (verse 1) and followed righteousness (verse 3) are protected from wickedness. God protects them lest they be tempted with iniquity. Notice that the righteous can reach out their hand to iniquity, which is why they need the Lord's protection.

In short, the protection provided by the Lord is protection from sin.

The Prayer of Believers (125:4-5) "Do good, O Lord, to those who are good and to those who are upright in their hearts" (125:4). The Lord has protected those who trust Him (verse 1) and live righteously (verse 3), so now the psalmist asks the Lord to bless them. Notice that their righteousness is internal ("upright in their hearts"), not just obedience to external rituals.

The psalmist adds, "As for such as turned aside to their crooked ways, the Lord shall lead them away with the workers of iniquity" (125:5a). Believers have a choice. They can trust the Lord, live righteously, and be blessed by the Lord, or they can turn aside to their wicked ways and the Lord will treat them the same way he treats the workers of iniquity. In other words, he will judge them. They are eternally secure (verse 1); they will never cease to be His people, but the Lord will judge them if they sin.

The psalmist concludes, "Peace be upon Israel!" (125:5b; see 121:6). One of the blessings of the Lord (see "do good, O Lord" in verse 4) is peace.

Summary: When you contemplate your security, remember that even though you are eternally secure, it is still possible for you to sin and if you do, God will judge you.

A point to ponder: Those who are trusting the Lord (verse 5) and living righteously (verse 3) can still be tempted (verse 3, 5).

One commentator says, "The psalmist praised God, saying that believers are secure in their salvation and that God will keep temptation from overwhelming them. However, he cautioned God's people to follow the Lord faithfully or lose His blessing for living as unbelievers do." He adds, "Those who trust in the Lord are eternally secure, but they can choose to follow Him faithfully and experience His blessing or depart from Him and suffer His discipline" (Tom Constable).

Psalm 126: When You are Restored #1

Psalm 126 is an ascent psalm written by an unknown author. The ascent psalms (120-134, see also 84) were songs sung by pilgrims ascending to Jerusalem for the annual feasts of Passover, Pentecost, and Tabernacles. In Psalm 126, the psalmist rejoices over being restored to Palestine (126:1; see Ps. 147).

Rejoicing over Restoration (126:1-3) "When the Lord brought back the captivity of Zion, we were like those who dream" (126:1). The author is among those who returned from the captivity in Babylon to Palestine. Acknowledging that the Lord made it all possible, the psalmist says coming back was so wonderful, marvelous, and exciting that it seemed like a dream rather than reality. It felt like it was too good to be true. They had not expected to see it.

"Then our mouth was filled with laughter and our tongue with singing" (126:2a). They were so happy they spontaneously laughed and sang songs of joy.

"Then they said among the nations, 'The Lord has done great things for them'" (126:2b). The people among whom they dwelt ("they") acknowledged that the Lord had done great things for them. This is significant because Cyrus, humanly speaking, gave them permission to return, but the people recognized that it was the Lord's doing.

The psalmist sums up the situation by saying, "The Lord has done great things for us and we are glad" (126:3). The great thing the Lord has done is bring them back from the "captivity of Zion" (verse 1). Their gladness is the overwhelming joy at returning to their homeland.

Request for Restoration (126:4) "Bring back our captivity, O Lord, as the streams in the South" (126:4). The South is a reference to the desert. In the summer, it was a dry, parched land, but during the rainy season, the streams were filled with raging torrents of water. Like those streams filled with water, the psalmist requests that the Lord bring back a flood of people from Babylon.

The Rule for Restoration (126:5-6) The exiles have returned and there is rejoicing (verse 1), but the restoration is not complete even for those who have made it back to the land. They must rebuild the homeland. It will be difficult, but it will be worth it. Hence the psalmist says, "Those who sow in tears shall reap in joy" (126:5). Farmers sow their crops in tears; the joy comes at harvest when they see the fruit of their tearful toil. Likewise, the restored Israelites will experience the tearful toil of reestablishing the homeland but will be joyful when it is done.

As he explains, "He who continually goes forth weeping, bearing seed for sowing, shall doubtless come again with rejoicing, bringing his sheaves with him" (126:6). They went forth weeping to Babylon. They have been restored. Now they must continually reap (toil) and continually sow to reconstruct the homeland and if they do, there is no doubt that there will be future rejoicing when they see the fruit of their labor. It is the law of reaping and sowing.

Summary: When you are restored to fellowship after wandering away from the Lord, rejoice, sing, pray for others who also need restoration, and go to work, toiling to rebuild your spiritual life and being assured that you will experience even more joy when you see the results.

A point to ponder: As joyful and exciting as restoration is, it is not the end; it is the beginning of the sometimes slow, hard, and discouraging work of rebuilding a spiritual life.

Psalm 127: When You Work Hard

Psalm 127 is an ascent psalm written by Solomon. The ascent psalms (120-134, see also 84) were songs sung by pilgrims ascending to Jerusalem for the annual feasts of Passover, Pentecost, and Tabernacles. In Psalm 127, Solomon talks about hard work with or without the Lord (127:2).

Dependence on the Lord (127:1-2) "Unless the Lord builds the house, they labor in vain who built it; unless the Lord guards the city, the watchmen stay awake in vain" (127:1). Three times in the first two verses, Solomon uses the word "vain." The Hebrew word translated "vain" means "emptiness, vanity, worthlessness." Building a house and guarding the city are worthless without the Lord's help. Their effort might not succeed because of a natural disaster (earthquake or a fire) or human destruction (an enemy attacking the city). The builder and the guard must depend upon the Lord for strength, health, and even life itself.

Solomon adds, "It is vain for you to rise up early, to sit up late, to eat the bread of sorrows; for so He gives His beloved sleep" (127:2). The Hebrew word translated "sorrows" means "pain, toil, hardship." Without the Lord's blessing, working hard from early morning till late at night is worthless. It is only earning a living by toil. On the other hand, the Lord gives sleep to His beloved people who trust Him while they work hard.

It is futile to be a house-builder, a city guard, or a hard worker without depending on the Lord. Jesus said, "Without Me, you can do nothing" (Jn. 15:5). Without dependence upon the Lord, believers cannot accomplish anything of spiritual, permanent, or eternal value.

The Blessing of the Lord (127:3-5) "Behold, children are a heritage from the Lord, the fruit of the womb is a reward" (127:3). Life's greatest blessings are gifts from God. The ancient Israelites were promised that one of the blessings of obeying the Lord was children (Deut. 28:4), which does not apply to believers because they are not under the Law (Rom. 6:14), but the principle does apply. Those who trust the Lord and obey His Word are blessed by the Lord (Jas. 1:25).

Using a figure of speech, Solomon explains part of the blessing of having children. "Like arrows in the hand of a warrior, so are the children of one's youth" (127:4). As arrows in the hands of a warrior defend against an enemy attack, so children born to people when they are young have someone to protect them when they are old. In ancient Israel, adult children cared for their parents in their old age.

Thus, "Happy is the man who has his quiver full of them; they shall not be ashamed but shall speak with their enemies in the gate" (127:5). A man with a number of children is happy because his children will distinguish themselves ("not be ashamed") in protecting not only their family but also their city.

Summary: When you work hard depending on the Lord, you are blessed with benefits that hard work alone cannot provide.

A point to ponder: The two possibilities presented in this psalm are doing something with or without the Lord. In both cases, the job gets done. The house gets built. The city gets guarded. The hard-working labor eats bread. Without the Lord, it is ultimately in vain. With the Lord, people are blessed with things money cannot buy.

Psalm 128: When You Reflect on Happiness

Psalm 128 is an ascent psalm written by an unknown author. The ascent psalms (120-134, see also 84) were songs sung by pilgrims ascending to Jerusalem for the annual feasts of Passover, Pentecost, and Tabernacles. In Psalm 128, the psalmist reflects on happiness (128:1, 4).

The Path to Happiness (128:1) "Blessed is everyone who fears the Lord, who walks in His ways" (128:1). The Hebrew word translated "blessed" means "happy" (see 1:1). The expression "the fear of the Lord" refers to those who know the Lord, reverence the Lord, and are afraid of the Lord when they are disobedient. Those who reverence the Lord and obey Him are happy.

The Particulars of Happiness (128:2-4) "When you eat the labor of your hands, you shall be happy and it shall be well with you" (128:2). The man ("you" in verse 2 refers to a man because verse 3 speaks of his wife) who walks in the ways of the Lord will be happy in his work and it will be well with him. The Hebrew word translated "well" means "good, pleasant, agreeable." He will enjoy his work and think life is good.

"Your wife shall be like a fruitful vine in the very heart of her house, your children like olive plants all around the table" (128:3). The man who walks in the way of the Lord shall be happy at home. His wife will bear children, which is one of the blessings of the Lord (127:3-5). The children sitting at the table are like olive plants, which are precious and will be productive.

"Behold thus shall the man be blessed who fears the Lord" (128:5). The point he made at the beginning (verse 1) and the point of this subsection (verses 1-4) is repeated, namely, the man who fears the Lord will be happy.

In this passage, the happy man is sitting at the table (verses 2, 3) with his family. This is one of the ascent psalms, one of the songs sung as people were going to one of the festivals in Jerusalem. During those festivals, the whole family gathered in Jerusalem. So it is not surprising to find the family at the table in this Psalm. It would be like the family gathering around the table at Thanksgiving or Christmas.

Prayer for Happiness (128:5-6) "The Lord bless you out of Zion, and may you see the good of Jerusalem all the days of your life" (128:5). At this point, the psalmist turns his attention from himself (verse 2) and his family (verse 3) to others outside his family. He prays that the Lord will bless them out of His Temple in Jerusalem ("out of Zion"). The Hebrew word translated "bless" in this verse is different than the one translated "bless" in verse 1. This one means to "bless." The blessing he desires for others includes seeing Jerusalem prosper all the days of their lives. He adds, "Yes, may you see your children's children" (120:6a). Seeing one's grandchildren is an indication of a long life. In other words, he prays that the people of Israel would see the goodness of Jerusalem all their lives (verse 5) and that their lives may be long (verse 6a). May the Lord bless Israel for many years to come. He concludes, "Peace be upon Israel!" (128:6b). The psalmist desires the blessing of the Lord on all of Israel.

Summary: When you reflect on happiness, you realize that when people walk in the ways of the Lord, they are happy in their personal and family lives, and you pray that the Lord will bless others.

A point to ponder: When we walk in the ways of the Lord, it affects not only us but also our family and others outside our family.

Psalm 129: When You Suffer a Severe Attack

Psalm 129 is an ascent psalm written by an unknown author. The ascent psalms (120-134, see also 84) were songs sung by pilgrims ascending to Jerusalem for the annual feasts of Passover, Pentecost, and Tabernacles. In Psalm 129, the psalmist is severely attacked (129:3, 5).

The Past Deliverance of Israel (129:1-4) Israel had been afflicted. The psalmist says, "Many a time they have afflicted me from my youth" (129:1a). The psalmist is not speaking about himself; he is speaking for Israel (see "Let Israel now say" in verse 1 and "Zion" in verse 5). Throughout their history ("from my youth"), they had often ("many times") suffered affliction. Then the psalmist says, "Let Israel now say, 'Many a time they have afflicted me from my youth'" (129:1b-2a). This is an antiphonal psalm (a verse sung responsively).

Israel had been delivered. The psalmist goes on to say, "Yet they have not prevailed against me" (129:2b). They had been afflicted and delivered many times.

Israel had been severely afflicted. "The plowers plowed on my back; they made their furrows long" (129:3). "Israel is pictured as a scourged man with welts on his back like *furrows* in a plowed field" (Ryrie Study Bible, italics his). For agricultural people, this was a vivid figure of speech of severe, brutal affliction.

Israel had been delivered. "The Lord is righteous; He has cut in pieces the cords of the wicked" (129:4). The cords may be a reference to the reins of the plowman (verse 3) or the cords may be another figure of speech indicating that Israel was bound. At any rate, the righteous Lord cut the cords; He delivered them.

The Present Deliverance of Israel (129:5-8) The prayer of the psalmist is, "Let all those who hate Zion be put to shame and turned back" (129:5). Pilgrims sang this song on their way to Jerusalem (Zion), the place where the Lord dwelt. Thus, those who hate Zion are also haters of the Lord. The prayer of the psalmist is that these haters would be put to shame and turned back from defeating Jerusalem. In other words, he prays that Israel would be delivered from them.

"Let them be as the grass on the housetop, which withers before it grows up" (129:6). In ancient Israel, the soil was on the top of some of the houses. After a spring rain, grass might begin to grow in the soil on the housetop, but it would wither under the summer heat. The prayer is that Israel's enemy would wither like the short-lived grass on a rooftop.

Continuing the figure of speech of grass, the psalmist says, "With which the reaper does not fill his hand, nor he who binds sheaves his arms" (129:7). May the grass wither (verse 6); may there not be enough grass for a reaper to have a handful nor enough for sheaves. In short, Israel would be delivered from her enemy.

Continuing the figure of speech of reaping, the psalmist says, "Neither let those who pass by them say, 'The blessing of the Lord be upon you; we bless you in the name of the Lord!'" (129:8). People passing a harvest field ("them"), where the reapers were reaping an abundant crop, express their congratulations by saying, "The blessing of the Lord be upon you." The psalmist says that the many enemies of Israel should be denied such a greeting. Instead, may they experience a crop failure. In other words, may Israel be delivered from their enemies.

Summary: When severely attacked, remember the Lord has delivered you in the past, so pray for the destruction of your enemy in the present.

A point to ponder: When being treated wrongly, remember the righteous Lord.

Psalm 130: When You Are Forgiven

Psalm 130 is an ascent psalm written by an unknown author. The ascent psalms (120-134, see also 84) were songs sung by pilgrims ascending to Jerusalem for the annual feasts of Passover, Pentecost, and Tabernacles. In Psalm 130, the psalmist discusses forgiveness (130:4, 7, 8).

An Entreaty for Forgiveness (130:1-4) "Out of the depths I have cried to you, O Lord" (130:1). Out of the depths of despair, the psalmist prays. First, he asks, "Lord, hear my voice! Let your ear be attentive to the voice of my supplication" (130:2). This prayer is an earnest plea for the Lord to hear him.

Then he asks, "If you, Lord, should mark iniquities, O Lord, who could stand?" (130:3). If the Lord kept a record of sin ("mark iniquities") and gave people what they deserve, who would survive ("stand")? The answer is no one.

Next, he says, "But there is forgiveness with You, that You may be feared" (130:4). People survived because the Lord forgives. As a result of the Lord's forgiveness, the forgiven will fear Him. The expression "the fear of the Lord" refers to those who know the Lord, reverence the Lord, and are afraid of the Lord when they are disobedient.

An Expectation of Forgiveness (130:5-6) The psalmist expects the Lord to forgive. So he says, "I wait for the Lord, my soul waits, and in His word do I hope" (130:5). He is confident that he will be forgiven because of the promise of forgiveness in God's Word. He trusts God's promise of forgiveness.

To emphasize the point of verse 4, he repeats it and expands it in verses 5-6. "My soul waits for the Lord more than those who watch for the morning, yes more than those who watch for the morning" (130:6). He eagerly and enthusiastically waits for the Lord's forgiveness as watchmen look for the dawn when other guards will relieve them.

An Exhortation to Trust the Lord (130:7-8) Assured of forgiveness, the psalmist exhorts Israel to seek forgiveness. "O Israel hope in the Lord; for with the Lord there is mercy, and with Him is abundant redemption" (130:7). Israel is encouraged to trust the Lord because He is merciful and because His redemption is abundant, meaning it is limitless. The psalmist is confident the Lord will forgive Israel. He says, "And He shall redeem Israel from all his iniquities" (130:8). God's redemption is so abundant (verse 7) that He redeems from *all* iniquities (verse 8).

Summary: When forgiven, tell others about God's abundant mercy and forgiveness.

A point to ponder: We can be assured of God's forgiveness, not because of our merit, but because of His mercy, not because of our performance, but because of His promise to forgive all iniquities.

Psalm 131: When You Trust the Lord

Psalm 131 is an ascent psalm written by David. The ascent psalms (120-134, see also 84) were songs sung by pilgrims ascending to Jerusalem for the annual feasts of Passover, Pentecost, and Tabernacles. In Psalm 131, David describes trusting the Lord (131:2).

Confession of Humility (131:1) "Lord, my heart is not haughty, nor my eyes lofty, neither do I concern myself with great matters, nor things too profound for me" (131:1). David tells the Lord he has a humble heart ("my heart is not haughty") and gives three indications of it.

His eyes are not lofty. A lofty look is an indication of a proud heart. It reveals an attitude of superiority that looks down on people.

He does not concern himself with great matters, meaning he does not take on projects that are beyond his ability.

He does not concern himself with things that are too profound for him. He recognized that some things were beyond his ability to explain; they were too profound. There are mysteries in life that defy explanation, such as why a young person dies in an accident. He was willing to say, "I don't know."

Proud people have an attitude of superiority. They think they know everything and can do just about anything. Humble people have a realistic view of themselves and they recognize their limitations. In the final analysis, pride and humility are spiritual issues. The proud are self-sufficient. In their opinion, they don't need God. The humble realize who they are before God.

The Claim of Trust (131:2) "Surely I have calmed and quieted my soul, like a weaned child with his mother; like a weaned child is my soul within me" (131:2). David is saying he is like a child who, after being restless, is now relaxed in his mother's arms. It is a picture of the contentment that comes from trust. Trust replaced tension. Trust has produced peace and contentment. "The ability to rest and be quiet rather than struggling for what we want is a sign of maturity as well as humility" (Constable).

The Call for Hope (131:3) "O Israel, hope in the Lord from this time forth and forever" (131:3). Having experienced what trusting in the Lord will do, David calls upon Israel to trust the Lord now and forever. He exhorts them to follow his example.

Summary: When you trust the Lord with a humble heart, you experience contentment and a desire to tell others to do the same.

A point to ponder: "Therefore humble yourselves under the mighty hand of God, that He may exalt you in due time, casting all your care upon Him, for He cares for you" (1 Pet. 5:6-7).

Psalm 132: When You Contemplate God's Covenant

Psalm 132 is an ascent psalm written by an unknown author. The ascent psalms (120-134, see also 84) were songs sung by pilgrims ascending to Jerusalem for the annual feasts of Passover, Pentecost, and Tabernacles. In Psalm 132, the psalmist contemplates God's covenant (132:11).

The Requests (132:1-10) "Lord, remember David and all of his afflictions" (132:1). The psalmist requests that the Lord remember David's affliction in finding a place for the Ark of the Covenant to dwell. He explains that David vowed (132:2) he would not sleep (132:3-4) until he "found a place for the Lord, a dwelling place for the Mighty One of Jacob" (132:5). The Lord dwelt in the Ark of the Covenant. David swore he would not rest until he found a place for the Ark to rest.

The people heard of it (the Ark, see verses 5, 8) in Ephrathah, another name for Bethlehem and they found it in "fields of the woods" (132:6). The Hebrew word translated "woods" (*jear*) is the same word that is used in the name of the town Kirjath Jearim, a town about 10 miles northwest of Bethlehem. The Philistines took the Ark and it rested in Kirjath Jearim for 20 years (1 Sam. 7:1-2). David moved it to Zion (Jerusalem; 2 Sam. 6:1-23).

Now the pilgrims on the way to Jerusalem sing, "Let us go into His tabernacle; let us worship at His footstool" (132:7). God's throne is in heaven; His footstool is Jerusalem (99:5). They request the Lord to arise (132:8), to clothe the priests with righteousness (132:8), to let the saints shout for joy because of His blessing (132:9), and, for David's sake, not turn away the face of His favor on David's successors who sit on the throne (132:10).

The Response (132:11-18) "The Lord has sworn in truth to David; He will not turn from it; 'I will set upon your throne the fruit of your body'" (132:11). The Lord will not forget His covenant with David; one of David's descendants will sit upon David's throne. The Davidic covenant was both unconditional and conditional. The unconditional promise of God was a descendant of David would sit on the throne of David, a promise ultimately fulfilled in the Messiah, Jesus Christ. Nevertheless, the covenant had a conditional aspect concerning individuals coming after David. Thus, the Lord says that if David's sons are obedient, they will sit on the throne (132:12).

Furthermore, "The Lord has (also) chosen Zion (Jerusalem); He has desired it for His resting place" (132:13) forever (132:14). The Lord will not only dwell in Jerusalem, He will abundantly bless her, including satisfying her poor with the food (132:15) and clothing her priests with righteousness (132:16a). Her saints shall shout for joy (132:16b). The Lord will make the horn (strength) of David grow and He will prepare a lamp (guidance) for His anointed (132:17). His enemies will be clothed with shame, but His crown (rule) shall flourish (132:18). These promises were partially fulfilled in some of the descendants of David who followed him on the throne of Israel, but they will ultimately be fulfilled in the coming of the Messiah, Jesus Christ.

Summary: When contemplating God's covenant, remember that God will fulfill His promises. For example, the covenant He made with David will be fulfilled.

A point to ponder: There are unconditional and conditional elements in God's covenant. God's covenant with believers today is unconditional (believers are eternally secure), but there are conditional aspects to it (believers are blessed as they obey).

Psalm 133: When You Contemplate Living in Unity

Psalm 133 is an ascent psalm written by David. The ascent psalms (120-134, see also 84) were songs sung by pilgrims ascending to Jerusalem for the annual feasts of Passover, Pentecost, and Tabernacles. In Psalm 133, David contemplates living in unity with the brethren (133:1).

The Benefits of Unity Stated (133:1) "Behold, how good and how pleasant it is for brethren to dwell together in unity!" (133:1). This is a topical sentence that summarizes the Psalm. It begins with "behold." Look at this. Think about this. This is a topic worth contemplating.

There are two benefits of unity among brethren. The first benefit of unity is that it is good. The Hebrew word translated "good" means "good, agreeable, valuable, benefit." Unity is valuable. The second benefit of unity is that it is pleasant. The Hebrew word translated "pleasant" means "pleasant, delightful, sweet." Unity is delightful. David is contemplating the benefits of living together in unity with the brethren. He was thinking about this as he was going to Jerusalem to observe one of the annual feasts with the people of God.

The Benefits of Unity Illustrated (133:2-3) Using two figures of speech, David illustrates the two benefits of living together in unity.

"It is like a precious oil upon the head, running down on the beard, the beard of Aaron, and running down to the edge of his garments" (133:2). The Hebrew word translated "good" in verse 1 is the same Hebrew word that is translated "precious" in verse 2. In other words, verse 1 is a statement of fact that unity is valuable, and verse 2 is an illustration of that.

The priests ("Aaron") were anointed with valuable oil (Ex. 30:30-33) (Ex. 30:22-25). It was poured on the head, ran down the beard, ran down the breastplate on which were inscribed the names of the 12 tribes of Israel, and ran down to the bottom of their garments. The fact that the oil ran over the breastplate containing the names of all the tribes of Israel and that it covered the priest from head to foot signified their unity, but the point David is making is that as the anointing oil used was valuable; unity is valuable.

"It is like the dew of Hermon, descending upon the mountains of Zion; for there the Lord commanded the blessing—life forevermore" (133:3). Hermon is a reference to Mt. Hermon, the highest mountain in the land north of Jerusalem. As the dew on Mt. Hermon refreshed the people there, unity was refreshing to the people on Mt. Zion (Jerusalem) because ("for") the Lord commanded the blessing of life to His people forevermore.

Summary: When contemplating living in unity, remember how valuable and refreshing it is.

A point to ponder: Believers are to "keep the unity of the Spirit in the bond of peace" (Eph. 4:3). Living together in unity is valuable and refreshing, compared to living together in discord and strife.

Psalm 134: When You See People Serving the Lord

Psalm 134 is an ascent psalm written by an unknown author. The ascent psalms (120-134, see also 84) were songs sung by pilgrims ascending to Jerusalem for the annual feasts of Passover, Pentecost, and Tabernacles. In Psalm 134, the psalmist sees the priests serving the Lord (134:1).

Servants, Bless the Lord (134:1-2) "Behold, bless the Lord, all you servants of the Lord, who by night stand in the house of the Lord!" (133:1). The psalmist calls upon the servants of the Lord to bless the Lord. The servants of the Lord who stand by night in the house of the Lord were the priests, who were on duty 24 hours a day (1 Chron. 9:33). They served as guards at night as well as priests offering sacrifices during the day. Therefore, this is an exhortation for the priests to praise the Lord.

"The psalmist adds, "Lift up your hands in the sanctuary and bless the Lord" (134:2). The lifting up of the hands signified offering up praise to God and receiving blessings from Him.

Lord, Bless Your Servants (134:3) "The Lord who made heaven and earth bless you from Zion!" (134:3). The psalmist then asks the Lord to bless the priests. As the Creator of the universe, He has the power to bestow enormous blessings on the priests, His servants.

This psalm is an appropriate conclusion to be ascent psalms (120-134). As the pilgrims, who had come to Jerusalem to observe one of the annual feasts of Israel, left for home, asking the Lord to bless the priests who had served Him by serving them was most appropriate.

Summary: When you see people serving the Lord, exhort them to praise the Lord and pray for the Lord to bless them.

A point to ponder: Thank God and pray for those people who serve God by serving you, such as your pastor who teaches the Word.

Psalm 135: When You Are Called to Praise

Psalm 135 is a praise psalm written by an unknown author. In Psalm 135, the psalmist exhorts the priests (135:1-2) and the people (135:20) to praise the Lord for His goodness (135:3-4, 8-12) and greatness (135:5-7, 15-18).

An Exhortation to Praise (135:1-2) The priests are exhorted to praise the Lord. They are called servants in verse 1 and those who stand in the court of the house of God in verse 2.

An Explanation for the Praise (135:3-18) The psalmist gives two basic reasons for praising the Lord (see "for" in verses 3, 5, 14).

1. The Lord is good (135:3-4). Priests are to praise the Lord because ("for") He is good, and sing praises because it is pleasant (135:3). The Lord is good because ("for") He has chosen Israel for Himself and for His special treasure (135:4; see Deut. 7:6). The Lord's goodness to Israel is further described in verses 8-12.

2. The Lord is great (135:5-7). The Lord is above all gods (135:5). He does what He pleases anywhere in the universe (135:6). He causes the vapor to rise, and makes lightning for the rain, and brings the wind (135:7). The Lord's greatness is also described in verses 15-18.

3. The Lord has been good to Israel (135:8-14). The Lord delivered Israel out of Egypt by destroying the Egyptians (135:8) and by sending signs and wonders to Egypt, Pharaoh, and all Pharaoh's servants (135:9). The Lord defeated many nations (135:10), including the king of the Amorites, the King of Bashan, and the kingdoms of Canaan (135:11). The Lord gave the land of Canaan to His people (135:12). Addressing the Lord directly, the psalmist says the Lord's name endures forever and His fame is spread throughout all generations (135:13), because ("for") the Lord will vindicate ("judge") His people and have compassion on His servants (135:14).

4. The Lord is great over idols (135:15-18). The living God is sovereign over nature (verses 5-7), nations (135:8-12; see also 115:4-8), and dead idols (135:15-18). The idols (gods) of the nations are made by man of silver and gold (135:15). They have mouths that do not speak (135:16a), eyes that do not see (35:16b), ears that do not hear (135:17a), mouths that do not breathe (135:17b). In short, they are dead; they cannot speak, see, hear, or breathe. The Lord is alive; He speaks, sees, and hears. Furthermore, those who make idols are like idols and so is everyone who trusts in idols (135:18). People become like what they worship, and idol worshipers are as powerless as their idols.

An Encouragement to Praise (135:19-21) Four times in the last three verses the psalmist says "bless the Lord." Israel, Aaron (135:19), Levi, and all who fear the Lord (135:20) are encouraged to bless the Lord, who dwells in Jerusalem.

This psalm begins and ends with the statement, "Praise the Lord!"

Summary: When you are called to praise the Lord; praise Him for His goodness and greatness.

A point to ponder: Believers tend to praise the Lord for His goodness more than for His greatness. Let us do both.

Psalm 136: When You Thank God

Psalm 136 is a thanksgiving psalm written by an unknown author. In Psalm 136, the psalmist thanks God for His work in nature (136:4-9), His work for Israel (136:10-24), and, above all, for His mercy (every verse). This psalm has been called the "Great Hallel" (Hebrew: praise; hallelujah means "praise the Lord"; for the other Hallel psalms, see 113-118).

An Exhortation to Give Thanks (136:1-3) In each of the first three verses, the psalmist exhorts people to give thanks to God. In each of these verses and in every verse in the Psalm, the reason for giving God thanks is "His mercy endures forever." Throughout this Psalm, the leader probably recited the first part of each verse and the people repeated the refrain, "His mercy endures forever."

An Explanation for Giving Thanks (136:4-25) The psalmist gives specific reasons for giving thanks to the Lord.

1. For His works in nature (136:4-9). The Lord does great wonders (136:4). He made the heavens (136:5), the earth (136:6), the sun and the moon (136:7), including the sun to rule by day (136:8), and the moon and stars to rule by night (136:9). After each verse, the refrain "For His mercy endures forever" is repeated.

2. For His works for Israel (136:10-23). The Lord struck the firstborn in Egypt (136:10), brought Israel out of Egypt (136:11), with His strong hand (136:12; compare with 8:3, where creation was the work of His fingers), divided the Red Sea (126:13), making Israel passed through it (136:14), overthrew Pharaoh and his army in it (136:15), led His people through the wilderness (136:16), struck down great Kings (136:17), slew famous kings (136:18), including Sihon king of the Amorites (136:19) and Og the king of Bashan (136:20; see Num. 21), and gave their land as a heritage to Israel (136:21-22). After each verse, the refrain "For His mercy endures forever" is repeated.

3. For His works of mercy (136:23-25). He remembered Israel in their lowly state (136:23; probably a reference to when Israel was in captivity in Babylon), rescued them from their enemies (136:24), and gave food to all living creatures (126:25). After each verse, the refrain "For His mercy endures forever" is repeated.

An Encouragement to Give Thanks (136:26) The psalmist concludes, "Oh, give thanks to the God of heaven" and one last time repeats the refrain "For His mercy endures forever" (136:26). The expression "the God of heaven" is unique in the Psalms; it was used, however, by the writers after the captivity, which suggests that this psalm was written after the captivity (see also the note on verse 23). It highlights the sovereignty of God. The psalm ends as it begins—with a call to thank God.

Summary: When you thank God, thank Him for His works in nature, His works on your behalf, and His works of mercy.

A point to ponder: When was the last time you thanked God for creation?

Psalm 137: When You Experience Severe Discipline

Psalm 137 is a lament psalm written by an unknown author. In Psalm 137, because of their sin, the children of Israel are experiencing the severe discipline of being captives in Babylon (137:1).

The Loss of Joy (137:1-4) When Babylon conquered Israel, many of the Israelites were carried captive into Babylon. There, the psalmist says, "By the rivers of Babylon, there we sat down, yea, we wept when we remembered Zion" (137:1). The rivers are the Euphrates, its tributaries, and canals. The memory of the destruction of Jerusalem ("Zion") was so painful they literally cried. There was no joy; there was no song. So they hung their harps upon the willows (137:2).

To make matters worse, those who carried them into captivity taunted them by requesting that they sing a song, "one of the songs of Zion" (137:3). Their response was, "How shall we sing the Lord's song in a foreign land?" (137:4). Experiencing severe divine discipline resulted in the loss of joy.

The Love for Jerusalem (137:5-6) The psalmist expresses his love for Jerusalem with several statements, each beginning with "if."

"If I forget you, O Jerusalem, let my right hand forget its skill!" (137:5). If he should ever forget Jerusalem, he prays that his right hand might forget how to play the harp.

"If I do not remember you, let my tongue cling to the roof of my mouth—if I do not exalt Jerusalem above my chief joy" (137:6). If he does not remember Jerusalem above his greatest joy, he prays that his tongue would cling to the roof of his mouth so he could not sing any song.

Israel's love for Jerusalem was so intense because the Temple was there, which housed the very presence of God.

The Longing for Justice (137:7-9) Turning his attention to the enemies of Jerusalem, the psalmist says, "Remember, Lord, against the sons of Edom the day of Jerusalem, who said, 'Raze it, raze it, to its very foundation'" (137:7). The men of Edom, a neighboring nation, cheered the destruction of Jerusalem by the Babylonians. They wanted it leveled to its very foundation. The psalmist is asking the Lord to remember them for their sin; he is asking for justice in their case (see Ezek. 25:12-14; Joel 3:19). He will remember Jerusalem (137:1, 5-6); he wants the Lord to remember enemies of Jerusalem (137:7). Remembering is referred to in each of the three stanzas of this Psalm (137:1, 6, 7).

Then he says, "O daughters of Babylon, who are to be destroyed, happy the one who repays you as you have served us! Happy the one who takes and dashes your little ones against the rock" (137:8-9). Addressing the daughters of Babylon directly, the psalmist longs for their destruction, suggesting that the ones who do to Babylon what Babylon did to them would be happy (see Isa. 13:1-22, esp. vs. 16). This is the law of strict retribution. It is the law of justice (see Gen. 12:3).

Summary: When you experience severe discipline because of your own sin, express your sorrow to the Lord, remember the joy of the Lord, and ask for the justice of the Lord.

A point to ponder: When the believers at Ephesus left (not lost) their first love (Rev. 2:4), the first thing the Lord told them to do was remember the place from where they had fallen (Rev. 2:5).

Psalm 138: When You Are in the Midst of Trouble

Psalm 138 is a praise psalm written by David. In Psalm 138, David is in the midst of trouble (138:7).

Praise (138:1-3) "I will praise You with my whole heart; before the gods I will sing praises to You" (138:1). David declares he will wholeheartedly praise God, even before idols.

David praises God for His mercy and truth. "I will worship toward Your holy temple and praise Your name for Your lovingkindness and Your truth; for You have magnified Your word above all Your name" (138:2). The Hebrew word translated "worship" means "to bow down, to prostrate oneself, obeisance" and the one rendered "lovingkindness" means "goodness, kindness" (BDB), "kindness, merciful" (Strong). David bows toward the Temple in Jerusalem to praise God for His lovingkindness and truth because ("for") God has magnified His word (His promise to be merciful) above all previous revelation of Himself ("name").

David praises God for answered prayer. "In the day when I cried, You answered me, and made me bold with strength in my soul" (138:3). David prayed for strength; God answered.

Prophecy (138:4-6) "All the kings of the earth shall praise You, O Lord, when they hear the words of Your mouth" (138:4). David is confident that when other Kings understand the Word of God, they will praise God and not idols (see "gods" in verse 1). This was the reaction of the Queen of Sheba (1 Kings 10:1-13). David adds, "Yes, they shall sing of the ways of the Lord, for great is the glory of the Lord" (138:5). The greatness of God's glory produces a spontaneous song, yet this exalted God, who is on high, "regards the lowly, but the proud He knows from afar" (138:6). God draws near to the humble and distances Himself from the proud. He resists the proud and gives grace to the humble (Jas. 4:6; 1 Pet. 5:5; see also Prov. 3:34).

Prayer (138:7-8) In the last two verses, David expresses what he is confident God will do (see "You will revive," "You will stretch," "Your right hand will save," in verse 7 and "the Lord will perfect" in verse 8) and asks God not to forsake the work of His hands.

"Though I walk in the midst of trouble, You will revive me" (138:7a). Although he was in the midst of trouble at the moment, David is confident that God will give him life and strength (see "strength" in verse 3).

"You will stretch out Your hand against the wrath of my enemies" (138:7b). The trouble mentioned in the previous sentence is now said to be the wrath of his enemies. David is confident that God will use His power ("hand") against the wrath of his enemies.

"And Your right hand will save me" (138:7c). Moreover, David is confident that God's power will deliver ("save") him from the wrath of his enemies.

"The Lord will perfect that which concerns me; your mercy, O Lord, endures forever" (138:8a). The Hebrew word translated "perfect" means "complete." David is confident that God will complete His purpose for him because of God's eternal mercy.

David concludes with a prayer, "Do not forsake the works of Your hands" (138:8b). David's prayer is that God will continue the works of His hand of delivering him (see verse 7).

Summary: When you are in the midst of trouble, praise God for His past mercy, pray for deliverance, and trust that the Lord will perfect His purpose in you.

A point to ponder: When in trouble, don't just pray for deliverance; ask God to use the trial to bring you to spiritual maturity (Jas. 1:2-4).

Psalm 139: When Someone Wants You Dead

Psalm 139 is a wisdom psalm written by David. In Psalm 139, David faces men who want him dead (139:19). They want to kill him!

The Omniscience of God (139:1-6) David says that God has searched him and knows him (139:1), including his sitting down and rising (139:2), his thoughts (139:2), all of his ways (139:3), and all the words he speaks (139:4). God has him hedged in (139:5). David says such knowledge is too wonderful, too high for him to attain (139:6).

The Omnipresence of God (139:7-12) David asks where he can go to flee from God's presence (139:7). If he goes from heaven to hell (Hebrew: Sheol, the place of the dead; 139:8) or from east ("wings of the morning") to the west ("uttermost parts" of the Mediterranean Sea; 139:9), God's hand is there to hold him and lead him (139:10). If darkness fell (Hebrew: bruise) on him, the Lord would see him as if he were standing in light (139:11) because for the Lord the night is light (139:12). Darkness does not hide anything from the Lord.

The Omnipotence of God (139:13-18) God knows David because He formed him (as a potter) and covered him (knitting him as a weaver) in his mother's womb (139:13). Hence he praises God because he is fearfully and wonderfully made (139:14). We would say, "Because he is awesome!" When David was being made in secret ("the lowest parts of the earth" is a reference to the womb), his frame (skeleton) was not hidden from God (139:15). God saw David's unformed substance (embryo) before he was born (139:16a). In fact, God knew David's whole life; it was in God's book before David was born. (God's knowledge of the details of David's life does not mean that David didn't have a choice.) God's work in David's life extends from conception to conclusion.

God's thoughts are great and precious to David (139:17). They are so great that if he counted them, they would be more than the sand (139:18a). They are with David when he wakes up every morning (139:18b).

The Opinion of David (139:19-24) In David's opinion, the wicked, those trying to kill him ("bloodthirsty men"), should depart from him and God should slay them (139:19), because they speak wickedly against God and take His name in vain (139:20). David confesses that he hates, that is rejects (Mal. 1:3), those who hate God (139:21); He counts them as his enemies (139:22).

David asks God to search him to know his heart and to try him to know his anxieties (139:23) to see if there's any wicked way in him and to lead him in the way everlasting (139:24). David was anxious because men were trying to kill him (139:19). He wants God to test him as a refiner tests metal to show that he is loyal to the Lord and to lead him in the way of the Lord.

Summary: When someone wants you dead, remember that God knows everything about you, is always with you, and has all the power to protect you; request their demise instead of yours, and rely on the Lord to refine you and lead you.

A point to ponder: The attributes of God are not abstract qualities; they are active characteristics. His absolute knowledge, assured presence, and almighty power are active on our behalf.

Poet Francis Thompson's expression "the hound of heaven" is based on this Psalm.

Psalm 140: When You Are Faced with a Slanderer

Psalm 140 is a lament psalm written by David. In Psalm 140, David faces evil men (140:1) who are slandering him (140:3, 11) and are planning his destruction (140:4-5).

Plea for Deliverance (140:1-8) David pleads with the Lord to deliver him from evil men and preserve him from violent men (140:1). They plan evil and continually gather together for war (140:2). They sharpen their "tongues like a serpent; the poison of asps is under their lips" (140:3). The asp is one of the most poisonous snakes. One killed Cleopatra. David's point is that the words of evil men are like the deadly bite of a snake. Paul quotes Psalm 140:3 in Romans 3:13 to demonstrate the sinfulness of humanity.

David pleads with the Lord to keep him from the hands of the wicked and preserve him from violent men who have purposed to make his steps stumble (140:4). These proud men have hidden a snare, spread a net, and set a trap for him (140:5). They were going to ambush him.

David pleads with the Lord to hear his prayer because the Lord is his God (140:6) and his strength, Who has covered his head with a helmet in battle (140:7). His prayer is, "Do not grant, O Lord, the desires of the wicked; do not further his wicked scheme, lest they be exalted" (140:8).

Prayer for Destruction (140:9-11) Turning his attention to these evil men who seek his destruction, David prays for their destruction (he uses the word "let" five times in verses 9-11).

"As for the head of those who surround me, let the evil of their lips cover them" (140:9). Luther rendered this, "The calamity which my enemies design against me must fall upon their own heads."

"Let burning coals fall upon them" (140:10a), like the fire that fell in Sodom and Gomorrah.

"Let them be cast into the fire, into deep pits, that they rise not up again" (140:10b). David's desire is that the fall of his enemies be irreversible.

"Let not a slanderer be established in the earth" (140:11a). His enemies were slanderers (see verse 3).

"Let evil hunt the violent man to overthrow him" (140:11b). David prays for their complete destruction.

Position of David (140:12-13) David's position is that he is confident that the Lord will do what is right. The psalm ends with two statements expressing that conviction.

"I know that the Lord will maintain the cause of the afflicted, and justice for the poor" (140:12). The Lord is a God of compassion and justice. Thus, David is certain He will act in his behalf.

"Surely the righteous shall give thanks to Your name; the upright and shall dwell in Your presence" (140:13). The result of God's deliverance will be praise and peace in God's presence.

Summary: When faced with slanderers, pray for your deliverance and their destruction, confident that God is compassionate and just.

A point to ponder: Praying for people's destruction is appropriate when they are evil (140:1, 2), wicked (140:4), violent (140:1), and 4) slanderers (140:11) planning destruction (140:5).

Psalm 141: When You Need Protection

Psalm 141 is a lament psalm written by David. In Psalm 141, David needs protection from wickedness and from wicked people (141:4, 9-10).

A Plea to be Heard (141:1-2) David pleads with the Lord to hear his prayer, saying, "Lord, I cry out to You; make haste to hear me! Give ear to my voice when I cry out to You" (141:1). He compares his prayer to incense burning in the Tabernacle and lifting up his hands as the evening sacrifice (141:2). He compares his plea to be heard with a sacrifice offered to God.

A Prayer to be Holy (141:3-7) David asks the Lord to guard his mouth, to put a watch over the door of his lips (141:3), to keep his heart from evil, to keep him from wicked works with wicked men (141:4a). He adds, "Do not let me eat of their delicacies" (141:4b). In other words, David is asking the Lord for the strength not to sin in word, thought, or deed, and not even to have fellowship (to eat with) with people who work iniquity. To help him be holy, he prays that the righteous would strike him, calling their rebuke a kindness and excellent oil he prays his head will not refuse (141:5a).

David explains ("for") that his prayer is against the deeds of the wicked (141:5b). He does not want to participate in the works of the wicked (see verse 4) and wants God to judge them. He says their judges are overthrown by the sides of the cliff (141:6a), meaning the leaders of the wicked would fall like an attacking army, throwing people off cliffs to destroy them. When God judges them, they will learn that David's words are true (141:6b).

Turning his attention to Israel (see "our" in verse 7), David says, "Our bones are scattered at the mouth of the grave, as when one plows and breaks up the earth" (141:7). Their bones are at the *mouth* of the grave. They are not in the grave; they are unburied. They are lying on the ground like a newly plowed field. The ground is plowed, but the seed has not been planted. This is a figurative way of saying that they are as good as dead—without God's help (see verse 8).

A Petition for Help (141:8-10) David declares, "But my eyes are upon you, O God the Lord; in You I take refuge; do not leave my soul destitute" (141:8). David flees to the Lord for protection. He needs this protection because the workers of iniquity (see verse 4) have set a trap for him (141:9). So, he asks, "Let the wicked fall into their own nets, while I escape safely" (141:10). David requests protection from death (141:7) and asks that the wicked be caught in their own snares (141:9), traps (141:9), and nets (141:10).

Summary: When you need protection from wickedness and wicked people, ask the Lord to give you what it takes to be holy and ask Him for help to be delivered from wicked people.

A point to ponder: In the Lord's Prayer, He taught us to pray daily for deliverance from temptation and the evil one (Mt. 6:13).

Psalm 142: When You Are Forsaken

Psalm 142 is a lament psalm written by David. In Psalm 142, David was hiding from Saul in a cave (see the superscription; see also Ps. 57) and was forsaken (142:4). In fleeing from Saul, David hid in a cave on two occasions: at Adullam (1 Sam. 22:1–2) and in En Gedi (1 Sam. 24:1–7). This psalm was written when David was in the cave at Adullam. Saul had come after him with 3000 chosen men (1 Sam. 22:2). A few of David's men were with him, but he had been forsaken by everyone else and was being pursued by an enemy who sought to take his life.

David's Cry (142:1-2) David says, "I cry out to the Lord with my voice; with my voice to the Lord I make my supplication. I pour out my complaint before Him; I declare before Him my trouble" (142:1-2). This was not a silent prayer that David prayed in his heart. It was an audible prayer, he said out loud with his voice. Instead of having a personal pity party or walking around complaining to anyone who would listen, David poured out his complaint to the Lord like pouring water out of a pitcher; He declared his trouble to the Lord.

David's Complaint (142:3-4) David explains his trouble, saying, "When my spirit was overwhelmed within me, then You knew my path. In the way in which I walk, they have secretly set a snare for me" (142:3). At Adullam, David and his handful of men faced Saul's army of 3000 men. His enemies have secretly set a snare for him, and he feels overwhelmed by it. He acknowledges that the Lord is aware of the situation.

Furthermore, he says, "Look at my right hand and see, for there is no one who acknowledges me; no one cares for my soul" (142:4). David's guards would normally stand at his right hand. Even though David had a handful of men with him, it was nothing as compared to Saul's army. The country did not come to his aid or care for his life. Forsaken by his friends and pursued by an enemy who sought his life, David feels forsaken and unprotected.

David's Confidence (142:5-7) So David says, "I cried out to You, O Lord; I said, 'You are my refuge, my portion in the land of the living'" (142:5). David took refuge in a cave, but he was aware that the cave was not his refuge; his refuge was the Lord.

"Attend to my cry, for I am brought very low; deliver me from my persecutors, for they are stronger than I" (142:6). When David says that his persecutors are stronger than he is, he is referring to the fact that he has a handful of men facing an army of 3000 disciplined soldiers. No wonder he is discouraged ("brought very low"). He feels forsaken.

"Bring my soul out of prison, that I may praise Your name; the righteous shall attend me, for You shall deal bountifully with me" (142:7). It was not his body that was in jail, but his soul is in prison, a reference to the restriction involved in hiding in a cave from Saul. Nevertheless, he is confident the Lord will deliver him and when He does, David says he will praise the name of the Lord.

Summary: When you are forsaken and desperately need help, pour out your trouble to the Lord, trust Him to deliver you, and praise Him when He does.

A point to ponder: Family and friends may forsake you, but your heavenly Father does not (Jos. 1:5; Deut. 31:6, 8; 1 Chron. 28:20; Heb. 13:5).

By the way, at Adullam, the Lord delivered David from Saul's hands (see 1 Sam. 22 for the amazing story of how He did it).

Psalm 143: When You Are Devastated

Psalm 143 is a lament psalm written by David. In Psalm 143, David is devastated (143:4).

A Plea for Mercy (143:1-4) Throughout this Psalm, David gives a number of reasons why God should answer his prayer for mercy. For example, he says, "Hear my prayer, O Lord, give ear to my supplication! In Your faithfulness answer me in Your righteousness. Do not enter into judgment with Your servant for in Your sight no one living is righteous" (143:1-2). Because God is faithful and righteous (143:1), David asks that he not be judged, indicating he is pleading mercy because of his sin.

David explains ("for") a second reason why he needs mercy. "For the enemy has persecuted my soul: he has crushed my life to the ground; he is made me to dwell in darkness, like those who have long been dead" (143:3). The Hebrew word translated "persecuted" means "run after, pursue, persecute." Notice the progression. David's enemy has pursued him, caught him and cast him to the ground, where he lies in darkness, like those who are dead. The word "long" indicates that he had been in this situation for a long time.

David concludes, "Therefore my spirit is overwhelmed within me; my heart in me is distressed" (143:4). The Hebrew word translated "overwhelm" means "to cover, be feeble, be faint, grow weak") and the one rendered "distressed" means "to be desolate, to be devastated." David is not just discouraged; he is devastated. David pleads for mercy because of his disobedience and devastation.

A Memory of the Past (143:5-6) David apparently had sinned (143:2), but he remembers "the days of old" when he meditated on all of God's works (143:5), prayed ("spread out my hands to You"), and longed for the Lord like a thirsty land longs for rain (143:6).

A Prayer for Guidance and Deliverance (143:7-12) David prays for the Lord to speedily answer his prayer because he is getting weaker ("my spirit fails") and because he is about to die ("go down into the pit;" 143:7). His prayer is for guidance (143:8, 10) and deliverance (143:9, 11-12), moving back and forth between the two requests.

David prays for the Lord to quickly ("in the morning") grant him grace ("Your lovingkindness"), because he trusts Him and <u>guidance</u> ("the way in which I should walk") because he lifts up his soul to Him (143:8).

David prays for <u>deliverance</u> because he takes his refuge in the Lord (143:9).

David prays for <u>guidance</u> ("teach me to do your will" and "lead me") because the Lord is his God and He is a good God (143:10).

David prays for <u>deliverance</u> ("revive me," "bring my soul out of trouble," "cut off my enemies and destroy all those who afflict my soul") for the Lord's name's sake, for the Lord's righteousness' sake, and because he is God's servant (143:11-12).

Summary: When you are devastated because of your disobedience and you face destruction, remember where you once were and ask God for guidance and deliverance.

Note the arguments David uses for God to answer his prayer: God's faithfulness (143:1), righteousness (143:1, 11), mercy (143:2, 8, 12), and goodness (143:10), and David's situation (143:3-4, 7), trust in the Lord (143:8, 9), and service (143:12).

A point to ponder: When we are devastated, we should not just ask for deliverance; we should ask the Lord to teach us what we need to learn from the experience.

Psalm 144: When You Are Doing Battle with Liars

Psalm 144 is a royal psalm written by David. In Psalm 144, David is facing foreigners in military battle who lie with their mouths and practice falsehood (144:7-8, 11)

Praise for Past Victories (144:1-4) David praises God for being his rock, who trained him for battle (144:1), his lovingkindness and fortress, his high tower and deliverer, and his shield, the One in whom he takes refuge and who subdues people under him (144:2). By His mercy ("lovingkindness"), the Lord prepared David for battle and protected him in it.

The Lord is to be praised for being mindful of mere mortals. David asks, "Lord, what is man, that You take knowledge of him? Or the son of man that You are mindful of him? (144:3; see 8:4). As compared to the eternal God, "man is like a breath; his days are like a passing shadow" (114:4). Humans are temporary as a vapor ("breath") and a momentary shadow.

Prayer for Present Victory (144:5-11) David prays for victory in his present battle using a series of commands and figures of speech. David asks God to bow down from heaven and touch the mountains (114:5), flash forth lightning (a figure of speech for judgment) and scatter his enemies (144:6a), shoot arrows and destroy his enemies (144:6b), stretch out his hand from heaven (144:7a), rescue him from the hand of foreigners (144:7b), who speak lies and practice falsehood (144:8). God uses rain, thunder, lightning, and hail to give His people victory (Josh. 10; Judg. 4–5; etc.). In praying for the destruction of his enemies (verse 6), David is praying for justice because his enemies speak lies and practice falsehood (verse 8; see also verse 11).

When the victory comes, David promises to praise God with a new song on a harp of ten strings (144:9), because He delivers David and his servants from the deadly sword (144:10). A "new song" (33:3; 40:3; 96:1; 98:1; 144:9; 149:1) is a song about His new blessings (98:1; see Lam. 3:23). David mentions himself by name (a rare occurrence in the Psalms), to remind future generations that their blessings (verses 11-15) came as a result of God's victories his life.

So David asks, "Rescue me and deliver me from the hand of foreigners, whose mouth speak lying words and his right hand is a right hand of falsehood" (144:11). They offer the right hand (handshake) of trust, but practice treachery.

Picture of Future Blessing (144:12-15) With a series of statements that all begin with "that," David pictures the blessings of victory. He asked God for victory that "our sons" may grow up like plants and "our daughters" maybe "as pillars, sculptured in palace style," that is, be beautiful (144:12), that "our barns" may be full, supplying all kinds of produce and that "our sheep" may bring forth thousands and ten thousands in our fields (144:13), that "our oxen may be well laden, that there be no breaking in or going out, and that there be no outcry in our streets," a picture of peace (144:14). David concludes, "Happy are the people who are in such a state; happy are the people whose God is the Lord!" (144:15). In other words, David pictures children growing up healthy and happy, peace, and prosperity for people whose God is the Lord.

Summary: When doing battle with liars, praise God for past victories, pray for a victory in the present, and focus on God's future blessing.

A point to ponder: When dealing with liars, focus on God's future blessing rather than fixating on the lies.

Psalm 145: When You Praise God as King

Psalm 145 is a praise psalm written by David. The last six psalms are praise psalms. The word "praise" appears 46 times in these [salms. Psalm 145 is an acrostic; each verse begins with a successive letter of the Hebrew alphabet, except for the Hebrew letter *nun*, which is missing between verses 13 and 14 but included in the Septuagint (the ancient Greek translation of the Old Testament) and added to verse 13 in the NIV ("The LORD is trustworthy in all he promises and faithful in all he does" is added). In Psalm 145, David praises God as King (145:1).

The Greatness of God (145:1-7) David declares that he will extol God as King and bless His name every day (145:2) forever and ever (145:1) because the Lord is great, greatly to be praised, and His greatness is unsearchable (145:3). One generation shall praise God's works to another generation (145:4). David promises to meditate on the glorious splendor of God's majesty and His wondrous works (145:5). Men will speak of the might of God's awesome acts, declare His greatness (145:6), and utter the memory of His great goodness and righteousness (145:7).

The Grace of God (145:8-9) "The Lord is gracious and full of compassion, slow to anger and great in mercy" (145:8). He is "good to all and His tender mercies are over all His works" (145:9). The great God (145:1-7) is gracious (145:8-9).

The Glorious Kingdom of God (145:10-13) God's works and God's saints shall praise Him (145:10) and speak of the glory of His kingdom and power (145:11) to make known to the sons of men His mighty acts and the glorious majesty of His kingdom (145:12), which is an everlasting kingdom (145:13). Saints should praise God for His eternal kingdom and make it known to others.

The Goodness of God (145:14-16) "The Lord upholds all who fall and raises up all who are bowed down" (145:14). As all look expectantly to the Lord, He gives them their food in due season (145:15) and opens His hand to satisfy the desire of every living thing (145:16). Since God's kingdom is over all, as the King (45:1), He provides for all by sustaining the fallen, raising up the oppressed, and giving them food.

The Generosity of God (145:17-21) "The Lord is righteous in all of His ways, gracious in all His works" (145:17). The Hebrew word translated "gracious" in verse 17 is different than the one translated "gracious" in verse 8. The one in verse 17 means "faithful, kind." The Lord is near to all who call upon Him in truth (145:18). He fulfills the desire of those who fear Him, hearing their cry and saving them (145:19). He preserves all who love Him, but He destroys the wicked (145:20).

David concludes, "My mouth shall speak the praise of the Lord, and all flesh shall bless His holy name forever and ever" (145:21).

Summary: When you praise God as King, praise Him for His grace, glorious kingdom, goodness, and generosity to all.

Notice how often this psalm refers to all [verse 9 (twice), 10, 13, 14 (twice), 15, 17, 18, 20 (twice), 21; see also 4, 6, 7, 12, 16]. God is King over all.

A point to ponder: As King who rules over an eternal kingdom, God is good and gracious to all and, therefore, all should praise Him.

Psalm 146: When You Praise the Lord for His Help

Psalm 146 is a praise psalm written by an unknown author. The last five psalms begin and end with "Praise the Lord" (Hebrew: *Hallelujah*). In Psalm 146, the psalmist is praising the Lord for His help (146:5).

An Expression of Praise (146:1-2) The psalmist declares, "Praise the Lord! Praise the Lord, O my soul! (146:1). At this point, the psalmist is exhorting himself to praise the Lord. Then he says, "While I live, I will praise the Lord; I will sing praises to my God while I have my being" (146:2). Looking into the future, the psalmist promises to praise the Lord as long as he lives.

An Explanation for Praise (146:3-5) Abruptly changing directions, the psalmist exhorts, "Do not put your trust in princes, nor in a son of man, in whom there is no help" (146:3). The implication is that we should praise the Lord and trust Him because there is no help in trusting people, not even influential people such as princes. To underscore the fact that there's no help in humans, the psalmist says, "His spirit departs, he returns to his earth; in that very day his plans perish" (146:4). People and their plans perish. God is eternal (146:6, 10); people are temporary.

On the other hand, "Happy is he who has the God of Jacob for his help, whose hope is in the Lord his God." (146:5). Those who trust the Lord find the help they need. Consequently, they are happy.

Examples of Help (146:6-10) Referring to God as the Creator of the universe and the eternal preserver of truth, that is, He is faithful to His promises (145:6), the psalmist gives nine examples of how the Lord helps. He <u>executes justice</u> for the oppressed, <u>gives food</u> to the hungry, and <u>gives freedom</u> to prisoners (146:7). He <u>opens the eyes</u> of the blind, <u>raises</u> those who are bowed down, <u>loves</u> the righteous (146:8), <u>watches</u> over strangers, <u>relieves</u> the fatherless and widows, and <u>turns the way of the wicked</u> upside down (146:9). Furthermore, "The Lord shall reign forever—your God, O Zion, to all generations. Praise the Lord!" (146:10). The Lord is to be praised because He not only helps, He reigns forever. His help is always available.

Summary: When you praise the Lord for His help, realizing that He helps when humans cannot, praise Him for specific examples of His help.

A point to ponder: Although there are times that people help, ultimately, help and happiness come from the Lord to those who trust the Lord.

Psalm 147: When You Are Restored #2

Psalm 147 is a praise psalm written by an unknown author. In Psalm 147, the psalmist is praising God for restoring the Jewish people of the captivity to Jerusalem (147:2; see Ps. 126). It contains three stanzas, each beginning with a call to praise followed by the causes for praise.

Praise for Restoration (147:1-6) "Praise the LORD! For *it is* good to sing praises to our God; for *it is* pleasant, *and* praise is beautiful" (147:1). The call is to praise the Lord. The reason ("for") is because praise is good, pleasant, and beautiful. To be more specific, "The Lord builds up Jerusalem; He gathers together the outcasts of Israel" (147:2). The Lord has restored the outcast to Jerusalem. Moreover, "He heals the brokenhearted and binds up their wounds" (147:3), counts the number of the stars; He calls them all by name" (147:4). "Great *is* our Lord, and mighty in power; His understanding *is* infinite" (147:5). "The Lord lifts up the humble; He casts the wicked down to the ground" (146:6). The Lord is so great He counts the stars, yet He cares about the outcast, the brokenhearted, and the wounded. In this case, praise the almighty God who has restored outcast, brokenhearted, and wounded Israel.

Praise for Mercy (147:7-11) "Sing to the Lord with thanksgiving; sing praises on the harp to our God" (147:7). Again, the psalmist calls people to praise the Lord, this time with thanksgiving. The reason is He "covers the heavens with clouds," "prepares rain for the earth," "makes grass to grow on the mountains" (147:8), "gives to the beast its food, *and* to the young ravens that cry" (147:9; ravens were especially vulnerable, because ravens do not provide for their young as other birds do), "does not delight in the strength of the horse," "takes no pleasure in the legs of a man" (147:10), but "takes pleasure in those who fear Him, in those who hope in His mercy" (147:11). With thanksgiving, sing praise on the harp to the Lord, Who not only takes care of the earth but is also merciful to those who trust Him. He does not delight in race horses or runners; He delights in those who rely on Him, who can take care of them.

Praise for the Word (147:12-21) "Praise the LORD, O Jerusalem! Praise your God, O Zion!" (147:12). For the third time, the psalmist calls people to praise the Lord. This time he specifically mentions the people of Jerusalem (Zion is another name for Jerusalem). The reason ("for") is "He has strengthened the bars of your gates," "blessed your children within you" (147:13), "makes peace *in* your borders, *and* fills you with the finest wheat" (147:14), "sends out His command *to the* earth; His word runs very swiftly" (147:15), "gives snow like wool," "scatters the frost like ashes" (147:16), and "casts out His hail like morsels" (14717a). At this point, the psalmist asks, "Who can stand before His cold?" (147:17b). Then he continues, The Lord "sends out His word and melts them; causes His wind to blow, *and* the waters flow" (147:18), "declares His word to Jacob, His statutes and His judgments to Israel" (147:19), "has not dealt thus with any nation; and *as for His* judgments, they have not known them. Praise the Lord!" (147:20). Along with protection, peace, and prosperity, the Lord is to be praised for giving His Word to Israel. Also, the snow, frost, hail, and wind obey His Word. So should His children.

Summary: When restored, praise God for His restoration, mercy, and Word.

A point to ponder: "God sustains both the creation and His creatures with His Word" (Constable).

Psalm 148: When You Are Strengthened

Psalm 148 is a praise psalm written by an unknown author. In Psalm 148, all of God's people have been strengthened (148:14).

Call for the Heavens to Praise the Lord (148:1-6) The psalmist commands, "Praise the Lord!" He calls for praise "from the heavens," "in the heights" (148:1), from "all His angels," "all His host" (148:2), the "sun and moon," "all you stars of light" (148:3), "you heavens of heavens, and you waters above the heavens" (148:4). With the use of the figure of speech known as personification, the psalmist calls on the heavens to praise the Lord as if they had the ability to do so.

Then, the psalmist gives the reason why the heavens should praise the Lord. He says, "Let them praise the name of the Lord, for He commanded and they were created" (148:5). He not only created them, "He also established them forever and ever; He made a decree which will not pass away" (148:6). The heavens should praise the Lord because He created them and established them forever by His word.

Call for the Earth to Praise the Lord (148:7-12) Turning his attention from the heavens to the earth, the psalmist says, "Praise the Lord from the earth, you great sea creatures and all the depths" (148:7), "fire and hail, snow and clouds; stormy wind, fulfilling His word" (148:8), "mountains and all hills, fruit trees and all cedars" (148:9), "beasts and all cattle, creeping things and flying fowl" 148:10). Again using personification, the psalmist calls on everything on the earth to praise the Lord.

Call for Humans to Praise the Lord (148:11-14) In a long list of all that should praise the Lord, the psalmist moves from the earth to humans. He adds to his list, "Kings of the earth and all peoples; princes and all judges of the earth" (148:11)," Both young men and maidens; old men and children" (148:12). All humans, from the high to the lowly and from the old to the young, should praise the Lord.

Then, the psalmist adds the reason for praising the Lord. He says, "Let them praise the name of the Lord, for His name alone is exalted; His glory is above the earth and heaven" (148:13), and "He has exalted the horn (strength) of His people, the praise of all His saints—of the children of Israel, the people near to Him" (148:14a). The psalmist concludes as he began with "Praise the Lord!" (114b). All humans should praise the Lord because His name and glory are exalted above the heavens and earth and because He exalts the strength of His people, Israel.

Summary: When strengthened, praise the Lord for creating and establishing the heavens and earth by His Word, for His name is being exalted, and for His strength being exalted.

A point to ponder: If the heavens and the earth are to praise God because He has created them and established them by His word, surely we should do the same. When was the last time you praised God for His creation?

Psalm 149: When You Rejoice in the Lord

Psalm 149 is a praise psalm written by an unknown author. In Psalm 149, the psalmist speaks of rejoicing in the Lord "in the assembly" (149:1), in bed (149:5), and on the battlefield (149:6).

A Call to Rejoice in the Assembly (149:1-4) "Praise the Lord! Sing to the Lord a new song, and His praise in the assembly of saints" (149:1). A "new song" (33:3; 40:3; 96:1; 98:1; 144:9; 149:1) is a song about His new blessings (98:1; see also Lam. 3:23). The call is for Israel to sing a new song that praises God in the assembly of the saints. The next two verses contain four statements, each beginning with "let."

"Let Israel rejoice in their Maker" (149:2a). God created not only the universe but also the nation of Israel.

"Let the children of Zion (Jerusalem) be joyful in their King" (149:2). Israel is to rejoice that God is not only their Maker, but He is also their King.

"Let them praise His name with the dance" (149:3a). This dance was not done by couples; it was a whirling motion done by individuals or by a large group (2 Sam. 6:16).

"Let them sing praises to Him with the timbrel and the harp" (149:3b). This joyful celebration should include dancing and music played on the timbrel and the harp.

The reason ("for") for this joyful celebration is, "The Lord takes pleasure in His people; He will satisfy the humble with salvation" (149:4). Salvation here includes all forms of salvation, including physical deliverance and spiritual salvation.

A Call to Rejoice on the Bed (149:5-6a) With three statements, each of which begins with "let," the psalmist calls "the saints" to rejoice with song on their beds.

"Let the saints be joyful in glory" (149:5a). The saints should rejoice in the glory of God's blessing on them.

"Let them sing aloud on their beds" (149:5b). The saints should rejoice by singing aloud, even in their beds. They should rejoice in public (149:1) and in private (149:5b).

"Let the high praises of God be in their mouth" (149:6a). The saints should rejoice by allowing the praises of God in their hearts to be expressed by their mouths.

A Call to Rejoice on the Battlefield (149:6b-9) In the middle of verse 6, there is an abrupt change from just rejoicing in the Lord to holding a two-edged sword. Instead of being "in the assembly of the saints" (149:1), or on their beds (149:5), they are now on the battlefield. The next three verses begin with "to," indicating the purpose of the warfare.

"To execute vengeance on the nations and punishment on peoples" (149:7). Vengeance and punishment indicate that this is the just treatment of nations who opposed the Lord. It is not personal or even national.

"To bind their kings with chains, and their nobles in the fetters of iron" (149:8). The leaders, as well as the people, must be stopped.

"To execute on them the written judgment—this honor have all His saints" (149:9a). They were executing the judgment as given in the Law (Deut. 7:1-2). Thus, they should "Praise the Lord" (149:9b).

Summary: When you rejoice in the Lord, do it with song in the assembly of the saints, on your bed, and even on the battlefield.

A point to ponder: Rejoice in the Lord with song, even in the shower.

Psalm 150: When You Publicly Praise the Lord

Psalm 150 is a praise psalm written by an unknown author. In Psalm 150, the psalmist calls on all humans (150:6) to publicly praise the Lord with musical instruments (150:3-5).

The Place of Praise (150:1) The climax of the Psalter begins with the words, "Praise the Lord! Praise Him in His sanctuary; praise Him in His mighty firmament" (150:1). Because "firmament" is parallel to "sanctuary" in this verse, "sanctuary" is a reference to heaven. This verse is a call for those in heaven to praise the Lord. This psalm is about praising God publicly from heaven (verse 1) to earth (verse 6).

The Reason for Praise (150:2) "Praise Him for His mighty acts; praise Him according to His excellent greatness!" (150:2). The two reasons for praising the Lord are what He has done ("mighty acts") and who He is ("excellent greatness").

The Means of Praise (150:3-5) The psalmist delineates various ways to praise the Lord. Except for "dance," all the means mentioned here are with musical instruments.

"Praise Him with the sound of the trumpet" (150:3a). The ancient trumpet in Israel was made out of a ram's horn.

"Praise Him with the lute and the harp!" (150:3b). The lute and the harp are smaller and larger versions of portable harps.

"Praise Him with the timbrel and dance" (150:4a). The timbrel was our tambourine. This dance was not done by couples; it was a whirling motion done by individuals or by a large group (2 Sam. 6:16).

"Praise Him with the stringed instruments and flutes!" (150:4b). The Lord is to be praised with stringed and wind instruments.

"Praise Him with loud cymbals" (150:5a). The loud cymbals were larger cymbals.

"Praise Him with clashing cymbals" (150:5b). The clashing cymbals were smaller than the loud cymbals.

The means of praising the Lord include playing music on wind, stringed, and percussion instruments, as well as dancing.

The Called to Praise (150:6) It is fitting that the Psalter should conclude with the words, "Let everything that has breath praise the Lord. Praise the Lord!" (150:6). By "everything that has breath," the psalmist is, no doubt, referring to all the people on the planet. The psalmist calls on those in heaven (148:1, 150:1), angels (148:2), Israel (149:2), Jerusalem 147:12), and all the people on the planet (150:6) to praise the Lord.

This psalm specifies the where, how, and who of praise.

Summary: When you publicly praise the Lord, praise Him for who He is and what He has done with all kinds of musical instruments and dance, and invite everyone to do the same.

A point to ponder: Everyone is to publicly praise the Lord enthusiastically, energetically, and exuberantly.

www.ingramcontent.com/pod-product-compliance
Lightning Source LLC
Chambersburg PA
CBHW081446070526
44586CB00019B/2247